The Atlantic Salmon

The
Atlantic
Salmon

Lee Wulff

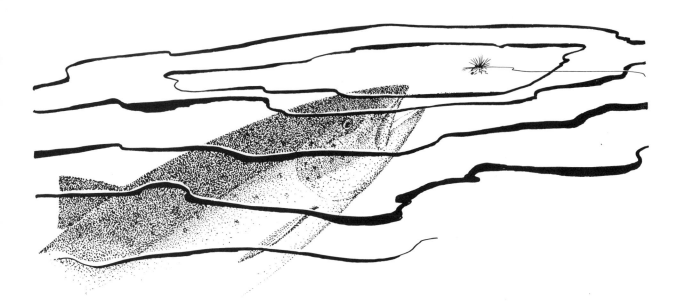

Nick Lyons Books

WINCHESTER PRESS

To all those who have given
love, work, or monies,
or have released their captured salmon,
and have thus worked to safeguard
and improve our magnificent sport.

Produced by
NICK LYONS BOOKS
212 Fifth Avenue
New York, NY 10010

Published and distributed by
WINCHESTER PRESS
New Century Publishers, Inc.
220 Old New Brunswick Road
Piscataway, NJ 08854

Library of Congress Cataloging in Publication Data

Wulff, Lee.
  The Atlantic salmon.

  ''A Nick Lyons book.''
  1. Atlantic salmon fishing. I. Title.
SH685.W797 1973   799.1'755 82-20253
ISBN 0-8329-0267-5

PRINTED IN THE UNITED STATES OF AMERICA
10 9 8 7 6 5 4 3 2 1

Contents

Foreword to the 1983 Edition

The first foreword was written for the initial publication of *The Atlantic Salmon* in 1958 and fitted to that year. Time moves on and it is time to write again to fit this date.

Because of the complexity of Atlantic salmon fishing I waited three years before writing my first magazine article on salmon. My first short book, *Leaping Silver*, came after seventeen years of salmon fishing. The first writing of this book came after twenty-eight seasons on the salmon rivers, and now, almost a quarter of a century later, I "take pen in hand" to mark in these pages the new knowledge of salmon and salmon fishing that has since become available and the greater understanding of these magnificent fish that has come to me as I continue to fish, enjoy, and learn, year after year.

In these intervening years salmon fishermen have increased manyfold while the numbers of salmon in the runs and the rivers suitable for their spawning have dwindled. Because there are so many more of us to call for good management of the salmon stocks we are certain to be heard and heeded. We can reclaim the salmon rivers. We can bring the runs back to something like their old-time glory. But we can never give again to anglers the opportunities available in my youth to catch and, if one wished to, keep or kill so many salmon. Even as we rebuild the stocks the number of anglers will grow at an even faster rate than the numbers of the fish.

The average angler cannot hope to increase his opportunity to take more salmon. His increase in pleasure must come from enjoying each salmon he catches more or by having each salmon spread the pleasure it can give to more than one angler. Each salmon angler needs to develop a deeper understanding of the fish and the intriguing angling problems involved to gain a growing pleasure from each fish as he casts and retrieves through his allotted time. Then his last salmon can give him as much pride, satisfaction, and wonder as his first. It is to this end that this book is taken through a complete revision and expansion.

Foreword to the 1958 Edition

Atlantic salmon fishing represents, in all likelihood, the highest development of individual angling. The tackle requirements and method of angling, as determined by law, are sporting in the extreme whereas other fish, like the tarpon and steelhead, which may in themselves be just as fine a trophy, may be taken by less sporting means. To fish for Atlantic salmon is to accept a difficult challenge; to capture one, barring an extremely lucky circumstance, certifies the ability to handle competently our most difficult fishing tackle. These conclusions come from one who has fished successfully for many types of fish in widespread waters and who was for twelve years a fishing editor for national magazines, and who has written on both fresh- and saltwater fishing for half a century.

It takes a lot of fishing as well as much listening and reading to understand the salmon. A top guide on his river may have a thorough knowledge of the habits of the fish in his stream yet this may be a confining and limited view. Limited, too, may be the angler who knows many rivers sketchily but none intimately through every flood and drought from spring to fall. A broad experience in salmon fishing with the opportunity for large catches on many rivers becomes ever harder to achieve.

Anglers hold widely divergent opinions about the habits and reactions of the salmon, much of whose life cycle is clothed in mystery, many of whose actions are contradictory. Few anglers agree completely about his needs and preferences. From such an audience an author can hardly hope for a universal acclaim for his work. Since salmon fishermen are relatively few in numbers, books on salmon fishing do not normally prove financially rewarding. Then why write one?

In half a century of salmon fishing, through season after full season spent on a wide range of salmon rivers in the taking of thousands of salmon, a competent angler with a questioning mind learns many things. If, with the judgment of maturity, he can present a picture of the art of salmon angling as he has found it, showing his own special beliefs and the circumstances that produced them against an undistorted background of the generally held conceptions, he may afford a new interest and a greater understanding of both fish and the sport to others. Such is the purpose of this book.

Though the great days of the turn of the century, when the commercial take was small, and when anglers were few, were before my time, I can be grateful for having lived during the past three quarters of a century. In this era I have seen many rivers when their runs were full and heavy and have watched, and been a part of, the development of the newer concepts of salmon fishing with lighter tackle, dry flies and nymphs, the hitched fly, and other basic changes from the traditional wet-fly fishing. I have known conditions on more than a hundred rivers when fishing was good, so good in fact that almost any day produced a few salmon and one in particular when I captured seventy-five (almost all of which were released, unharmed). Atlantic salmon fishing is for me, as I hope it will be for you, an intriguing thing which is not only a sport but an integral part of the joy of living.

These salmon are making one of the spectacular leaps they are famed for over the Humber Falls as they head upriver to spawn.

1

The Paradoxical Fish

he essential differences between angling for Atlantic salmon and for other game fish had their beginnings long before man ever thought of fishing. Over endless years in the slowly changing world, Nature's pattern has fitted this salmon into its own special niche, bestowing upon it interesting traits and characteristics quite at variance with our normal conception of how a fish should live and act. These living habits are of interest not only to the scientists who are ever asking the why and how of things but to every angler whose thoughts or efforts may turn toward this unusual and paradoxical fish. Without a basic understanding of this background no salmon angler will be very good at the sport or have the ability to enjoy it to the fullest.

The salmon is anadromous. He is one of that select group of fishes able to move from fresh water to the sea and back again, surviving a change which would be fatal to all other fish. He not only adapts organically to this sudden change but varies his coloration to match his surroundings. His life cycle takes him from the headwaters of the North Atlantic rivers to the broad expanses of the sea where he roams beyond the reach of man's most careful watchings.

The rivers are his nurseries and the sea his major source of food. In the flowing freshwaters the young salmon find suitable nourishment and hiding places, and the streams become crowded with their numbers. But in the sea they are a few among the throngs of regular sea inhabitants such as the cod, the mackerel, the herring, and similar species. For some strange reason Nature was not content to leave the streams to the trout, the largest of which would maneuver well in shallow inland waters and survive upon the food the streams produce. Instead a species was developed that returned hordes of mature salmon to the streams at spawning time. These salmon were too large to maneuver perfectly in confined waters and to support themselves upon the limited small forms of food available there.

Having brought these great, swift fish back to their rivers after a sea sojourn of ravenous feeding, it was essential that their appetites be curbed lest they try to live on their own young, which form the greatest share of the available food, and so contribute

Salmon in various stages of growth: The tiny parr (lower left) *may actually be between 3 and 5 years old, while both the grilse* (top) *and the adult salmon* (center) *may range between 4 and 7 years of age.*

to their own extinction. So we find great hordes of salmon, ranging in weight from a few pounds to more than forty, settling into the freshwater pools, sea-fed fish which the rivers themselves could not produce except by sending them out to board on the bounty of the sea.

The appetites of these returning, mature salmon are curbed to a very great degree but not so completely that they do not, on rare occasions, take a fly or bait. Therein lies the paradox that created fishing for a fish devoid of hunger, a fish larger and stronger than his surrounding waters could produce, confined to narrow pools and river channels where he cannot escape the sight of the fisherman's fly.

Throughout the spawning run the salmon loses strength and weight and, if he survives the long starvation and the strenuous spawning, he returns to the sea to enter another period of heavy feeding and further growth in preparation for an additional spawning visit to his river. The Atlantic salmon, *Salmo salar*, may survive to spawn a number of times while his namesakes, the Pacific salmon group, made up of five different species with the basic scientific name of Oncorhynchus, die of organic changes developing within their bodies during their first and only spawning cycle.

To look more closely at our Atlantic salmon let us begin with the egg lying in a typical streambed where it has just been deposited, fertilized, and covered over with gravel. The spawning time is the late fall. The days are growing short and the waters chill. The parent salmon have left, turning toward the comparative safety of the deeper pools or the greater safety and abundance of food to be found in the sea.

The development of the egg begins immediately after fertilization. During the cold months of winter such development, however, is very slow. In early spring, with the gradual warming of the water, the tail will break through the skin of the egg and the salmon enters upon his mobile stage as an alevin, a big-eyed baby less than an inch long with a great stomach formed by the egg sac from which he has hatched. He wriggles rather than swims at this stage and moves through the interstices in the gravel, developing his muscles. The contents of the egg sac nourish him as he strengthens until, when the sac is empty and he has assumed a more normal shape, he is able to fend for himself and feed on the microscopic life of the stream.

His early life parallels that of the small trout with which he shares the shallow waters and minor currents of the rivers. His back is brownish with a series of transverse bands or fingermarks extending down across his sides where bright red spots dot the iridescent silver. As he grows, he feeds ever more ravenously both underwater and on the surface. Small insects, both flying and aquatic, become the mainstay of his diet.

His stream growth is relatively slow, slower than that of his stream-mates, the trout. The average "parr," as the salmon of this primary freshwater stage are called, usually takes three or four years to develop. A very few salmon may complete the parr stage in slightly over a year; others may require five years or even longer to attain readiness for the trip to the sea. The growth is rapid at the start of the parr stage, tapering off occasionally toward the end of the period when a degree of maturity is reached and milt often develops in the male parr.

Much has been written of the speed, power, and leaping ability of the mature Atlantic salmon. The parr, for its size and weight, is perhaps even more wonderfully endowed with these attributes. On a still evening when the insects are hovering above the water one may see these salmon-in-miniature clearing the water in prodigious leaps to capture their winged food. A parr of four or five inches may leap well over three feet. They will attack a moth or butterfly almost as heavy as they are, leaping on it repeatedly, forcing it down into the water where it becomes sodden and unable to rise again. Then, when it is helpless in the water, they will tear it to shreds and devour it.

Parr will attack almost any small thing in the water that lives or moves, including the artificial flies of the anglers fishing for mature salmon. Some of the incongruity of salmon fishing becomes apparent with the realization that a 2-ounce parr will readily take a fly which at the moment is "too large" to entice a 20-pound salmon.

In fishing for salmon many parr are caught inadvertently, and a fair percentage of them are fatally wounded in the process. It is unfortunate that some careless salmon anglers, anxious to perpetuate their sport, should so often injure the young fish upon which they must depend for a sport a few years later. However, the loss of parr caused by anglers in not the major one. There are other enemies of many sorts at hand.

Parr live in the elemental world of eat and be eaten. The maturing parr is not discriminating in his diet. He will eat not only insects but small fish whether they be baby smelt, baby trout, or baby salmon sufficiently smaller than himself. Meanwhile mergansers, kingfishers, trout, eels, and other fish prey on the parr. Let us take an average egg, one of the 7,000 fertilized eggs of an average female of 9 pounds. Of these about 6,000 alevins hatch out. The loss during river life is estimated at about 90 percent. Our parr becomes one of only 600 survivors to complete the parr stage of development and start the journey to the sea.

With a little over three years of stream life behind him, a sudden change comes over our parr as the April waters rise. His dark fingermarkings begin to fade. His red spots grow dim and disappear. The mottled coat designed to blend in with the shifting shadows of the stream changes mysteriously until he becomes a miniature sea salmon, silvery of the sides and belly, darkly bluish black along the back. This is his protective coloring for the sea, as out of place in the river as his normal parr coat would be in the saltwater.

He makes the color change in advance because, apparently, the dangers of the river are far less for him in blue-black and silver than would be the dangers with his stream coloring in an unfamiliar sea. So, as he drifts and swims with the flooding waters of the spring freshets racing downstream to the sea, he is as prepared as Nature can make him to be invisible to his enemies in those vast expanses where there is nothing to hide behind and no mottling pattern of mixed sun and shadow in which to disappear. His back is shaded to dissolve into the darkness of the deep, deep waters below him when he swims beneath the preying seals. His belly is colored to lose itself against the silvery, light-reflecting surface of the water when some large and predatory fish looks up from below.

The toll by predators of this concentration of trim 5- to 7-inch baby salmon with their rounded tail lobes and overly large eyes is heavy, but at any other time of the year it would be heavier. As a favorable factor there is more water in the rivers at this time of melting snows to build a great cushion of brackish water at the river's mouth into which the true saltwater inhabitants dare not enter.

Our bright, new smolt has the coloring, speed, stamina, and foraging ability to survive. He and his family group of 600 and other groups of his year's crop, as well as precocious parr of shorter river life and laggard parr of earlier spawnings, ride in and out with several tides to adjust to the shock of changing from fresh water to salt water. This variation of the time parr spend in freshwater and the time the salmon spend in the sea forms one of Nature's safety factors. Even if one year's run of salmon or of smolts were to be completely annihilated there would still be others in the sea and stream to carry on.

The smolts, leaving the river, spread out into the sea. On one tide the brackish water will be swarming with them and on the next they will have gone.

No one knew where they went or why until, in the late 1950s, the sea feeding grounds of many of the Atlantic salmon were discovered. Gill nets spread out in the sea off Greenland captured Atlantic salmon that had come there to feed from both sides of the North Atlantic. The Greenland cod fishery was in a decline, and Greenland's commercial fishermen turned their efforts to the taking of Atlantic salmon. With the success of the Greenlanders, other nations joined in to capture these valuable fish. Those were the days of the 3-mile and 12-mile limits (3 miles in Greenland), and great fishing ships of many nations, regardless of whether their rivers produced any of the salmon which came to this rich feeding grounds or not, joined in a race to see how many they could catch while the stock lasted.

Fortunately, through the efforts of American anglers and commercial fishermen, an American threat to boycott Danish goods (Denmark controlled Greenland), and the establishment of the 200-mile limit stabilized the situation. Now the Greenland's territorial waters extend out to cover the salmon's feeding grounds there, so that the catch is now shared between those who produce and those who feed these salmon, and out of necessity, catch rules are more reasonable.

The salmon taken in the nets off Greenland are basically fish in their second year of sea feeding, weighing in the neighborhood of 8 pounds. Fish not captured off Greenland will increase their weights by about 40 percent between the fishery period of August and September off Greenland and the return to their native rivers the following spring. Their food off Greenland's southern shore is mainly shrimp and capelin, a small smeltlike fish that flourishes in the North Atlantic and is also a basic food of cod, whales, and sea birds. It is the shrimp-feeding that gives the salmon flesh its reddish color.

We still have much to learn about the habits of the salmon in the sea. We are finding that there is another sea feeding ground, similar to that off Greenland, located northwest of the Faroe Islands, another Danish possession which lies northwest of Scotland. Salmon from the rivers of northern Europe which were previously free from sea harvest are being taken there in considerable quantities with drastic results to the angling in their native rivers.

Sea-ranching of salmon is now going on in the Faroes (and at other places). Atlantic salmon are reared to the smolt stage in captivity, released into a stream at a point close to the sea, and then, true to their homing instincts, they return to their point of release where they are harvested. They return, that is, if they are not intercepted at the feeding grounds some 70 miles northwest of their home base on the Faroes. The salmon ranchers, quite naturally, do not enjoy having their "private stock" taken over by someone else far away at sea in a net many miles long.

All this calls for international treaties and agreements among the salmon-producing and salmon-feeding nations. The feeding grounds of the salmon may change. New ones may be discovered. Fairly dividing the capture of salmon among the involved nations will be a problem far into the future. Not only commercial but angling interests are involved.

One great puzzle still remains. Where do the grilse, the one-year sea-feeding salmon, spend their time in the sea? During the fishery period—August and September—in Greenland and the Faroe Islands, these little salmon would be about the size of full-grown mackerel. Their whereabouts are still as much of a mystery to us as the sea locations of all salmon were a quarter of a century ago. It is almost certain that with our increasing technologies for tracking and location we will soon find out.

Grilse have become an increasingly important segment of the total salmon stocks. Our netting and angling laws have caused the taking of the big fish and a decrease in their numbers and breeding power while the number of the heavily protected grilse has increased inordinately. A severe sea harvest of grilse would be a heavy blow to the salmon stocks and to salmon anglers in particular.

The smolts that will become grilse are so few compared with the other fish of the sea's great expanse they become lost in its vastness. Only scattered reports come in to tell us where one salmon—or a few—passed by and were seen or captured.

OPPOSITE PAGE LEFT: This smolt was intercepted on its way to the sea in early June on Portland Creek in Newfoundland. Smolt are distinguished from parr in part by their coloration, which consists of silver sides and belly and a bluish back. RIGHT: Sexually ripening male and female grilse.

Occasionally salmon are seen near shore and near the surface during their sea period on movements not connected with the spawning run. Near Twillingate on Newfoundland's northern shore and along the Labrador side of the Strait of Belle Isle large salmon in the 20-pound range have been seen hugging the shore rocks in December. Some localities report good catches of such mature fish at off-seasons and in sections far from any salmon river.

Codfish, caught many fathoms down off the mouths of rivers, have had smolt in their gullets indicating that some, at least, follow the lower levels of the sea. A further indication of their deep travel lies in their choice of food. Scientists attribute their red-pink flesh to a diet of crustaceans of a shrimplike nature, which in northern waters may be found at a considerable depth.

Salmon are active fish and excellent leapers. They will jump freely when played on angling tackle. Tuna and mackerel, which do not jump when played by anglers, often drive schools of baitfish to the surface and come clear of the water when they rush up toward the surface through the schools. It is reasonable to believe that salmon, if they fed on school fish near the surface, would also be seen breaking the water as they fed but that is not the case with the grilse. We do know at what depth they travel and feed.

A study was made involving the tagging of smolt on certain rivers and tabulating reported captures. In the case of tagged fish from three New Brunswick rivers—the Pollet, the Dungarvon, and N. W. Miramichi—the results of 1,452 recaptures showed the salmon taken over a wide area of the ocean in nets but *only in the river of their origin* by anglers. The bulk of the fish reported were taken in the New Brunswick areas, but almost a third were taken on the northeast shore of Newfoundland, 600 miles away by airline and far, far more by the shortest sea route. Fifteen were reported from Labrador. Inasmuch as the New Brunswick fishery check was relatively complete while the check of the Newfoundland and Labrador fisheries comprised only 85,000 out of a total 1953 catch of 310,000 salmon, it is likely that four times as many fish would have been reported in a complete coverage of those areas. This indicates that perhaps half or more than half of the fish of a given river may be taken in nets in another province 1,000 miles away.

Salmon, almost without exception, return to their native rivers for spawning. Within the rivers themselves there is reason to believe that salmon return to the particular branch of the stream where they orginated. There are streams in which salmon run up two out of three branches but not the third, though to the human eye all three are similarly suitable for spawning of salmon. Only on rare occasions do salmon become lost at sea and fail to find their way back to their own streams. This homing instinct is a thing we humans find hard to understand. We try to reduce it to a simple basis but the salmon's secret has so far eluded us.

The salmon of each river or part of a river seem to operate as a group. They will normally be very similar in physical characteristics. The fish of one river may be uniformly chunky and heavy for their length while those of another river, emptying into the sea only a few miles away, will be consistently slim.

An excellent example of this is to be found in the North River and the Eagle River of Labrador, both of which empty into Sandwich Bay. The North River is filled with fast-water runs and very few quiet resting places. There are no lakes in its drainage. The Eagle in contrast, rises in a great network of lakes and flows in a smoother fashion

Spectacular leaps at the Humber Falls.

A male (top) and a female (bottom) that were caught at the Humber Falls in Newfoundland in July 1938.

with very little white water. The salmon of the North River are long and lean, designed for hard travel. Those of the Eagle are typical of most Labrador salmon, neither lean nor chunky. There is no mistaking the North River fish.

Where introductions of salmon spawn are made to a river, a type of salmon at variance with the original stock may be established and they will be recognizable among the returning fish in the years that follow the stocking. Eventually they will merge.

Salmon have well-developed senses of smell or taste. The parr have spent several years in the river environment. The taste of the water must become as familiar to them as the air we breath. They can be depended upon to recognize the mixture of smells of their particular watershed as well as we can recognize the smells of our own surroundings. The smell of newly mown timothy hay or the fragrance of a pine forest are examples. Anyone brought up in a country of pine woods would certainly know he was not at home in a grove of maples and would recognize the pine scent again when he found it. We can be certain that the waters of no two salmon rivers will be exactly alike.

We do not know whether salmon remember their route to sea and follow it back or whether they cut across the seas directly in their migrations after the fashion of a homing pigeon, whether they follow the ocean currents or, occasionally, fight them.

In the nature of their specialized lives a homing instinct is important and we know they manage it somehow. If salmon did not return to their native rivers but went where convenience or flow of tides took them each season some rivers would be overcrowded and spawn would be wasted, while still others would be almost barren of fish with a consequent waste of good reproductive potential. Since it is most important to their survival to have a homing instinct, salmon have it.

Even more amazing, perhaps, than the homing instinct that brings the salmon back so unerringly to his own river is the special knowledge that lets the fledging salmon, the smolt, find his way among the varied ocean currents to the richest feeding grounds for his species in the whole North Atlantic. The understanding of this amazing ability still remains beyond us. Just how it works we may one day discover.

The tagging of fish and their subsequent recapture have given us but a very slight knowledge of the grilse's travels in the sea. Where the grilse spend most of their time and why remains a mystery. They disappear into the darkening depths of the ocean without a trace to reappear miraculously changed. In the interim they have grown from smolts of an ounce or two to salmon of anywhere from 2 to 7 pounds. At the end of slightly over a year's sea feeding, our 6-inch smolt has becomes a 2-foot salmon, small of head and with a slight V in the back of his tail, and many salmon of this size enter the rivers in their spawning run.

The salmon at this stage of development are amazingly swift and are ready leapers. They range in weight from 2 pounds to as much as 7 depending upon such factors as heredity and feeding. The bulk of them, however, will be in the 4- to 5-pound category. A grilse by definition is not a salmon below a certain weight but a fish with approximately thirteen months sea feeding. There may be 7-pound grilse in one river and 3-pound "salmon" in another. Grilse from one section of a river may be uniformly large while those of a different and more difficult-to-reach spawning section may run uniformly small although the two groups work up through the better part of the stream's length together.

Not all salmon return to their rivers after only thirteen months at sea. Others, our particular smolt among them, stay on longer in the sea. They continue to grow at a rapid rate. Two full years of sea life will give them a weight of from 8 to 15 pounds. Three years can turn a smolt into a twenty-five-pounder. Others, continuing on with their sea feeding, will be even larger when they return to their rivers.

Our smolt-become-a-salmon returns to the river with a run made up of several variations of the cycle. The first wave of fish to enter, predominantly two-sea-year fish, have entered the river two weeks earlier, not long after the current crop of smolts had disappeared in the sea. Our fish, after three sea years, weighs 20 pounds and enters just as the main run of grilse is returning. In one pool he rests beside two 5-pound grilse, one of which is his own age, the other two years younger. At another time he was the largest of a group, the others all two-sea-year fish with a nearly uniform weight of 11 pounds. Once he lay in the shadow of a forty-pounder that had spent four solid years of feeding in the sea, then spawned and was returning for a second spawning.

In late October our big male salmon finds a mate and together they move to the gravel beds well upstream in the main river. He fights with other males when necessary and drives away sea trout and eels bent on eating up the spawn. When the female has brushed a depression in the gravel and deposited a few eggs in it, our male moves in and spreads milt to fertilize them. The eggs are covered up, the spawning continues. Little by little the mound of gravel is built up. Periodically both fish return to the pool to rest. They return again and again to the gravel until all their eggs and milt are spent. Spawning activity takes place both in daytime and at night with by far the greatest activity taking place at night. Salmon are extremely vulnerable while working thus in the very shallow water which may only partly cover their bodies, and they prefer the cover of night's dark blanket.

Should either male or female have eggs or milt remaining when the other's supply has been exhausted he or she will seek a new mate and continue the spawning to make a maximum contribution to the future. Although salmon normally pair up with others of proportionate size, there may be small males attending large females and even well-developed parr may hover near the beds to spread their milt precociously on the eggs of a mature female. The spawning action extends over a period of a week or more and, when both fish are spent, the female drops back to the pool while the male stays on near the eggs for some time longer. Perhaps he stays to guard the eggs a while, perhaps for some strange reason beyond our ken. Eventually he, too, drops back to the greater safety of the pool. His mate survived and soon returned to the sea but our male, weakened beyond recovery by his exertions, his work done, saw the eels close in to tear at his gills and stain the water with his life's blood.

Spawning costs the surviving salmon about 40 percent of their weight. The ordeal coupled with the long period of starvation which accompanies it is so rigorous that only a small percentage of females and an even smaller percentage of males survive to spawn again. In a given watershed the mortality rate may be as high as 95 percent and is rarely lower than 80 percent. In general, not one salmon in ten of the spawning run will have spawned before. Salmon die from the rigors of floods and from attacks of enemies within the rivers. They are killed by otters, eagles, and eels, yet on rare occasions salmon have been caught when on their way upriver to spawn a fifth time.

This trim female salmon was caught on Fox Island River in 1940. The dark spots near the anal fin of this hen fish, blown up in the right-hand photograph, are sea lice, often found on salmon fresh from the sea.

The descent to the sea is a critical period. Rivers with an easy return to the salt water have a higher rate of survival. Some salmon are able to return to the ocean in late fall before the rivers freeze over and the ice locks them in pools till spring. Descending salmon are normally so weak they head upstream into the current but are washed slowly downstream because their swimming speed is less than the speed of the flow. There are few birds or animals large enough or fierce enough to catch and kill a salmon in the stream when he is strong, but when he is thus weakened a bear, an eagle, even an osprey or mink can manage it. An eel, biting deep and twisting away with a small chunk of flesh, may kill a salmon by attrition. There is danger from disease in their weakened condition. Even anglers, fishing for the early, fresh-run fish may hook and play these tired fish, some of which may still be backing down the rivers as June wanes into summer. In one province fishing for these spent and hungry "black" salmon is permitted. Even though released after being played the effort may be great enough to preclude survival. Dangers in the stream are many but they are few compared to the saltwater predators who gather as the remnants of the previous spring's full run come drifting back, exhausted, to the sea.

Those who make it safely to the sea mend swiftly. Strength and speed return and they resume their sleek and solid look. Being mature they rarely wait more than a year before the spawning urge drives them back to the river again. The nature of this cycle makes it plain that the grilse or smaller salmon on their maiden spawning venture have but the slimmest chance of ever becoming sizable salmon. Assuming a grilse enters the river at a 5-pound weight, if he spawns and survives to return to the sea the following spring, he will have lost nearly half of his weight and will drift downstream, spent and worn as other fish of two years' sea feeding that went to sea when he did will be ascending the streams for the first time weighing in the neighborhood of 10 pounds. If he does survive the recuperative period in the sea and ascends the river a second time in the following summer he will be in company with maiden salmon who went to sea when he first went but their weight, instead of being about 8 pounds like his, will be 20 or 25. Discerning anglers will keep grilse for food but return the large salmon to the river in order to let these big fish spawn and so provide more future fish with a tendency for a longer initial stay at sea and a greater weight when they come back to the river.

An example of the adaptability of salmon to their surroundings is seen in the rivers of Ungava Bay. Fishing the Delay (a tributary of the Kohsoak, one of the great long rivers) I found that the salmon of this far-north open country had insects or other food in their stomachs. This was in late June, in the mid-1970s. I caught one female fish with half-developed eggs in her. Inasmuch as the runs of fresh salmon from the sea occur in that area in late August or September, this had to be a fish that had come in the previous summer. Far-northern fish are slow in growing and require longer to develop. The fact that these fish, or at least some of them, take two years to complete their river spawning run is quite interesting. Studies are continuing. These salmon are probably unique in this characteristic, which is fortunate. If all salmon took two years for their spawning runs and fed to a greater degree in the streams, they'd be much more vulnerable to anglers, and the sport of bringing them to a fly would be far less challenging.

How big do salmon get? Records have not been well kept on this side of the Atlantic, and one is never safe in assuming the largest authenticated catch is truly the largest. A friend who fished the Humber in the old days, showed me a picture of a salmon taken by Dr. Jack Fisher that he said weighed 57 pounds. There are probably many instances on many other rivers where great salmon were taken by anglers who did not certify or even photograph their catches. The largest certified catch of an Atlantic salmon on tackle in Canada or the U.S. is 55 pounds, caught in 1939 by a lad of fifteen—his first salmon. Many fish of this approximate size have been taken, but they are scarcer now than they were years ago.

European records are better. Largest rod-and-line fish for the British Isles, though perhaps not taken on a fly, is 67 pounds for sure, with a possible 69-pound-12 ounce top. In Norway there is a 79-pound-2-ounce record. There is also a record of a 103-pound-2-ounce salmon taken in a net on the Devon River in Scotland. Our own salmon taken by nets often include very large fish which are not recorded. It is probable that if the whole of New England was still salmon territory, the world's largest recorded salmon might have come from this area and we, too, might have 70-pound salmon on rod and line to boast about. Perhaps, in some far future day, our grandchildren may see them.

Although we know little else of the salmon's sea life we know these things for certain. A salmon's scales grow in rings like the trunks of trees and just as we can tell a tree's age by counting the annual rings, we can read on the scales of each salmon the general picture of his growth.

There is no uniform time period for the rings on a salmon's scales. The average is about twenty-six a year, although the number may be either more or less. In every case the rings on a scale represent equal intervals of time. Thus when the fish is growing rapidly, the spaces between the scale rings are relatively wide apart. When he is growing slowly they are relatively close together. Since the summer is the period of greatest and the winter the slowest growing period, the former is represented by a series of widely

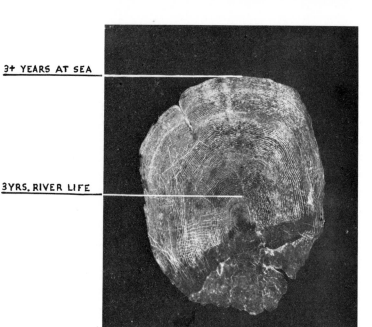

3+ YEARS AT SEA

3 YRS. RIVER LIFE

LEFT: A 31-pounder from the Lower Humber. RIGHT: A salmon's scale reveals a life history in much the same way that the rings in the trunk of a tree show its stages of growth. The outside, widely spaced rings indicate that this 31-pounder spent three or more years at sea; the close inner rings, that it swam the river as a parr for around three years. It was hooked on the Lower Humber in 1944.

spaced rings and the latter by a series spaced together. These dark and light bands are readily seen and each pair of them represents a full year's life. It takes a microscope to read the parr section when the fish is small and the rings are very fine and close together. The sea growth can be distinguished with a magnifying glass. Scales will tell us how many years a fish stayed in the stream, how many years in the sea. They can tell us, too, whether or not a salmon has spawned, and, if so, how many times.

The spawning period for a salmon is a period of starvation. From the time he leaves the sea until he returns to it again the salmon loses weight. His body shrinks and when he goes back to the sea again he may weigh little more than half as much as when he left the sea to spawn. His body has changed its shape. Because of his bone structure he can not shrink lengthwise. His head seems abnormally large, his tail massive, his fins outsized. All his shrinking is done in girth rather than in length.

His scales, too, have shrunk to fit his body, being absorbed in part during his period of fasting. Because his length remains unchanged the lateral dimension of the scales also remains the same. As his girth becomes less and less the scales are reduced in that dimension to fit his changing shape. In this process the outside rings are eaten away on the sides but not at front or back. The cut-off ends of the rings on the side of the scales are quite noticeable in a spawned-out fish as it returns to the sea.

When the hungry fish starts his heavy feeding again in the sea he not only fills out to his former well-rounded shape but begins to grow in length as well. The new growth rings begin around the outline of the shrunken scale just as the salmon wore it back to sea, preserving the spawning mark permanently where the original rings end abruptly at the new growth. Each spawning is marked indelibly in the scale's record of any salmon's life.

Salmon return to their rivers supercharged with energy, bringing in with them from the sea a store of strength great enough to power them through a hundred miles of upstream travel against rapids and over falls, through an arduous period of spawning activity, and then through a bitter cold winter. We think of a bear which simply fattens up, crawls into a cave and sleeps for three months as being unusual. The salmon dwarfs this feat by storing up enough energy not just for three months sleep but to maintain his activity for a period three times as long.

The salmon returning to his river from the sea has known its limitless space where he could swim for days on end without turning a corner, where his only safety lay in being able to outdistance his enemies or outmaneuver them, for in the sea there is nowhere to hide. These factors have added length to his runs and height to his leaps. He has a sense of space and distance no fish whose entire life has been spent within a small body of water can hope to attain. He has also a store of power no fish that renews his strength by day-to-day feeding can hope to equal.

Other fish may be bigger and stronger than the Atlantic salmon but none requires more delicate tackle to overcome the same amount of fighting fish. He is more likely to be caught on a fly less than an inch long than on a larger one. His choice of flies may be as small as a common mosquito tied to a leader as fine as sewing silk and breaking under a pull of no more than a pound and a half. Because of his life in the open waters, speed and agility have been the primary keys to his safety. He has no sanctuary but the deeper waters of the pool and must depend upon its length and breadth to insure his continued existence.

When hooked the salmon will not rush to wrap the line around a snag. At the end of a line he will sweep from one side of the long pool to the other, breaking into high, towering leaps. If a line is fouled it is only because, on one of his wild runs, some snag happened to lie between him and the angler, intercepting the line, not because he was trying to hide. In the wild recklessness of their struggles for freedom salmon have leaped clear of the streams out onto the banks and into the thickets of alders along the shores. It is not their instinct to seek shelter but to run and leap and run again. To a fish of the open sea any hiding place would seem like a trap.

A fresh-run salmon is likely to streak 150 or 200 yards of line off the reel in a single steady surge. The small head and shapely body are driven swiftly by his powerful tail. The broad pectoral fins give him great maneuverability, and help in making his amazing leaps that may carry him 10 feet or more into the air. When one considers the lure to which he rises, a small artificial fly which may be only one hundred thousandth part of his own weight, it is easy to understand why his devotees put him at the pinnacle of all angling.

When a salmon travels the river it is usually at night, except through high water after a heavy rain. In the evenings, when the river is in shape to run, there will be renewed activity among the salmon. They often circle the pools, swimming along just beneath the surface to mark the still waters with the sweeping wakes they leave behind them. With the settling of darkness they will work to the heads of the pools and move upstream, leaping as they go.

For generations salmon have rested in the same pools and pockets, choosing the same resting places year after year, hanging in the current almost motionless for hours,

A windless, misty morning holds the promise of a beautiful fishing day on the Moise River in Quebec.

or dropping to the streambed to rest on their broad pectoral fins with their bodies stretched out behind in readiness for an immediate getaway. A salmon may stay for days or even weeks in a single pool.

Back again in the narrow channels of his baby days a restlessness stirs him. He leaps from time to time and sometimes, for no apparent reason beyond the sheer exuberance from his own well-being, will make a sudden circuit like a young girl in love who breaks into impromptu dancing. He feels the gentle movement of the remembered but now unfamiliar fresh water as it caresses his body. The same restlessness leads him to rise now and again to take a floating bit of wood or catch an insect, perhaps to hold it, perhaps to spit out.

It is these rare periods of restlessness the angler must depend upon for his rises. In salt water salmon have been taken in nets and occasionally fresh-run fish in tidal pools have their stomachs crammed with food. Their rapid saltwater growth is a testament to their voracity at the sea but when the salmon settle in streams again their hunger leaves them. Nature takes away their ability to digest any food.

As he reaches the narrower sections of the river our salmon becomes shyer, more aware of the danger of his position. While it is possible to approach quite close to a fresh-run fish, a salmon that has been in the river for a while is prone to slip off into deeper water at the first movement toward him from the shore. The gaudy, brilliant fly-patterns, often deadly with the bright fish not long away from the sea, tempt the old fish little, and the smaller flies of neutral coloration, most like the insects of the stream, are those he will prefer. The longer a salmon stays in fresh water the less likely he is to rise to any of the angler's flies.

The Atlantic salmon is a leaping fish. He leaps over the falls and obstructions lying between the sea and his spawning grounds, sometimes making a clean leap of as much as 12 feet. He leaps when pursued by an enemy, a practice he shares in common with many other game fish. He leaps quite frequently for no apparent reason while resting in the pools during the long days and nights between his entry into fresh water and the spawning time. Anglers have long wondered about this apparently unnecessary leaping and tried to explain it to themselves.

It has been said salmon leap to settle the developing milt and spawn within their bodies. This may be true but other spawning fish like the trout and walleye have spawn develop, too, and find no such need to leap. There is a feeling in some quarters that salmon leap in order to shed parasites like the sea-lice that cling to their sides when they enter the rivers from the sea. These tiny parasites die within from a day or two to ten days after entering fresh water, and the salmon continue to leap just as freely after the sea-lice have died and fallen off.

The salmon's leap may be a symbol of repressed energy, an automatic release of tension for a high-strung and powerful fish forced by the nature of things to remain inactive while at the very peak of its physical well-being. Most logical of all is the theory that salmon as a species must be able to leap in order to ascend the turbulent waters and get up over the falls. An all-American football player doesn't make his rating by sitting on the bench, and a salmon, to become an expert leaper, must leap for practice. He must leap by the very nature of things. Even if all the other suggested reasons for salmon's leaping are true—or if none of them are—the salmon would still jump as he does, without apparent reason for it, so that when the need arises he will have the strength and the ability to climb the cascading white waters.

Although the heaviest run of salmon normally enters the rivers in the high-water periods of late spring, other lesser runs will follow. The later runs may reach the river mouths at a time when the streams are too low to travel, and then the salmon spend the waiting time cruising in and out with the tides in the brackish waters of the bays waiting for the rains to freshen and raise the river to a suitable traveling state. Delayed by stream conditions or for other reasons some part of the run may not enter the rivers until late in the fall, just in time for spawning.

When the early fish come from the sea the spawn and milt within them have just begun to develop. It hasn't grown to a point where its weight makes them heavy and

One of the thrilling leaps of a hooked salmon; the photo was taken by the author while playing the fish. River of Ponds—1941.

awkward. They are at top strength and fresh in their mind is the endlessness of the sea. Salmon reaching their spawning rivers later in the season are more nearly ready for spawning than were the early fish when they entered. Regardless of the time of entry into the river they will all spawn at about the same time for, in the continuing cycle of reproduction, it is essential that the eggs have the best chance of maturing. There is one best time for salmon to spawn in a given river and over the thousands of years of their existence it is certain they have settled on it.

Man has changed the salmon's life patterns drastically. In some of the smaller rivers, where poaching has been heavy, the salmon no longer come into the rivers early and rest in the pools to await the spawning time. If they did they would be vulnerable to nets and snagging. Instead, they develop their spawn and milt while still at sea and only enter the rivers in late fall, just in time to spawn. They come in on the fall spates that make the rivers high and dark, and they find safety in that darkness and in the heavy flows. This gives the angler little time to fish for them. They are dark and not as active as the bright spring fish, though they may bear sea-lice when caught. It is unfortunate that we cannot hook and play them at their best. It is better, though, that they have adapted to survive in spite of the poacher's treachery and that we still can catch these dark, reluctant risers at their own best time than have had them eliminated because they could not make the change.

The first signs of the spring run will be the sight of the silvery forms of the salmon as they flash into the air in the waters just off the coast, their backs dark with a rich, blue-black brilliance, their sides and bellies shimmering silver. They leap as they swim, throwing their sleek, hard bodies into the air as if revelling in their escape from the heavy pressure of the dark waters. They enter the rivers and slowly change their coloring. They do not, like a returning sea-run trout, revert to their early stream coloration. They will never again develop the red spots and brownish bandings of the parr, but they do take on a darker tone, losing the hard demarcation between the back's blue-black and the side's clean silver. In clear streams they turn a blend of gray or brown or reddish, mottled and sometimes spotted, dark above and light below. In the dark, peat-stained waters they may eventually become almost entirely black.

The male fish develops a hook on his lower jaw which fits against or into a corresponding recession in the upper one. This hook may become quite large and ungainly in some old males and is thought to be an aid in fighting off other males or in digging at the spawning beds. The heads of the males are larger than those of the females of the same weight. They are usually stockier and often deeper from dorsal to belly than females of the same length.

Both sexes lose weight proportionately as the days go by and their stored up fat is absorbed and used. The flesh, a brilliant red-pink when fresh run, slowly loses its tone and turns white. As spent spawners returning to the sea, they will be gaunt caricatures of the sleek, firm fish of the earlier season. Yet even as they ready for the trip back to the sea, while still in fresh water, their sides and bellies will suddenly brighten again to silver. Touch the silver and the light coating will come off. Place the silvery spent fish upon the bank and in half an hour its skin will dry and turn quite dark again. But the silver is there. Before they reach the sea and start their ravenous recuperation Nature touches them with her magic and makes them ready.

2

Salmon Fishing—Yesterday and Today

Salmon fishing goes back at least as far as the year 1426 when, in the *Treatyse of Fysshynge wyth an Angle*, an unknown writer put down: "The Samon is the moost stately fyssh that ony man maye angle to in fresshe water" and went on to describe the taking of salmon "wyth a red worme" and also "wyth a bobbe that bredyth in a dunghill and specyally with a souerayn bayte that bredyth on a water docke." His "it is seldom seen (taken) wyth a dubbe" tells us that fly fishing had begun but was not yet popular.

Thomas Barker, describing the art of angling in his book, *Barker's Delight*, had this to say in 1659 about playing a salmon: "You must be sure that you have your line of twenty-six yards of length, that you may have your convenient time to turn him; or else you are in danger to lose him. . . . You must forecast to turn the fish as you do a wild horse, either upon the right or the left hand, & wind up your line as you finde occasion in guiding the fish to the shore, having a good large landing hook to take him up." A salmon rod of Barker's day consisted of a 10-foot butt joint and a 6-foot tip. We can assume that the hook and the 26-yard line that "turned" his salmon were stout in proportion.

Today's leader may be as delicate as a cobweb, its hook a tiny bend of barbed steel. Today's line is long enough to let a salmon run his fill. Yet in this ancient sport there has been little real change save that the salmon have grown much scarcer and the erstwhile few salmon fishermen have become legion. The thrill of catching this "moost stately fyssh" has in no way lessened.

A Philadelphian once told of his efforts to lease some excellent salmon water in Quebec. He had learned of two anglers who were searching for a third to share with them the expense of a lease and the subsequent fishing. After a quick study of the situation, it became apparent to him that, in order to enjoy this superb angling, he would have to sell his house and Cadillac and get a loan against his salary. Inasmuch as his house is a large one in a fashionable section of the city and shelters his mother, son-in-law, and daughter as well as his wife and son, he regretfully decided to continue taking his salmon fishing where he could find it, in competition with the nets near the mouths of the rivers, and an ever increasing number of anglers on the pools. When the chips are down, it is dollars rather than words that determine what types of fishing are best. The Atlantic salmon fishing tops the list. It is wonderful and it is scarce.

Fishing for salmon is quite different from fishing for other stream fish. A given stream may produce a certain poundage of trout which live and forage within its length. They will spread all through the waters, and there will rarely be more than a dozen yards of stream length where a trout may not lurk to take an angler's fly. A trout stream may be fished anywhere from top to bottom with chances of success, while an average salmon river will have a pool only every mile or so, at best. A hundred anglers could fly fish for trout successfully and pleasantly on a stream where, if the waters were to contain salmon instead of trout, only half a dozen could have a comparable chance to catch a salmon. Furthermore, while the trout of the streams are reserved solely for the anglers, the stream's salmon must be shared with a commercial fishery which takes the lion's share of the annual production.

There is considerable conflict of ideas as to whether Atlantic salmon fishing waters should be open to the public, owned outright by individuals, or controlled in some manner between these two extremes. Less than half of the salmon water still existing in eastern North America is either under lease or ownership. That under public access has the poorer fishing, although those waters previously had an overwhelming share of the western Atlantic's salmon.

In private fishing the angler knows he will have certain waters to fish, either entirely for himself or as one of a controlled group. He knows in advance who his stream companions, if any, will be. He knows, too, that the fishing is fairly expensive and, if he leases it, feels it is worth the investment.

Public fishing is cheaper. It is of poorer quality per individual angler. For some it is excellent; others fish with almost no hope of catching a salmon. It is a rule of economics that eventually costs and prices seek their proper level. It can be expected that in the long run both types of salmon anglers will get just about what they pay for. This is only as it should be. The great danger is that in this conflict or in another between commercial netters and anglers there will be too little consideration given to the salmon's side of the story.

Unlimited public fishing for salmon, where the license fee is low and wherever salmon waters are readily accessible to anglers, soon results in very poor salmon fishing or none at all. There simply is not enough salmon fishing to go around. The salmon fishermen must be held within the numbers the pools can accommodate, or the quality of the sport suffers. The quantity of salmon taken from the rivers must be dictated, not by the number of anglers who want to take a certain number of salmon home, but by the number available without impairing the residual breeding stock. It is not a question of whether or not salmon fishing, or at least the killing of salmon must be limited, but of how it can be done with fairness for all.

There is a continuing movement by anglers to curb the take of the commercial fishermen through legislation. This is predicated on the basis that a salmon taken in the river brings a greater return to the province than it does when taken in a net. With the take in the rivers increasing through more widespread fishing by many more anglers, it would be necessary to reduce the sea catches by the increased river take in order to maintain a level. This has been resented by the sea fishers who are also endeavoring to increase their own take. They fail to see why the status quo should not be maintained. Neither group is particularly happy, and meanwhile the salmon are diminishing.

Fly-Fishing Only

Many a new Atlantic salmon angler is surprised to find the taking of these fish restricted to "fly-fishing only." Often a rebellious feeling is engendered. Why should we, the bait casters or the spin-fishermen, be discriminated against? There are good and logical reasons for the ruling.

The salmon is not a feeding fish and consequently is not attracted in anywhere near the usual degree by lures proportionate to his size. The lures most efficient in taking salmon are no larger than those used for trout in the one-half- to 2-pound class. They are far smaller than the lures in normal use for bass, pickerel, pike, walleyes, lake trout, and all the other major game fish commonly taken by bait casting or spinning. The most efficient and exciting way to present a small artificial fly is, unquestionably, with fly-fishing tackle.

Fly-fishing is not the easiest method to learn. It requires greater delicacy of movement, more accurate timing, and the coordination of both hands in the casting, stripping, and shooting of line. It takes months or even years of practice to learn to do it well. Bait casting takes a much shorter learning period, and spinning may be learned in a matter of minutes. It is this difficulty of learning the necessary coordination that brings forth the objections, but that is compatible, too. Atlantic salmon fishing is a sport to which one should graduate from lesser problems. It requires an understanding not usually found in beginners. The tradition of salmon fishing is of small flies, gently handled. The largest fish may rise to remarkable small flies which are beyond the bait caster's or the spin-fisherman's capabilities to present well.

The caster of metal lures may then say, "Ah, but in Europe they fish by spinning and bait casting with both lures and baits. Won't these western Atlantic salmon take a spoon or worm?"

The answer must be that these Atlantic salmon, too, will take a spoon, a worm, a bass bug, and other lures. They will not, however, in the broad picture, take them as well as flies. And by limiting the take to fly-fishing only, the take is slowed down and spread to more anglers over a longer period of time.

Atlantic salmon are in a serious decline. They once spread as far south on the Atlantic's western shores as the Delaware River. They were so plentiful in New England in the early 1800s that work contracts sometimes contained stipulations that men should not be fed salmon for more than a limited number of meals per week. The Connecticut River system, hundreds of miles long, was probably the finest salmon river on the continent, with the greatest run of salmon.

But the rivers were dammed up to run the mills, and both main rivers and tributaries were dammed for the driving of lumber and pulpwood. Pollution poured into the rivers from the mills as New England became highly industrialized. The salmon were considered expendable. They were spent so thoroughly that none but stray salmon were caught south of the Penobscot and, for a long period, few other than strays were caught in any Americn river until the recent restorations.

The recent restoration of salmon to the Connecticut and the Penobscot rivers

ABOVE LEFT: The first fly-fishing vest, short and many-pocketed, was designed and sewn by the author to keep flies ready-to-hand and out of the water. The photo was taken in 1933. ABOVE RIGHT: Before the vest: Arthur Sarkisian wearing what was then classic angler's garb.

The author in 1939 with a late-run salmon from Harry's River.

A salmon grievously wounded by net or seal bite will press on—and still take a fly.

from which they were extinct has been the result of a massive effort on the part of anglers and state and federal governments. Long years of work by anglers as well as dedicated people within the management groups to start the action have gone into the effort and, at this writing not only are the fish coming back and the rivers being freed from pollution but dams are receiving fish ladders to make entire watersheds available. The year 1981 showed a run of more than 500 salmon in the Connecticut and a capture by angling of over 1,000 salmon in the Penobscot. Fertilized eggs from the spawn of the Connecticut fish are building up a stock of truly "native" fish with maximum homing instincts and the ability to survive in that environment. The salmon restoration program in New England now assures fishing availability and a great promise of pleasure to both anglers and salmon watchers of the future.

Heavy netting, reaching to all the salmon shores with more and more efficient equipment, takes an increasingly heavy proportional toll of the salmon population. Anglers have multiplied nearly a hundredfold since the turn of the century. They are able to reach more rivers and cover them more thoroughly. Not only industrial wastes but the chemical sprays used to save the forests kill young salmon and their food. Salmon fishermen, in general, are agreed the very existence of their sport is threatened. Why, then, when too many salmon are already being taken from the spawning run before they have a chance to spawn, should we break tradition and permit additional methods of fishing which would mean the taking of even more fish?

The main reason for the fly-fishing-only rule lies in the difference between the European system of leased waters and the western Atlantic systems which permit public fishing to a considerable degree. Where an individual or a group control certain salmon waters, patrol them, and are responsible for their future, great care will be taken not to take too many fish and so endanger the breeding stock of the watershed. Where individuals or groups have a considerable investment involved and enjoy firm controls, they can be depended upon to guard their investments and keep the salmon populations up. Where waters are owned and the fish belong to the owner, there is every reason to fish them wisely.

However, when the average individual fishes for salmon under an inexpensive license, he has no such feeling of personal responsibility for the future of the fishing. If his license permits him to take six salmon in a day or week and there are only six in the stretch of river he fishes, he is likely to try to get them all, not knowing, and sometimes not caring, whether they are just a few out of an abundance or the sole remnant of the entire river's run. Not being motivated by a deep concern for the future, he may even be willing to fish in an illegal manner in order to get what he feels is his share of fish. If the salmon should disappear from the river, as they have from many streams in the past fifty years, he has lost no tangible investment. He simply doesn't buy a license when they are gone, and neither he nor anyone else fishes salmon there.

Where the river is under strict control and wisdom dictates a certain number of salmon can be taken without damage, it is of little import to the future of the sport whether they are taken by fly-fishing, spinning, or spearing. But in the case of public fishing, or where numerous unorganized owners must share a river's run, it is reasonable to insist on the taking of the fish by methods best fitted to give a fair distribution of the sport and the fish to all and to attempt to hold the catch within certain limits. If the unscrupulous angler were permitted to fish with weighted flies or other heavy lures commonly used in spinning and bait casting, he could foul-hook salmon after salmon and it would be very difficult to prove these fish had not made a rush for the lure, missed it, and were hooked by the angler, inadvertently, in the side or belly. Because salmon are so large and conspicuous in the pools they rest in, so easily seen, and, in most cases, so easily approached, this "jigging" of salmon, as it is often called, is relatively easy to accomplish.

Jigging is like an unclean disease. It is an easy way of taking fish and many an unworthy angler takes advantage of it. There is no salmon anywhere in fresh water but may be caught fairly on a fly if certain conditions are met. Admittedly there are places where salmon are extremely hard to take. There were more of them before dry flies came into use. It is impossible to say that any salmon under any stream conditions cannot be drawn to some type of fly. This being so, it is difficult to condone the foul-hooking of salmon, or even consider the relaxing of a ruling which holds the angler to fly-fishing and greatly deters the foul-hooking of fish, for under the present ruling, the user of weighted flies or heavy lures is open to prosecution.

The angler who foul-hooks a fish admits to himself he is not good enough to hook that salmon with a fly and is selfish enough not to give anyone else a chance. Perhaps the worst part of jigging lies in the false impressions it can create.

A story of a personal experience will illustrate how sport may be spoiled. Many years ago I happened upon a well-known guide in the act of playing a fish he had foul-hooked. Before he knew I was present I had taken a photograph of him with his rod bent double and the twenty-pounder up on the surface with the fly and sinker showing at his side. How good the photograph was he couldn't know, but he was quite worried lest I report him. A stranger in a foreign land, I did not. After that he went out of his way to be friendly and amazed me with his fishing skill and understanding. He pointed out the best places to fish, explaining his hard-won knowledge of the river. He fished regularly when not employed as a guide but because he was known to foul-hook fish frequently, his local reputation was bad. He had a family and was poor, and he just couldn't pass up a chance to foul-hook a fish once he's located him and made a few passes over him with a fly, provided, of course, no one was watching.

He told me of the lengths to which he had sometimes gone to avoid detection as a "jigger," carefully pasting down scales from another part of the body over the telltale wound in the salmon's side, back, or belly, after sewing the skin back together with painstaking care. One day, he found conditions just right. In a particularly good pool a new group of fish had just come up from the sea and, within the first few casts, he hooked and landed a fifteen-pounder on one of his favorite flies, a small Blue Charm. Continuing to fish in a proper and gentlemanly way he was able, within a two-hour period, to take three more fine fish by his skill and tackle artistry.

This time there was no need to repair the fish. All four were without a hookmark save in their mouths. No one else had been on hand to witness this wonderful catch in a hardfished river, where taking four such big salmon in a morning was a most unusual feat. If he carried them proudly back to the settlement, no one would believe he had caught them honorably. Furthermore he was sure there would be talk, and that an increase of vigilance on the part of the warden would follow. Instead of enhancing his standing as a guide such a display would only add to the unsavoriness of his reputation. Instead of showing his catch and getting the praise and acclaim the accomplishment deserved, he hid three of the fish in the bushes beside the pool and sneaked all four

ABOVE: Angler and quarry on Fox Island River in 1940. RIGHT: Guide Ned Brake holds a 42-pound salmon taken by angler Harold Butler on the Lower Humber.

home, one at a time, over a thirty-six-hour period, during which he didn't dare fish for fear of complicating his problems by catching still another salmon.

Unfortunately, the foul-hooking of salmon may not be difficult and the deliberately foul-hooked fish is usually landed. In the first place, fine leaders and small hooks, the factors calling for utmost skill in playing a salmon, are rarely used by the outlaws who have little difficulty in getting their weapons close to the fish. Although a salmon hooked in the body is harder to pull in because he cannot be headed toward the angler by the tackle's pull, the poacher's heavier gear and larger hooks more than offset that advantage for the fish. If the tackle is strong enough to hold a foul-hooked fish he will drown swiftly after his first wildness.

The basic reason why the fly-fishing-only regulation exists on our rivers is because not all licensed fishermen can be trusted. Any angler with a weighted lure or fly, a fly with more than two hook points, or any device designed to foul-hook a fish, is automatically suspect and subject to prosecution. If anything heavier than a regulation fly were permissible for salmon fishing, the problem of protection would be insurmountable.

A word about illegal netting may be fitting at this point. Obviously, if it were legal to stretch a net completely across a salmon river, the entire run of salmon for that river could be wiped out within a few years. Nets, therefore, are limited to the salt water beyond the "caution boards" or markers which are set by officials at the point within which they feel the salmon do not have a fair chance of escaping them as they approach the river. These markers may be as close as 200 yards on either side if the river flows directly into the sea on a straight shoreline, or perhaps as far away as a mile or more when the bay into which the river flows is narrow and the salmon inside the markers would be channelled too effectively into nets, were they permitted closer.

Illegal netting is done by poachers in the pools of the rivers. This activity is carried on discreetly, occasionally in isolated sections by day, but for the most part at night. It is difficult to net a river when the water is very high for the fish are not concentrated and it is hard to keep the net in place. When the water is low, it is easy to take every salmon in a pool, leaving it completely barren. A salmon river without salmon is a sad thing. As long as the fish are there the angler can have his sport whether he catches one fish, several, or none at all. In an empty pool there is nothing for the angler to enjoy.

The problem of control and protection of salmon waters is far from simple. If it were possible to set a yearly quota of salmon for each river, and once that number had been taken, rigidly protect the rest, we might well permit the use of many types of tackle and lures, even to the use of spears which call for a skill and judgment often greater than that demanded of an angler. As long as we operate on a system of open and closed seasons, or allow fishing for salmon whenever or wherever they are in the rivers, without sufficient sanctuaries, the catch must be limited by the fishing methods permitted, by the number of anglers, or by the individual's catch limit, a system far from perfect.

Black Salmon

There is some argument as to the relative merits of the fresh-run, or "bright" salmon in comparison with the spring, spent, "black," or slink salmon which are those caught on their way back to the sea after spawning. One advocate of fishing for black salmon in the early spring was even more convinced of the quality of that sport after he caught his first bright, fresh-run fish. He took that well-rounded silvery fish during a severe dry spell in a small pool. Since it had nowhere to run, the fish was landed—after a long time—without having taken any backing off the reel. At lunch that day he remarked that his fish of the morning had been nowhere as difficult to take as the spawned-out fish he had caught in the early season's high waters.

He might well have clung to that belief indefinitely had it not been for a three-day rain that brought the river up to bank-full running. On his last morning, he hooked another bright salmon in the same pool, which by then was filled with a raging flow. Not only did the fish get into his backing, but when it came to the end it snapped it neatly and departed with everything except the rod and reel. Only then did the angler realize that in flood waters even a tired and hungry spent fish will put up a good scrap, but that a bright salmon under the same conditions will make the black fish look like a piker.

Black-salmon fishing is permitted on some of the New Brunswick rivers. Everywhere else it is prohibited. The spent fish, having wintered over in the rivers, has taken on a light coat of silver and is headed for the sea. He has regained his hunger and takes a big fly readily. The spring rains and the melting snows have built the rivers up to heavy volume, and when hooked he does the best he can to escape. He will jump a few times. He will run a little but, for the most part, the angler is pitting his tackle against the power of the current. Even a completely dead salmon or a wooden replica of one would take a bit of time and work to bring in through such heavy water.

Black salmon are hungry and for them large flies are better than small ones. Streamer flies, long slender imitations of small fish, are most commonly used. If large spoons and bass plugs were permitted, they would be very effective. A whole capelin or a herring would be even better. The spent salmon would strike them eagerly. Then, after they'd spent their small store of energy, they would come to shore. Almost without exception those anglers who have experienced the capture of more than a few bright

The still waters of Western Pond.

salmon will admit there is no comparison as to their fighting qualities and that far greater skill is required for the bright fish.

If an angler keeps a spent fish and throws it on the bank, its silver will soon fade and it will turn dark and drab. Its flesh will be white and poor. It is edible, but most anglers don't and won't eat it. If the fish is returned to the water, he may survive and get back to the sea but, because he is already weak, he well may not. The law limits an angler to a daily take of one black fish and lets him hook only five fish, the latter being a difficult rule to enforce. No gaffing is allowed.

Is there nothing good to say about black-salmon fishing? There are these things to say. In answer to the bright-salmon partisan who says that taking a spent fish which would come back in a year or less weighing nearly twice its weight is a move against conservation. "You are right. But the taking of a bright salmon on its way to spawn is an even greater move against conservation. The bright salmon on its way to the spawning ground has a very good chance of getting there to spawn. The spent fish has less than one chance in twenty of living long enough to get back to the river where it then stands the same chance the bright salmon has to make the spawning grounds safely. If there is any question about which angler is taking a heavier toll of the future salmon population, the odds are all in favor of it being the bright-salmon angler."

Studies on the Miramichi indicate the great bulk of the black salmon taken by anglers is of the previous season's late run, entering the rivers in September, October, and November, almost half of the total coming in after the legal fishing season has closed. If they were not fished for as black salmon they would not be fished for at all.

Black-salmon fishing was inaugurated in 1939. Its popularity has grown and the tourist return from the spring fishing season in New Brunswick is considerable. With bright-salmon fishing falling off in quality in recent years, an increasing number of people have a much better chance of getting black fish than the bright-salmon anglers do.

Black-salmon fishing is more fun than catching some of the other game species. They have more fight, or at least as much as a lake trout or a pike. They leap, which is always a thrill for an angler. They are big, a far bigger fish than most anglers are able to catch on a fly rod in a stream in any other way. They're caught in a swift flow of water which makes landing them a fair tackle problem. It isn't even necessary to be able to cast to catch one, as they may be taken by simply trailing the line behind the canoe.

For spent-salmon fishing, a heavy fly rod is in order. Other requirements are good reel and adequate line and backing, a good stout leader of any convenient length, and a streamer fly from size 2 up to 2/0. It is doubtful if the pattern is very important. Take along a few Mickey Finns—or some tarpon flies. One can buy suitable flies at fishing camps or stores in the area. The biggest problem will be locating the fish. They're ravenously hungry, like a bear in the spring. One final recommendation: if you like to eat fish, take along some canned or smoked bright salmon—or a good recipe for an all-disguising fish sauce.

3

Why A Salmon Takes A Fly

f it could be proven absolutely that the Atlantic salmon never feed in fresh water on their spawning run, there would be no attempt to tie flies as insect imitations. If it were not extremely difficult, if not impossible, to prove that they do feed at all in fresh water, then salmon fishing would not be the remarkable sport it is. In truth, scientists say, an Atlantic salmon returning to fresh water cannot physically digest food, though he may try.

Consider these returning hordes of fish which have fed in the sea to such advantage. Is there anything in fresh water to approximate the vast shoals of shrimp or capelin or herring they are accustomed to feed upon? The salmon rivers have little to offer except a few insects and a fair quantity of salmon parr or lesser trout, and the eels, large trout, kingfishers, mergansers, and others are already preying upon all these smaller forms of life. If the salmon tried to maintain their strength by feeding, they would not only clean up almost all the immature salmon but would eat all the small living things on which the parr feed and still be hungry. To say that they do try to feed in fresh water but are balked by their size cannot be true. Trout of 5 pounds and larger manage to feed quite regularly, but smaller salmon, swifter and more able physically, are always empty-stomached. Fish a 6-inch smelt through a pool, and trout after trout will try to take it. Almost never a salmon.

When caught in fresh water, the stomachs of salmon are consistently empty. In not more than one salmon in many thousands will the slightest trace of food be found. The arguments that the salmon empty their stomachs, ejecting the contents when hooked, or that their digestive processes are so fast nothing can hope to be found in them, do not hold true. In the first place, anglers who have caught thousands of salmon, many of them in clear water from a vantage spot, would have seen the salmon eject food, and this has not been the case. Secondly, if the processes are so rapid, then nothing would be found in salmon taken in the salt water or brackish water, which is not the case. This poses an insurmountable problem to many a beginning salmon fisherman. To them it is inconceivable that a fish that will take a fly will not take other food and is not a "feeding fish."

A big fish on a big river.

Of considerable interest in this regard was the catching of a 5-pound grilse with four 6-inch capelin in its stomach. Digestion had barely started. Arthur Sarkisian caught that fish while we were fishing the Tidal Pool of Castor's River in 1954. Obviously the salmon had been feeding heartily in the nearby salt water (capelin are never found in the streams) just prior to his entering the river and stopping to rest in the Tidal Pool. The fact that his stomach was thoroughly filled had not prevented his taking a #8 Blue Charm. His interest in the fly would hardly seem to have been hunger, and the capelin indicated no ultrarapid process of digestion.

One of the most diligent fishermen I ever met was a novice at salmon. The water was high and the run just in from the sea. He hooked a number of parr on his first morning, and as he brought one of them skittering in for releasing, a good-sized fish made a pass at it. It may have been a salmon but it is a little more likely to have been a big sea-run trout that had swirled up out of a very real and well-established hunger. But the angler was convinced it was a salmon and his guide, a bit diffident about contradicting him, let him think so. He became convinced salmon wanted food and, though it was illegal, he bribed his guide with rum to let him use bait.

He ran the gamut of all the baits he could lay his hands on, including worms, salmon eggs, pork rind, bacon, beef, and lamb. These were usually offered in good-sized chunks on the "big bait, big fish" theory. He did hook a fish briefly, but it never jumped and held to the deep water. It showed a flash of silver just once before it got away. It could have been a salmon, and again it could have been a big sea trout come into the river earlier than usual. Had there been many big sea trout in the river, I'm sure he would have caught quite a few. They do not respond well to the small salmon flies, and, since no one else was breaking the law to fish with bait, none were caught. At any rate, that angler never wavered in his belief he had hooked a salmon.

He fished with flies when other anglers were around but as soon as he and his guide were alone, one or another of his assorted baits went splashing out to where he'd seen salmon leaping. Twenty-two good fish were caught during his week on the river, but only one of them fell to him. He caught it while others were watching and he had to fish with a fly.

A salmon can store up enough energy to climb rivers and go through an arduous spawning period without feeding for an incredibly long time. Once an angler accepts this fact he can begin to understand salmon fishing. If he keeps thinking that food interests salmon he will, in all probability, remain ever utterly bewildered by this swift and beautiful fish.

After having been convinced a salmon does not feed in fresh water to any appreciable degree, the fisherman may discover one rising to an occasional mayfly or flinging himself wildly in the air for a small white butterfly. Such an angler once said to me, "You say they don't feed, but the big one I've been trying to catch took three bugs off the water."

"You've been fishing for that salmon for a week, all day and every day," was the reply. "Do you think he can live on those three little bugs?"

He shook his head and I continued, "Of course he'll take a fly or two in his mouth, but are you sure he didn't spit them out? Even if he doesn't, it would be something like your rationing yourself to only three blueberries a week. It still doesn't make the idea of using bait look very attractive."

Another angler expressed great surprise because after he had fished a pool without results for several hours a salmon rose where he had been casting and took a small insect down from the surface. When it was pointed out that since all his efforts with a dry fly that afternoon had been to make a perfect imitation of such a suitable fly, he should not have been surprised. He had reduced the fineness of his leader till it was as small in diameter as he dared go, yet it was still visible and his fly was no match in actual practice for the real insect which floats free without a leader's attachment or control. He had tried flies of many sorts, each imitative in its way of an insect supposedly native to the area and of interest to the salmon. None had been able to compete with the true mayfly the salmon had taken, an insect so perfectly representative of the artistry of Creation that every fly in his tackle box was but a crude travesty of the winged insect's delicate grace.

Salmon occasionally will chase and capture natural insects. Fortunately, they will, at times, also take an angler's spurious imitation. What they do with the natural insects they take is still debatable. Most anglers hold that if a salmon does catch a natural insect he immediately ejects it. Others are certain he takes the fly for food. Their consistently empty stomachs tend to prove they rarely eat insects for, if they did, occasionally some of the less digestible remains would be found inside their stomachs. Someone came up with the suggestion that the salmon take the fly into his mouth and squeezes out the juices of the bug, which he swallows, then ejects the carcass. These juices, according to the claim, contain the vitamins a salmon must have if he is to stay alive.

Unfortunately for this theory, if we follow the same line of reasoning a little further, it becomes obvious that a 30-pound salmon would need six times as much in the way of vitamins as a 5-pound grilse and, therefore, would have to catch and swallow the juice from six times as many insects. The bigger the fish, if the theory holds, the more likely he would be to rise to a fly and the more often he would be seen feeding on insects. Experienced salmon fishermen know this is not the case. They have learned that 5-pound fish are more readily brought to the artificial fly and are more active in any *apparent* feeding than are the larger fish.

The solution of why a salmon rises to a fly is not so simple. The urge to rise seems more a matter of something in the mind of the salmon than of any real physical need he has. If the salmon can store up enough energy, why cannot they store up enough vitamins, too? Because our doctors tell us we humans cannot do it for any great period of time does not necessarily mean a salmon cannot. Nature is full of strange patterns, and where the seemingly impossible must be accomplished to safeguard her wild things, sometimes it is accomplished in a way we find difficult to explain. A heavy downpour in Death Valley's perennially desert areas recently created pools of water for the first time in the memory of man. Suddenly there were frogs in the water, from eggs that had lain dormant and dehydrated for longer than man thought possible. Some female spiders devour the males after mating. Nature's ways are not always our own.

It is logical to conclude the salmon's hunger leaves him and he has no essential need of vitamins and food. He shrinks in size, changing physically. This shrinking of size alone is fairly convincing. Salmon do not try to avoid or retard it by foraging in the manner typical of feeding fish. They do not make a practice of cruising the pools to round up minnows. They cling to the safe and comfortable waters without foraging in the more productive shallows that hold the bulk of the river's sources of food. If they were seriously interested in the river's food supply they could be depended upon to make a systematic search for it. No fish eager to feed would allow so large a share of the available food to remain untouched.

Salmon entering rivers from the sea are sometimes infested with tapeworms. Salmon are caught with tapeworms in them soon after they reach the rivers, but when the salmon reach the fresh water, the tapeworms soon starve to death. They may be seen on occasions partly ejected and trailing behind as the salmon swims. We kept salmon captive in a small, dammed-up pool at the Portland Creek camps. Salmon that had been caught on a fly and released there for the guests to watch ejected several such starved-out tapeworms which were either picked up off the bottom or taken from the fish. When the parasites cannot live on what a salmon eats, it is certainly not enough to support the fish himself. All logic points to a loss of appetite or nausea which Nature induces for the benefit of the species and adjusts for in her own special way. To this moment, it is beyond our understanding.

Under the circumstances, if a particular salmon were to feel that not once during the entire period from the entry into the river till he drifted back toward the sea after spawning need he take the slightest morsel of food, it should not be surprising. It is certain that few of them do have any signs of an avid hunger, and the urge to rise to a fly or to any other bait or lure comes rarely.

Rare as the urge may be, it does come and upon its coming is based the sport of salmon fishing. It may come because of a conditioned reflex. During the several years the parr spend in the streams, they feed eagerly on insects. Their taking of food of this type becomes instinctive. When a bumbling fly touches the water just above them, the parr will make a rush for it before there is any time for conscious thought. It is as instinctive as our swatting at a hornet suddenly buzzing by our ear, or putting our hands out for protection when we fall. This reflex action is so ingrained in the parr after a few years of competing with other parr to be first to reach any moving, living, edible thing coming within range that it may well be the major factor in their rising to a fly when they return again to the same environment from the sea.

Canadian salmon—strong and
lively leapers.

Coming back from the sea, where their feeding reflexes have been maintained, to rest again in the turbulent flow of sweet fresh water, there must be a remembrance of many things. When an insect comes wandering by there can reasonably be a deep and basic instinct to make a pass at it. It should be remembered, the period of parr feeding in most cases is longer than the sea-feeding portion of a salmon's life. Its effect must be a strong one.

Large salmon, long away from previous freshwater influence, are slow to rise, but small salmon, or grilse, only a little over a year removed from this intensive freshwater feeding, rise much more readily. If a grilse and a salmon that had spent two years at sea were alone in a pool, the probability would be about four to one the grilse would take the fly before the larger salmon, a ratio varying as the square of the time away from the river rather than a simple two-to-one probability.

Salmon on their spawning run are deeply affected by the overpowering urge of sex and reproduction, like moose during the rut. Their entire lives up to the point of entry into their rivers has been a preparation for reproduction. Physically, they are at the highest point of their strength. They are like a young betrothed couple, physically ready but restrained, eager yet thwarted.

They have within their firm bodies a tremendous strength, yet they must nurse it carefully if it is to last through the spawning and perhaps beyond. They are a restless fish, tense and jittery. They seek the eddies where they need not spend their store of strength needlessly, yet where the soothing flow of passing water will ease their tension. Periodically they seem to feel the need for a burst of physical action, perhaps to relax, perhaps to reassure themselves of their own physical capabilities. They leap, or make a sudden, swift surge for no other apparent reason. Or they rise to a fly, a maneuver calling for a nice turn of speed and timing. Any trivial thing like an artificial fly swimming tantalizingly within range may trigger the action that will demonstrate against their speed and coordination of movement. Why does a salmon rise? Why does a small boy cross the street just to kick a tin can?

If hunger was an important factor in a salmon's rise, it would be reasonable to expect them to prefer large flies or lures over small ones in their aim for a bigger and better meal. A herring-sized plug would be far more attractive than a mosquito-sized fly. Then, too, salmon would take the fly on the first cast over and would not, as is so often the case, require hours of fishing with the same or similar small flies directly in front of them before they finally make up their minds to rise. It is difficult to reconcile the need for a perfect presentation and cast after cast after cast, all very similar, with a hunger urge.

With many salmon, the fly to which they rise must hit a certain spot in their vision to draw any reaction. Watching from a bridge or similar point of vantage it is possible to see simultaneously a salmon and an angler's fly as it swings across the current directly in front of the fish. In many cases with a certain swing of fly, when it reaches a definite point, the salmon will be seen to move up toward the fly on a short, false rise. The casting continues and the salmon remains undisturbed until the fly, affected by the imperfections of casting and the vagaries of the current, again hits the identical swing. Again the salmon will move. It may take a great many casts and several false rises before the salmon is hooked. Often there will be only a number of false or short rises and the salmon will never touch the fly. Can this be hunger?

Salmon lying in pools at the foot of a falls are poor risers. Perhaps the imminence

Salmon fishing is usually best 50 to 300 feet below the falls rather than immediately below it. These are the famous Humber Falls.

of the falls and the problem its ascent presents fill their minds. Being preoccupied with it, they are less likely to be affected by a passing fly. At the Big Falls of the Upper Humber, it is easier to catch salmon a hundred yards or more below the falls though there are usually more fish nearer the falls. If preoccupation with anything else is a factor in taking away a salmon's impulse to rise, it is further evidence of the lack of effect of hunger and a greater effect of restlessness.

Some guides believe certain color combinations will cause a salmon to rise while others will depress him. Such a belief in color's effect places importance on a reaction of the esthetic nature rather than of hunger. The New Brunswick and Nova Scotia guides find the Durham Ranger a very effective fly, but the Newfoundland guides, almost to a man, shun red in a fly and think the Ranger would poison any salmon waters they cast it into. Strong feelings about color have developed in some localities. They do not always hold when skillful and unbiased fishermen undertake to fish with the supposedly offending shades. However, there does seem to be a definite basis for color preference in flies and for the supposition that color does affect and interest these unusual fish.

I recall one of the oddest situations illustrating the unpredictability of Atlantic salmon. It centered around a gentleman from Texas whose entire previous fishing experience had been at Wedgeport, Nova Scotia with big tuna. He only half believed the tales about the salmon's poor appetite.

One lunchtime he and his guide boiled the kettle at a falls where salmon nosed up close under an overhanging ledge beside the cascading water. Struck with a sudden notion to try "chumming" for them, as for tuna, he crept out with a supply of bread crumbs and gently dropped them over one at a time. Eventually a salmon rolled up to inspect one closely. The Texan then got his rod and crept back to his vantage point. Twelve inches of leader extended from his rod tip and a bread crumb was hooked on his fly. Like an Apache stalking a deer, he eased the rod tip out over the water for a foot or two and touched the crumbed fly to the surface.

A salmon took it and dashed off with the bread, fly, and half the leader, because half the rod was still in the bushes and the line, tangling with a branch between the guides, jammed up and could not pass. I know this happened, and it remains a favorite story of the guides. It can no more be explained in simple terms than can any other salmon rise. It is as paradoxical as the salmon itself. In this fishing there simply are no hard and fast rules.

Men have fished for days to catch a single large salmon or a conspicuous one, sometimes successfully, more often not. Salmon, especially the very large ones, rise rarely. Yet every true salmon angler knows that any salmon may rise at any cast. On this slim hope he is willing to spend day after day on a given fish. When a salmon will rise up under a fly to inspect it closely, time after time, without taking it, the capture of such a fish becomes a challenge, a personal duel between the angler and the particular salmon. Where salmon can be recognized and identified, the fishing takes on an extra intensity. Barring a serious change of river conditions, a settled-in summer fish will remain in his lie for days, and the fisherman may cast to him until his arm aches and his head swims. There is no other fishing quite like it.

When the river waters are warm and the salmon have been lying for days or even weeks in the same pools, a lethargy seems to come over them. It is as if the realization of the futility of any action on their part had been brought home to them and caused a sort of semihibernation. Their restlessness becomes less acute, their senses dulled. It is at such times that the angler may cast and cast without the slightest results. The salmon seem to be wooden. They stir little and leap scarcely at all. Under these conditions the problem confronting the angler is not so much one of tackle or fly presentation as it is of waiting for a cool snap in the weather, or a shower of rain to bring new hope and new energy to the salmon. Only rarely by some effort of his own can he pierce their apathy.

Under such circumstances, the use of an extremely large fly will sometimes do the trick, especially if it is slammed down on the water with quite a commotion. When one angler on such a pool containing many listless salmon hooks a fish, it is the rule that within a short time several others will have been raised or hooked. The explanation for this seems to lie in the stirring up of the other fish by the one that was hooked as he rushed madly about the pool. Perhaps the salmon were asleep and this commotion awakened them. This is the basis for the logic of "stoning the pool," a process in which a dead pool is pelted thoroughly with rocks from one end to the other in an efffort to stir up the fish and scare them into activity. An hour or more later, when their fear has subsided, the angler may find some of their old recklessness revived and with it, a will to rise to a fly.

An amusing incident illustrating this point occurred on the Dennys River in Maine one July day some years ago. Three of us were fishing a long pool in the meadow. We had been fishing steadily and unsuccessfully since early morning. One salmon was lying in plain view on a shallow bar near the head of the pool, and one of my friends had been casting to him for some time. The other man was across the stream and a little above him, while I was across the stream and below him perched on top of a pile of logs to do my casting. While my fly dragged listlessly through the water, a small chub affixed himself to it and was pulled in. These nuisances are often possessed with a desire to rise just in time to keep a salmon from taking the fly and consequently are held in very low esteem. Confronted with this chub, I was overcome, for some strange reason, with a wild desire to throw it at the fisherman who was casting so seriously, though fruitlessly, for the visible salmon on the bar. Something, I felt, should be done to break up the monotony of the situation in which three of us fished doggedly without any conversation and without any results. I pictured the 6-inch chub landing at the feet of the engrossed

A rise often occurs during that still and magic time between dusk and darkness.

angler with a startling splash and heard, in my imagination, his surprised outcry. The chub somehow slipped from my hand as I threw it and, instead of carrying to the shallow water of the far bank, it fell at the precise spot where the salmon lay.

If I have ever been embarrassed, it was then. The water a man fishes is sacred. His prospective fish is his as long as he cares to cast for it. But upset as I was at the slip of the chub, my mortification was nothing to the emotion that swept over the object of my throw.

"Good God, man! Don't ever do that. You might as well run the Queen Mary through the pool," he shouted, and then went on to utter a long series of not-so-nice things about me. When he finally ran out of words, he picked up a long trimmed sapling from the shore and, wading out, thwacked it down on the water he had been fishing. He twisted it in the current and worked it back and forth like a giant toothbrush. Tiring of that, he let the sapling float off downstream while he clambered up the bank to return with a log which he dumped from his shoulder into the sacred spot so recently despoiled. As a final gesture, he resorted to throwing stones of all sizes into the rest of the pool.

In spite of my embarrassment, I joined the others in laughter as we reeled in our lines. Wordlessly the three of us walked upstream to the next pool, only to find two men already fishing it. The shadows were piling up on the far bank, so we decided to call it a day. Accordingly, we turned downstream again on our way to the road.

Passing the pool that had been so thoroughly stoned, we were surprised to see the same old salmon in the same old spot, and as we watched he rolled up to the surface to take a leaf floating down with the current. My brooding, mistreated friend stripped off some line and, casting out, hooked the fish, our only salmon for the day. It was less than twenty minutes since the last stone had been thrown. A disturbance that would have ruined the chances for practically any other kind of fish was just what was needed to make that salmon rise.

There is no question but that the occurrences of a salmon taking a fly a second time are rare, but it is also certain they do occur. On the River of Ponds, Connie White, having just tied up a different and unusual fly, left the lodge to try it out while the evening light lasted. A salmon took it and, after a minute or so of play, the leader parted at the halfway mark. The next morning, another angler caught the fish and returned her fly to her.

A few days later General Thomas D. White, her husband, raised a salmon to a #4 Jock Scott, which, at the sudden strike, was left instantly in the fish's jaw. He put on another identical fly and started fishing again a few feet upstream. A minute or so later,

he reached the fish's previous location and was greeted with another strike. The fish was hooked and played and finally beached. Side by side in his jaw were my friend's two #4 Jock Scotts. Not long afterward on another river late in the same season, one of the listless salmon in a pool rose to my #8 low-water Silver Gray. He struck the fly shortly after it touched the water at the end of a long cast. The rod snapped into a deep arc to give a solid pressure on the hook and as quickly straightened out as the hook pulled free. Twice more on the fly's swift journey toward me, the salmon rushed it wickedly and missed, lifting himself clear of the water in a mass of spray the final time. A quick cast, and the fly dropped over the gray shadow as he eased back toward deeper water. It was immediately engulfed in the salmon's maw with a voracious surface rush.

I also recall catching two fish each of which had hook marks on its jaw. One may well ask, is a hook mark distinctive enough so that nothing else could make it? There might be some question on this score, but there can be none at all about leader cuts across his snout and lower jaw. When a fish is played on a fine leader that comes out of his jaw on the opposite side from which he is being played, the marks left by the cutting pressure of that leader are readily recognizable. Nothing else I know of could make those marks. Both fish had leader cuts, and since the only previous fishing of that river that season had been less than a week earlier, the time was fairly well set. An occasional salmon has so deep an urge to take a fly that he will still rise if caught and released. It is my belief that occasionally, on the River of Ponds over the length of a season, we caught quite a few fish twice and some of them three times. It would be difficult to explain the holding up of the consistently good fishing during the late days of the season any other way. We had released more fish than could be located in the pools we fished, and, even allowing for migration of many of them, there could be no doubt but that more than half of the fish in some pools had been played and released. To top it all, a captive salmon, caught and released there in a small dammed-up stream at the camp, rose to a fly dropped over him from the bridge above.

I still have a vivid mental picture of a salmon that came to my fly years ago on a dreary day at the Blue Pool on the upper reaches of the Northwest Margaree.

A cliff rises sheer and steep directly in the path of the sliding water, churning it over in huge boils and turning it away at a sharp angle. The salmon lie against the cliff farther down where the river has once more regained its composure and smoothed its surface. Fishing has been slow. The rises have been few in the hours preceding the moment when the fly settles to the water at the edge of the slightly overhanging rock wall and swings slowly toward me. The air is still and heavy; the water as dark as bitter tea from the heavy rains on the peat bogs of the weeks before. A few of the first bright, frost-fallen leaves are floating down. One moment the scene is quiet with the hush of Nature's animated stillness. In the next there is a shining salmon on the surface, a tug at the line that draws the rod down sharply as his full, silvery body wrenches spasmodically and then . . . slacks as he is gone.

Had the hook found its hold, the chances are my fish would have been conquered and released again because there were enough salmon at camp. The struggle might have been more or less routine, but that rise was brilliant and memorable and needs no photo of a vanquished fish or trophy on the wall to keep its memory untarnished. Looking back, it has been the rises more than anything else that have formed the high points of my salmon fishing memories. It is at the moment of the rise when the angler gets his first solid contact with a fish that may often seem to be only a phantom, everpresent, leaping here, there, and everywhere, but somehow intangible for much of the time.

4

Tackle

The subject of salmon tackle is a profound one. The development and tradition of salmon angling and its required equipment covers the whole span of modern fishing. For centuries anglers have been devising tackle delicate enough to hook and powerful enough to sometimes land Atlantic salmon. The Gods of Sport have watched with pleasure as, under the long refining process, rods and reels have become possessed of an amazingly delicate strength and precision, lines have reached a new pinnacle of soft and velvety action, leaders a new range of invisibility, and flies have developed into works of art whose full glory can only be blended from the bright materials of many far-off lands. An afternoon on a salmon river with today's tackle would have been absolute heaven to a Waltonian angler, and for us to look into the future is no more availing than it was for him. In this chapter I can hope to do little more than skim lightly over a subject whose intricacies would fill volumes and whose conflicting standards will continue to be the subject of serious discussion, while salmon remain to climb our northern rivers.

Rods

In the Atlantic provinces of Maine, Atlantic salmon fishing tackle is limited by law to fly-fishing tackle. In discussing rods for this area we need consider only those useful in fly-fishing.

Fly rods have been made of many materials. Originally they were made of solid woods, with lancewood and greenheart being preferred. Some of these rods are still in existence. They are heavy and bulky compared to our more modern instruments, for the newer ones are made of stronger materials with a lesser cross section for equivalent strength.

First of the innovations to become popular was the split-bamboo rod. The outer surface of bamboo is extremely tough and durable. By cutting long, tapering strips with a triangular cross section and gluing them together so that each outer side is made up of the outside of the bamboo cane, a rod with virtues never before attainable was made.

The bending strength of a solid wood rod varies as the angle with the grain is changed. The resistance to bending on a pull across the grain is not the same as it is when the pull is on the same plane with the grain. Rods of solid wood tended to stay bent or "take a set" in the direction of maximum bending, or in any direction in which they were particularly weak. Split-bamboo rods are without this directional weakness and are lighter and more durable.

The bamboo canes have nodes in them which are spots of weakness in the triangular sections and must be smoothed out. But this weakness is minimized or overcome by varying these nodal points in each of the six sections of a hexagonal split-bamboo rod so that no two of them come at the same point in a rod's length.

The skill of the early artisans who made split-bamboo rods was amazing. They contrived tools to make sections of bamboo so perfectly uniform that at the tip of the rod the cross section might be as small as a sixteenth of an inch, yet each of the six bamboo sections was identical. They compared with the wooden rods of their day as did the Eiffel Tower with the solid masonry structures above which it rose. Split-bamboo rods came into popularity late in the nineteenth century and held preference till the late 1940s.

Bamboo, like any naturally grown material, varies from stick to stick and rod to rod. Untreated bamboo rods are subject to weathering, and the original glues will sometimes lose their grip. Bamboo softens when wet, and if the protective coating of varnish on a rod is broken, dampness can seriously weaken it. The source of bamboo suitable for rod making is limited, and during the Second World War, good bamboo became almost impossible to obtain. These factors, in addition to man's natural inventive progress, led to experiments in rods made up of solid steel, solid glass fibers, tubular steel, beryllium copper, and other materials. Out of these experiments came in the 1940s the hollow glass rod which was the favorite until the mid-70s.

Glass, though stiff and brittle in large pieces, is almost perfectly elastic within its bending range. When worked into fine filaments or fibers and molded into a tapering hollow shell it provides an excellent rod. The material is uniform and once the manufacturing processes are set up, the making of good glass rods becomes a matter of routine.

Glass rods are inexpensive, impervious to dampness and relatively free from any flaws. The design can be established for any particular rod length and action, and if the processing is equally well done, all the rods produced will be as good as the pilot model.

One development came along which was a boon for the bamboo rod, the impregnation of bamboo with Bakelite. This strengthened and unified the individual sections and made the whole impervious to moisture. The rods made by this process have all the life of fine babmoo and few of its previously encountered weaknesses. The action of the fine split-bamboo rod is still considered by many fly fishermen as the best obtainable, and the impregnation gives the rod a new durability and permanence. The split-bamboo rods are preferred in the higher price brackets where the finest craftsmanship and selection of materials are utilized. In the middle and lower price brackets the glass rod took over.

The Space Age brought us graphite fibers which have a far better strength-to-weight ratio than does bamboo or glass for fly rods. "Graphite" rods cut the weight required for a rod of a given length and power to almost half. With them, tournament casters have added yards to their fly-casting distances. These rods, like those made of glass fibers, are hollow. They are made of fibers bonded together over a mandrel which is later withdrawn.

Graphite rods have a faster reaction time than those made of glass or bamboo. They return more quickly to the normal, straight position. Like glass rods they have almost no tendency to take a "set" from constant bending in one direction. They are impervious to the elements although dampness can affect the windings and reel seats. Graphite is close to perfection as a fly-rod material. Still, anglers will always be trying to improve their tools, and a new material, boron, is being used both mixed with graphite fibers in hollow rods and alone in solid form to make rods that are claimed to be superior to graphite.

Each material has a charm and a special capability. The "feel" of their actions and the love of the artistic craftsmanship involved in the split-bamboo rods lead many anglers to prefer them over all others. The fiberglass rods, the least expensive but capable of excellent actions, are favored by the majority of those who fly fish. However, as time goes on, graphite or a mixture of boron and graphite can be expected to become the favored rod material.

The rod and line are the keys to fly casting. The rod is selected first and the line then matched to it. Early rods were long and, being made out of solid wood, were quite heavy if judged by today's standards. Half a century ago the average salmon rod was 15 feet long. In 1933 when using a 5-ounce, 9-foot rod in bold defiance of tradition, I can recall seeing a 19-foot rod in action. When I asked the old gentleman who was using it how much it weighed, he replied airily, "I don't know what it weighs exactly, son, but it's fairly light, under two pounds, I'm certain."

LEFT: The author experienced a tense moment in 1964 just before the scale needle came to rest on 24 pounds, marking his first 16-20 salmon. (A 16-20 catch is an Atlantic Salmon taken on a #16 fly and weighing 20 pounds or more.)
RIGHT: "Jock Scott," a.k.a. Donald Rudd, and the author being interviewed during a long rod/short rod contest on the Dee in Scotland.

Rods over twelve-and-a-half feet are becoming relics now, used for sentiment. In their time there was no other way to cast a fly as far as easily. Modern rod materials and modern line tapers have increased the casting distance of the shorter rods and made the very long rods no longer necessary.

Long salmon rods are built with a double handgrip. They are called "two-handed" rods because both hands are required for casting with them. Because two hands are required on the rod, it is more difficult to handle the stripping line for shooting on a long cast and for the stripping in and out usually necessary in dry-fly fishing. With the long, two-handed rods, the cast is usually made to a given length of line and each subsequent cast is made to that length without any stripping in and out of line.

This makes for simple fishing. The wet fly is cast at a quartering angle downstream and across the current. The current sweeps the fly across the flow, then it is picked up with a single back cast and rolled or cast forward again on a fishing cast. Three factors were of major importance in changing preference from the two-handed rods to the single-handed type. The first was the advent of the dry fly, the second a great increase in fishing pressure, the third the forward tapered line.

With increased fishing pressure salmon became harder to catch. A fisherman accustomed to fishing but a few hours a day with a two-handed rod began to find that day-long fishing was often necessary to hook what he considered to be his quota of salmon. Lighter tackle made these long fishing days more pleasant. The shorter, single-handed rods were not only less work but less expensive and easier to carry.

Dry-fly fishing, which first entered the salmon fishing picture seriously in the late 1920s, called for a good deal of stripping in and out of line. After the dry fly has floated down toward the angler it is picked up and the line must be lengthened again for another upstream cast. This stripping in and out of the line is much more easily accomplished with a single-grip rod which leaves one hand free for the necessary line manipulations.

The design of lines called "forward tapers" made it easier to shoot line through the guides on the delivery cast. It made possible longer casts with shorter rods and was a major factor in the reduction of the average length of fly rods for salmon fishing. It, too, added yards to the existing fly-casting distance records. Lines of this type have a taper from the fine forward end to the diameter of the heavy forward section, or belly, which after a distance of from 20 to 40 feet is reduced to a "shooting" section of about .035 inches in diameter. This shooting section follows the heavy belly out on a forward cast much more readily than the continued heavy diameter of the double-tapered line and gives a longer cast for the same effort.

A compromise came into vogue to fit the changing picture. The lower grip of the two-handed rods was made detachable to permit the use of a suitable rod with either one or two hands as desired. When using a wet fly where the retrieve does not call for shortening the line between casts, the two-handed rod is the simplest to fish with. When a dry fly is to be used, or whenever there is considerable stripping of line to be done, the single grip is preferable.

The removal or addition of the butt to the basic single-handed rod has another advantage. By far the larger percentage of fishermen use their best trained hand for the reeling. In order to do this they must transfer the rod from strong hand to weak one as soon as the fish has struck. Holding the rod is simplified if the butt can be rested against the body with the weaker hand holding the upper grip. Without a lower grip the reel is pressed against one's clothing and becomes difficult to operate. With a detachable lower grip in place or with the double-grip rod, the reel is held away from the body and from any interference with buttons or pocket flaps on the clothing.

Rods of less than 9 feet are so light and so easily handled they are rarely combined with a detachable butt. Rods of 10 feet or over are heavy enough to call for two-handed casting and are normally made two-handed or with a detachable grip. Rods of 9 or 9½ feet (without butt) are light enough to cast single-handedly, and not all anglers feel the need of the extra grip for them, either for casting or the playing of the fish.

How light can a rod be and still be adequate to handle a large salmon? There used to be agreement that a certain minimum length or weight of rod was essential for properly handling these fast and powerful fish. Little by little the acceptable length of rod has come down. As a pioneer in the use of extralight tackle for salmon, by 1940 I had come down to a 7-foot, 2-and-a-half-ounce fly rod, and since then have rarely used anything heavier. In 1943, in order to demonstrate to the most confirmed doubter, I eliminated the rod entirely from my tackle. Casting some 30-odd feet by hand, I hooked a 10-pound salmon and played it by holding the reel in my right hand, reeling with my left, until I could finally reach down and tail it with my own hand, ten minutes later. Witnesses were present and pictures were taken to prove that a salmon rod may be as light as one wishes, even to the point of none at all. This experiment was the basis of an article in *Field and Stream*.

To catch a salmon without a rod, I needed a certain type of pool where I could find salmon lying within reach of a hand cast, with fairly open water in which to play the fish. The rod, in the playing of a fish, is a cushion which takes up the shock and keeps the fish from getting a solid pull at the leader before line can be released from the reel. To fish without a rod calls for reactions fast enough to take up those shocks with the extended arm. Any angler with adequate reactions can duplicate the feat, but at that time there was no record of its previous accomplishment. I have done it several times since and on one unforgettable occasion had a salmon of approximately 25 pounds played to exhaustion. A movie camera was on hand and just as I was about to tail the fish the cameraman asked me to hold off with the tailing for a minute while he changed a lens setting. I let the fish take one more swing into the current and he fouled the light leader around a snag. The #12 dry fly lost its grip, and with it went my only opportunity to take a salmon of that size by hand casting without a rod.

The rod is more necessary for the casting than for the playing of the fish. It is easier to land the average salmon without a rod than it is to cast out and hook him without one. Any sort of wind, a very heavy fly or a long, light leader make casting without a rod next to impossible. Yet any one of these things can be managed with no more rod than the tip joint of a three-piece nine-footer.

The no-rod demonstration served to prove a point and lay to rest certain taboos once firmly held. The rod has two main purposes, to cast the fly and aid in the playing of a fish. The angler should choose his rod with an open mind and a realization of his own abilities and requirements, letting temperament and experience be the deciding factors. Those without previous fly-fishing experience who are generally conventional should follow precedent with a 9-foot rod or longer. If they plan to fish big rivers and will be

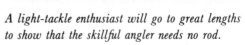

A light-tackle enthusiast will go to great lengths to show that the skillful angler needs no rod.

accompanied by old-time guides, they may well choose two-handed rods but should stay within the nine-and-a-half-foot length plus detachable butt. Longer rods should be decided upon only after actual experience in the field as they are losing popularity and are harder for one's widow to sell.

For anglers with considerable trout-fishing experience, a rod a little heavier and longer than they use for trout fishing is in order. If playing a large trout taxes one's skill then a detachable butt will be an advantage. It is easier, physically, to reel in and exert a pressure on the fish when the rod is butted against the body with a detachable grip, than when the rod is equipped with a single grip and held in the hand.

The gain of easier reeling and exertion of pressure on the fish by using the detachable grip may be offset by the extra weight and the loss of mobility. Though it takes more strength to exert the same pressure with a single-handed rod, the angler can move about more freely than if he must hold a rod pressed tightly against his body as he walks or runs to follow a fish. When fishing from a canoe, a two-handed rod is a distinct advantage, while on foot it is likely to be a handicap.

For those who are accustomed to fishing with single-handed rods and who favor lightness in their tackle, there is no need to buy a new rod. The identical rod used for trout fishing will serve for salmon. Given the same terminal tackle the rod's job is the same with salmon as with trout, except that the time required to subdue the fish will be proportionately longer. The maximum safe strain on the rod is no greater with a 20-pound salmon on the line than with a 2-pound trout. It can be broken by either yet is adequate, properly handled, for both.

The major factor in rod length is the casting distance required. To have a rod with which one cannot cast far enough to reach the fish is a serious handicap. This situation is present where wading is difficult and boats or canoes are not used. With the smaller rod the canoe or boat must be moved more frequently to cover the same amount of water. With salmon lying far out in deep pools, an angler may have to wade more deeply to make up the difference in distance. It is possible to cast a long line with short, light rods, as explained elsewhere, but unless an angler is trained for this casting, he will find it difficult. The rods of less than eight-and-a-half feet are for those with special qualifications both in casting and in the playing of fish.

Rod action is a mysterious thing, difficult to describe. A paragraph or two can do little toward explaining the range of rod actions but it may simplify the approach. "Wet-fly" and "dry-fly" action are two terms very loosely applied to rods and not explained frequently enough. The dry-fly fisherman usually casts his fly at an upstream angle, lets it float while he gathers in the slack until, at the end of the drift, he picks up the fly again and lengthens the cast to its orginial extent. This demands a certain minimum backbone in a rod. Wet-fly fishing usually requires little change in the line length from one cast to the next and can be managed with a rod of very soft action. The type of rod so soft that it is suitable only for wet-fly fishing, a typical wet-fly rod, is rarely manufactured now, and not many of them are still in use. Any good fly rod with a little backbone can be used alternately for both wet- and dry-fly fishing. When asked to explain the difference, I often say hold a fly rod out above the water and it is a dry-fly rod—let it down into the water and it becomes a wet-fly rod. A rod that cannot be used for both types is hardly worth having.

There is a class of rods, often referred to as "parabolic" in action, which tend to bring the bending down closer to the butt. Once in casting motion they tend to develop a rhythm, like a pendulum. This makes it easy to time the casts while slowly extending line, but since the rod has a tendency to cling to its rhythm, it is impossible to change the length of extended line as quickly as with a rod which is somewhat stiffer in its lower half. Parabolic-action rods are very easy to cast with but not quite as effective in casting power or in adapting to varying line pressures.

Long rods offer a greater cushion than short ones against sudden movements of the fish. The length of rod affects the pull at the grip. The same pressure that will pull a 7-foot rod down to its limit of resilience will still leave some resilience in a 9-foot rod of similar taper. Short, stiff rods are particularly awkward to use, and delicacy in the tip is essential to the handling of swift fish on very small flies and light leaders regardless of rod length.

The soft rod holds the fish more gently. The hook is less likely to wear a hole in the salmon's mouth but there is not quite as much control available for turning the fish or lifting the line over obstructions. When the leaders to be used are fine, the advantage lies with the softer, more delicate rod. All other things being equal, the rod, to give the best results in playing a fish, should have the softest action compatible with the required casting qualities.

Although the casting of the line is usually the deciding factor in choosing a rod, its effectiveness in playing the fish is almost as important. The long rod has greater leverage in directing a fish when he is more than two rod lengths away. The reverse is true, close in. When the fish is within 10 feet of the angler the short rod is of great advantage. Thus, for those who beach or bring their fish to a guide or companion for netting, tailing, or gaffing, the longer rod is preferable. For those who like to or must land their own fish, the short rod has so much advantage for the close-in playing that this overbalances any gain in controlling fish at a distance.

When buying a rod, the integrity of the maker is the best recommendation for quality. Look at the trim and the ferrules for careful finish. The rod material should not be reduced in diameter where it goes under unyielding steel. Ferrules should overlap for a short distance before the rod material is reduced in size. Guides should be of tough, wear-resistant metal. Locking reel seats are excellent where weight is not a factor, but the cork grip is best when overall lightness is a point to be considered. The testing of a rod should be done with a balanced line by actual casting. The handling of a rod without a suitable line load gives little information about its fishing capabilities.

Rod weights are important as a measure of skill. The weight of a rod is the total weight, equipped with guides, butt, reel seat, etc. A few manufacturers list only the weight of the glass or bamboo which gives a false impression.

Fly rods are delicate and should be protected by a metal carrying case. More rods are broken by accidents like being stepped on or caught in closing doors than in actual fishing. The care of rods calls for keeping them clean and, where possible, keeping them dry whenever they are not in use. Split-bamboo rods, unless impregnated, are susceptible to continued dampness. A strip of bamboo, immersed in water for a few days will become as limp as spaghetti. A crack in the finish of an unimpregnated split-bamboo rod when steadily subjected to moisture will allow a weakening at that point

and often cause the rod to break there when under strain or strong flexing. Split-bamboo rods that are not glued up with modern waterproof glues may come apart in continued dampness if there are breaks in the finish. To avoid trouble with such rods, check the varnish coating and replenish when necessary. A frequent waxing of the rod will cover up minor breaks in the varnish coating and help maintain a complete waterproofing.

All rods, in addition to being kept clean and dry, should be kept away from extreme heat. Salt water or salt spray can cause corrosion of metal guides, ferrules, and reel seats. The ferrules of a good rod are fitted with care and precision. Even a small amount of grime and dirt will keep them from seating properly. A bit of gasoline-soaked cloth rubbed over the male ferrule and inserted into the female ferrule around a matchstick will clean them.

Rod guides and tip-top should be checked occasionally to see if they present a smooth surface to the line as it whips through them. Any roughness of the guides can roughen up and ruin a good fly line in a matter of minutes. Guides of agate or glass are likely to have cutting edges when cracked, but metal guides, if soft, can be equally damaging.

This pair of 30-pounders from the Moisie were taken on a 6-foot, 1¾-ounce split-bamboo rod in well under a minute to the pound.

Reels

A good reel is essential in salmon fishing. No other part of the angler's equipment is more important in playing a fish or requires more precision in its manufacture and dependability in its performance. The runs of the Atlantic salmon are long and fast. They create a serious test for any reel. A reel of poor design or inferior materials or workmanship will not stand up. A poor rod, a weak line, a poorly balanced or a very ordinary hook may be favored in the fishing and will do its part in the capture of a salmon, but when the fish makes his long, swift run there is no escaping its full job by the reel. Any failure to operate perfectly usually results in the fish's escape.

For Atlantic salmon fishing with its fly-fishing-only regulations we need consider only fly reels. They are usually single acting, making one revolution of the spool for each turn of the handle. The spools are deep and narrow and have no gearing. Such reels are of the simplest construction. The spool rides upon a shaft (usually steel) with the inner spool surfaces (normally bronze or another metal) riding directly upon it. The shaft must be of good steel and rigidly set in the reel's frame. The spool must be light but strong with a smooth, hard-bearing surface.

A well-built reel of this elementary type, if properly used and cared for will last indefinitely. One of mine, a three-and-three-eighths-inch Hardy St. George which has been in use for more than thirty years, has taken part in the capture of well over 2,000 salmon. It is still in use and in excellent condition. This establishes the simple, single-acting reel of good design and materials as adequate for the fishing. Any improvements and variations are not essential and must be judged by any additional effectiveness or pleasure of possession they can contribute.

Weight is an important factor, and fly reels are made to obtain maximum line-carrying capacity with minimum weight. The spools are usually perforated on the outside to permit more rapid drying of the line while on the reel and to reduce the weight of the spool. The inner plate of the spool remains solid to prevent dirt and grit from entering the back of the reel where the click and drag are located. Basic single-acting reels are very easy to take apart. A spring catch or a short screw holds the spool in place on the shaft and, when released, the spool and its complement of line and backing slip readily out of the frame. This makes for ease of cleaning, oiling, and rapid replacement of a broken part. Interchangeable spools, each carrying a different type of line, make the change from a floating to a sinking line easy to manage.

The handle of this type of fly reel protrudes directly from the outside plate of the spool. The surface which the fingers grip rotates upon a shaft so the finger grip need not be changed as the spool is turned. There is no friction or slipping of the fingers over the handle's surface. A round handle will do, but a grip of slightly triangular section is easier to hold. The handle should be short, just long enough to provide a good grip. There is always the possibility of the line's being loose enough to catch around a long handle when the salmon makes a sudden surge. The shorter the handle, the less likelihood there is of losing a fish in that manner.

The fly reel should be equipped with a click and an adjustable drag. The resistance of a spring and tooth to the turning of the cogged wheel attached to the spool tend to keep the reel from overrunning under a rapid removal of the line. As the reel spool turns, there is a clicking noise proportionate to the speed of the line's withdrawal or taking in. This sound tells the angler just how fast his fish is running, and from that he can judge whether to follow the fish or hold his ground. He can estimate how much line he has lost without turning the reel over to look at the spool. Some reels are made without clicks to operate silently, in which case this important advantage is lost.

The click also acts as a drag to keep the reel from overrunning when the fish takes line rapidly. The simplest clicks are not adjustable and offer a uniform resistance to turning. This type is not recommended for salmon fishing. Improved reels have a knurled screw or level with which the tension of the tooth may be varied. This, in turn, proportionately retards the turning of the spool. The heavier the drag, the more certain it is to prevent overrunning which, if it occurs, causes a tangle on the spool and lets the fish break away. A light drag is essential when using small hooks or fine leaders. Sometimes the minimum drag required to keep a reel from overrunning when a particularly fast fish draws off line with a sudden burst of speed is great enough to break a fine leader. To solve the problem of variable tension many anglers keep their reels set at a low drag tension but apply extra drag at the critical moments by either holding the line between the fingers with varying degrees of pressure or by applying braking pressure against the reel spool in just the right degree with a finger. A pressure-type braking device is used in some reels and is of the adjustable type, but no adjustment can be used quickly enough to release line when a fish runs suddenly and the tension has been set in advance.

In the mid-60s I invented a new type of fly reel. It eliminates the frame within which the spools of all previous reels rotated. I felt that with a strong center shaft a frame was not needed, and without one, an angler could put finger-pressure on the outside rim of the fly reel for maximum sensitivity and braking power. A hundred of these reels, called the "Lee Wulff Ultimate," were made by Farlow in England and stand as a major development in fly-fishing reels. The best drag possible is one that can be put on or taken off instantly, which is best done by finger-pressure. Drags that must be screwed on or off take too much time and may leave an angler with a heavy drag when a sudden, fast run calls for a light one.

The better reels are designed with a greater resistance against turning when the line is going off the reel than when it is being wound in. This makes reeling line in easier than it would be if the same drag were maintained for both directions. This factor often is built into the reel and makes it advisable that the purchaser be certain the reel is either right-handed or left-handed.

Similarly a line guide, which is an aid in guiding the line onto the spool of the reel uniformly, is placed either for right- or left-hand use. The usual placement is for right-hand reeling, although left-hand reeling by right-handed fishermen is growing more and more popular. Line guides may be in the form of a large ring of hard metal or of agate. Hard metal is to be preferred, for there is always risk of the agate's cracking and damaging the line as it passes back and forth over the sharp edges.

The deep, narrow spool is preferable in the single-action reel. The larger the diameter of the line-filled spool, the more line each turn of the reel will bring in. Since most of the reeling is done with relatively short line out, the narrow spool is most efficient. When a great deal of line is out and the line-filled diameter of the spool is cut in half, a single turn of the spool will only bring in one-quarter as much less line.

Similarly, the effect of the drag is proportionate to the diameter of the line on the spool. If the reel is 3 inches in diameter when the drag is set with the correct tension then when the diameter is reduced to one-and-a-half inches, the pull required to turn the spool has doubled. If a drag is adjusted properly for a full spool, it must be slackened as the line diameter decreases, or else it will become too heavy for the leader to stand. When the line on the reel builds up again, it must be readjusted to its original position.

Ball bearings have been incorporated into fly reels. They are most often installed only as thrust bearings at the base of the shaft, which gives the reel a slightly longer life but scarcely increases its performance though increasing the size and weight considerably. If incorporated into the spool to make its rotation around the shaft create less friction, ball bearings would increase the weight and bulk even more. The reel would require much more careful cleaning, would be much more expensive, and, inasmuch as a completely free-running fly reel is of no value, there would be little point to such an installation. There must always be a certain minimum turning tension to prevent overrunning.

Multiplying reels which make two or more turns of the spool for every rotation of the handle are sometimes used for salmon. They are heavier and bulkier due to the gearing required. The spool of the multiplying reel is wider but not as deep as a comparable single-action reel. The greater speed of bringing in line is advantageous on the larger rivers where the fish are played at long distances for a good portion of the time, and a rapid enough take-up on a half-filled spool is not possible with the single action. The extra weight is not a problem with heavier rods but with medium or light rods it becomes a serious handicap.

In choosing a multiplying reel for fly-fishing, care must be taken to avoid any protruberances or undercuts which might cause the line to catch and tangle. An angler has only to lose one big fish because a loose loop of line caught in the reel just as the fish was hooked to realize how important it is that a reel be snag free in design.

Automatic reels may be satifactory for other types of fishing but they are not truly suitable for Atlantic salmon. A one-armed angler may of necessity need one. A normal fisherman will do much better with a conventional reel. In the first place, automatic reels are heavy for their line capacity. Secondly, their normal spring retrieve is short, not long enough to bring in a salmon's run in its entirety. If a spring great enough to retrieve a salmon's run were installed in a reel, it would be much too heavy for comfortable casting. Thirdly, as the fish takes line the tension tends to build up, and as the line comes in again, the tension decreases. A constant tension at the fish, which is never exceeded, is the general aim of the angler and the automatic reel doesn't fit into this pattern.

For many years the best fly reels have been made in England. Only a few U.S.-made reels are of comparable quality, the bulk of them being made for less difficult fish. Reels satisfactory for bass and trout are not necessarily adequate for salmon.

The fly reel must be big enough to hold a fly-casting line and a certain amount of backing. How much backing is needed depends upon the waters to be fished. In large, fast rivers a longer backing line is needed than in the smaller pools or in low water. Salmon in a lake or at the tidehead where there is a wide expanse of water may take advantage of it to make a long run.

An angler has only to lose one salmon because it ran out all his line to become acutely aware of the amount of backing he carries on his reel. Like an airplane pilot who insists on having a bit more gas in his tanks than he expects to use, the experienced salmon fisherman has enough line on his reel to anticipate any fishing condition he may encounter.

One hundred and fifty yards of backing line is a good basic figure. It will do for most fishing, though there are very large rivers where it is impossible to follow a fish swiftly or at all, and twice that much may help to save a fish. The backing, being fine, will take up less reel space than the fly-casting line which, though shorter, is much more bulky. Nylon is relatively impervious to rot and need not be dried each time it gets wet.

The fly line should match the rod with which it will be used. As rods get heavier, the fly lines increase in diameter. Where there is only one rod in question it is fairly easy to decide what reel is necessary or how much room there is on a given reel for backing. If a single reel is to serve on two rods it will be necessary to get a reel big enough to serve both. In choosing such a reel, combine the backing and the heavier of the two fly lines and make sure they fit on the spool comfortably.

The three-and-three-quarters-inch reel is a very popular size with the 4-inch diameter running a close second. Narrow-spooled fly reels of this diameter are suitable for use with rods ranging from 8-and-a-half to 9-and-a-half feet (without butt) and will accommodate the lines they require with adequate backing. The 3-and-a-half- or 3-and-three-eighths-inch diameter reels are about the minimum in order to accommodate the necessary casting line and backing required to play a salmon.

It is generally accepted that a single-handed fly rod with reel (and line) in place should balance at a point at or near the forward end of the grip. The concentration of weight at the reel balances the forward weight of the rod. This balancing of reel to rod is often spoken of as a very difficult thing. Actually it is not. There are fairly wide limits within which a reel's weight may fall while still permitting the angler to cast with effectiveness and comfort. Balance of line to rod is extremely important, balance of reel to rod is as much a matter of comfort as effectiveness. Balance is a little more critical with single-grip rods than with double-handed rods.

In order to play a salmon, a certain amount of line and backing must be held by the reel. With extremely light rods this reel and its line load are obviously heavy and, in the conventional view, out of balance. However, by shifting the grip of the casting hand down against the reel this imbalance is completely offset, and the new position of the hand requires a shorter cork grip which, in turn, is advantageous in the design of a short, very light rod. A three-and-a-half-inch reel with a #7 line and a hundred and fifty yards of backing can be used on a 6-foot, ounce-and-three quarters rod comfortably and effectively. It is easy enough to adjust the same reel with a slightly heavier casting line to a 9-foot, 6-ounce rod.

The place on the grip at which the angler holds the rod is not rigidly prescribed. Beware of tailored grips which were designed for another's hand. By shifting the hand toward or away from the reel, the fly caster can adjust for a lighter-than-usual or heavier-than-usual reel or for different weights of line on the same reel.

How the rod is gripped as well as where it is gripped is important. The conventional grip is to surround the cork with four fingers and press the thumb atop the rod grip, pointed toward the rod tip. An equally effective grip especially favorable for light rods is to have the cork grip lie across the hand from the index finger to the heel of the palm. The index finger lies atop the grip and extends up over the graphite, bamboo, or glass and is pressed against it. The other three fingers hold the grip tightly against the palm from below and the thumb presses against the grip horizontally from low on the opposite side of the fingers. This forefinger-atop-the-rod grip is preferable when arm action is to be incorporated into the cast. The conventional grip allows freer play of the wrist. The forefinger on top may give better direction and accuracy.

The best of reels will fail to function properly if neglected. The entire back cavity between the spool and the reel's frame should have a thin coating of oil or grease on it at all times. Oil is essential to prevent wear and cut down friction on the click, the shaft, and upon any bearing surfaces. Elsewhere oil will prevent rust or other corrosion. Reels should be cleaned and oiled every week or two during periods of use and at the end of every season before they are put away.

Normal use has very little effect upon a reel if it is clean and well oiled, but grit and sand will cause excessive wear and can ruin a reel in a very short period. Avoid placing a reel in sand or letting it touch the bare ground. Immersion in cloudy or muddy water may cause particles of dirt to get into the reel's action. If there is any sound or feeling of "grinding" in a reel, it should be cleaned immediately.

Lines and Leaders

The reel, while extremely important in the playing of the fish, becomes a simple carrier of the line during the casting. It is the rod and line upon which the angler must depend for putting his fly to the fish and they must be teamed up in balance to do their best job.

Proper balance of rod to line is, to a fair degree, a personal thing, affected by how a particular individual grips the rod, what his casting action tends to be, and how far he wants to cast. Mainly, however, it is a matter of efficiency. The most efficient combination is the one to be preferred. The poor caster really needs a well-balanced outfit. Without one he'll be severely handicapped. The more capable a caster is, the better he can cast with a mismatched outfit, but the better he is able to appreciate a good rod-line team and get the most out of it.

To work at its peak, a rod needs enough line-weight in the air to flex it to a maximum safe working strain under the power of the caster using it. The weight should be distributed over from 25 to 50 feet, depending upon the length of the rod. The heavier the line per foot of length the shorter the line that may be cast well; the lighter it is, the longer the extending line must be to reach efficient casting power (except in wind). There is not much leeway. Too light or too heavy a line will not work at all.

A powerful caster may tax his rod to the utmost and use a heavier-than-usual line to get long casts. A very gentle caster, to whom the extra ten or twenty feet is not important, will be better satisfied with a line generally accepted as "light" for the rod. It is possible to list the lines most suitable for a given rod. Such a listing is for the average rather than the individual.

A fly line must be fairly heavy since it provides the weight to make the cast possible. It must be bulky, flexible, and soft, yet have a good wearing surface. Fly lines must remain free of tangles and a line of small diameter tangles readily. The line must not be stiff or tend to hold its shape. A stiff line will not flow readily throughout the cast, and a very soft line will not flow at all, being too limp. The degree of flexibility must lie within certain limits. If the line, after being coiled up on the reel for some time, tends to keep the shape of its coils, that tendency will interfere with casting. The surface of a fly line must be smooth and fairly hard. A soft surface will soon wear away. A rough surface will not slide readily through the guides, nor will a sticky one.

Fly-casting lines were made up of woven fibers impregnated or coated with a plastic substance to give them weight and good surface. Nylon, Dacron, and silk were among the preferred fibers. Impregnated lines, in which the plastic substance penetrates the line completely, were the longest wearing. Plastic coatings, once they crack or break, create a very rough surface and make casting difficult, but as long as the surface remains unbroken they offer no problem.

Modern fly lines are made up of a plastic coating extruded over a woven core, usually nylon or Dacron, of a uniform diameter. The thickness of the plastic coating is varied to create desired taper.

The simplest fly lines are of uniform diameter from end to end or "level." In order to let the fly drop delicately to the water at the end of the cast, and to avoid having a heavy line-end splash near the fish, the better fly lines are tapered. The line at the point nearest the fly, where the leader is joined to it, is much smaller in diameter than is the main working section. There are many tapers on the market, but they fall into three main classes—the single taper, the double taper, and the multiple taper, or forward taper line.

The single-tapered line simply tapers from the reel to a fine diameter at the forward end. It is valuable mainly for roll casting. The double-tapered line has a similar taper at each end permitting the reversal of the line when one end has been worn out. This gives twice the fishing life. The multiple-tapered line is of fine diameter at the forward end, tapers to a maximum diameter, which it maintains for a certain length, before tapering down to a shooting line or running line which is smaller than the maximum but larger than the fine point at the line's front end.

LEVEL LINE

DOUBLE TAPER

BALANCED MULTIPLE TAPER

EXTREME MULTIPLE TAPER

Types of tapers.

Multiple-tapered and double-tapered lines with identical tapers will cast identically up to a point. The forward tapers of both may be alike, and for the first twenty feet of heavy line, or belly, they may match up. Beyond that point, as the line goes out of the guides, there will be a distinct casting advantage with the multiple, or forward, taper. It will be easier to draw line out beyond that point because the additional line is lighter. For a given total weight, it will extend farther for the same energy by the caster. The ultimate cast that can be made with it will be longer. There is no good casting quality inherent in any of the double-tapered lines which cannot be matched by a multiple taper, and no single- or double-tapered line can match a well-designed multiple taper for overall casting performance.

In general, the forward end of the line should taper up from .025 inch to about .040 in 6 feet and increase in diameter about .005 for each additional 2 feet until maximum diameter is reached. The heavy section of the line should be from 18 to 40 feet depending upon the diameter and the rod with which it is to be cast. The taper down to the running line in the rear will be at about the same rate as the front taper. The shooting line should be about .035 in diameter.

Many of the multiple-tapered lines on the market are too extreme for good salmon fishing. Some have front tapers which are too short and drop a heavy section of the line too close to the fish. Others have short, heavy working sections which lack delicacy or control. Still others have shooting sections which are too small in diameter, excellent in a dry and windless gymnasium but sure to tangle when exposed to wind and waves.

A shooting line of smaller diameter will allow longer casts, but it is so fine that retrieve loops gathered in the left hand while casting will tangle in the wind. Consistent use of a shooting line of .025 or .030 inch is sure to produce tangles. When a salmon takes a dry fly and starts his wild rush, the least tangle of the hand-held line reaching the first guide will set him free. A shooting line heavier than .040 inch is not necessary and the extra diameter will only cut down casting distances and take up extra space on the reel.

A too-light running line takes away from the angler the control of his cast once the final forward motion is made. If this running, or shooting section as it is called, is of a reasonable diameter (.035 inch), it will have weight enough so that a pressure by the rod in any direction as it goes shooting out of the guides will have an effect on the cast's direction. Accuracy in casting often depends upon these last-minute touches of control. To sacrifice them for an extra few feet of distance will not pay off in fish caught. Placement of the fly must always take preference over sheer distance.

There is another type of line used in fly casting but rarely for Atlantic salmon. It is the "shooting head." It was originated and is used by distance fly casters in tournaments. This type of line is also used on the Pacific Coast and in many western rivers for steelhead fishing and often for fishing in the sea where fast and extralong casts are particularly valuable.

A short, heavy section of fly line, usually with a short front taper, called the "head" is attached to nylon monofilament shooting line (usually .020 inch in diameter). The head is of the right weight to use the power of the rod at maximum. On the cast the line can be "shot" for a great distance. The smooth, light monofilament slides through the guides with a minimum resistance and provides maximum distance.

The nylon, however, is more difficult to handle. It tangles more readily and twists in the wind. To counteract this most shooting head casters wear a basket on their chests in which they coil their retrieves and from which the line will shoot out readily on the next cast. Deep-wading anglers often hold long loops of retrieved line between their lips. They are held out downstream by the current and then released when the cast is made. Braided line, which is light and very slick, is being used with shooting heads by some casters. It shoots almost as well as monofilament and is much less likely to tangle. Shooting heads are trouble, but the longest possible casts can be made by them.

Lines used to be calibrated in letters. An HDH is a double-tapered line varying from H (.025) to D (.045) and back at the far end of H (.025) again. A GBF line is a multiple taper ranging from G (.030) at the forward end to B (.055) at the belly and back to F (.035) for the remainder of the line.

Since the early 1960s fly lines have been designated by numbers. This may well be because of the manufacturers' inability to make their lines to the specific standards of the old letter system where an A line had a diameter of .060, a B of .055, a C of .050, etc. The line numbers represented the weight of the first 30 feet of the line in grains with the following categories.

Lines of different manufacturers will vary. One company's #7 may be almost a #6, another's almost a #8. Another disadvantage of the number system is that if the belly of the line continues beyond the 30-foot mark the extra casting weight is not recognized in the line's number designation. A 10-foot front taper and a 20-foot belly will cast far differently than a 10-foot front taper and a 30-foot belly. The specific gravity, an important factor in air resistance and rapidity of sinking, is never given except in general terms like slow sinking, fast sinking, floating, and the like.

Any photographer can get the specific shutter speed, the particular lens opening, and the particular magnification he desires. It is unfortunate for fly fishermen that they cannot go into a store and get a line with a specific taper and a particular specific gravity.

Two lines identical in dimensions but varying in specific gravities will not have the same casting qualities. The lighter line, lower in specific gravity, will weigh less. It will float better, but it will not cast the same way. Being lighter, it will have equal wind resistance but less weight and inertia than the heavier line.

For those who want a line to sink, a high-specific-gravity line is preferable. It will take a wet fly farther under the surface than a floating line. It will be less conspicuous to the fish as it travels under the surface than a floating line would be. It will cast a little better due to lowered wind resistance. It will fit on a slightly smaller reel. Those who wish a floating line will find it in a low-specific-gravity type, sacrificing a little in casting distance, space on the reel spool, and invisibility to the fish, for their ease of flotation.

A line with a specific gravity of from 0.95 to 1.00 will either float or sink, depending upon whether or not it is greased and how it is fished through the water. Such a line has maximum utility. It can be made to sink or float, but the decision must be made well in advance, as it is difficult to ungrease a line, and it takes time to grease it. A pair of matched interchangeable spools or matched reels, one loaded with a floating line and the other with sinking, will let a fisherman change from floating to sinking line quickly and give him the best possible performance in each case.

One of the most important points to check when rigging out with a new line is the point of the forward taper. Some manufacturers, unfortunately, leave a level section of smallest diameter at the forward end which should be cut off. Any extra length of fine line at the front end is a disadvantage. It has no appreciable casting weight but is fairly visible to the fish. It should be cut off and replaced by the leader which should start at about the same diameter and is almost invisible to the fish.

It is easy to determine the end of the taper with the naked eye by creating a loop and comparing diameters a foot apart on the line but placed side by side for comparison. By shifting the comparison point, you can find out just where the taper ends. If, after testing the line with leader attached, it does not straighten out or work well on short casts, trim back gradually to a point where the casting improves, but do not exceed .030-inch diameter at the forward point if you can help it.

Line Weight Equivalents

AFTMA Code	Weight (Grains)
1	60
2	80
3	100
4	120
5	140
6	160
7	185
8	210
9	240
10	280
11	330
12	380
13	450
14	500
15	550
16	600
17	650
18	700
19	750
20	800
21	850

How to determine the end of the taper.

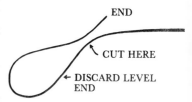

END

CUT HERE

← DISCARD LEVEL END

There are a good many variations of sinking fly lines on the market. They have some advantages but often the advantage sought is an illusion. There is no question but that a high-density, fast-sinking (high-specific-gravity) line takes up less space on the reel, will have less air resistance when casting, and will retrieve at a lower level in the water. Against that one must consider that the sinking line is much harder to pick up from the water for a back cast. It will require from one to five extra strips of line more than a floating-line pickup will. This takes time, requires energy, and cuts down the angler's actual fly-in-the-water fishing time.

Another consideration is that the line will sink at a given rate, say 4 inches per second. If the fly is cast into water moving at a rate of 5 feet per second then in the 10 feet of current movement the line will sink to only 8 inches below the surface. To a salmon lying in 6 to 10 feet of water that may not make much difference in his decision to rise. Consider, too, that if you are using a 12-foot leader and have a 12-foot front taper, while the belly of the line may sink at its prescribed rate the fly and the leader will sink only at the same rate they would if cast on a floating line. The tapered section of the line sinks at a varying rate from the forward point to the belly. Only the belly section sinks rapidly. In other words, the angler must let his line sink, then draw the fly 24 feet toward him to get it down to the level of the belly of the line. That's quite a handicap. Sinking lines work well in still waters, but where the water is moving normally or where the fish are at a distance a sinking line is a lot of trouble and will not catch more fish for you. The sinking line's real advantage is in the still or slow-moving waters.

Heat and humidity cause some lines to rot and deteriorate. Whenever they are to be stored, and periodically when in use during the season, lines should be taken from the reel, cleaned, and dried. If lines are used as floaters, they should be greased. Occasionally this grease should be removed with a rag and new, clean grease applied. Sinking lines need not be greased but should simply be kept clean.

Lines should be checked every few days for roughness on their surfaces. If any roughness is noted, the guides should be checked to see if a roughness in one of them is causing the trouble. Lines should also be checked for strength, especially as they get older. A break in the surface can be the opening for rot and a subsequent breaking of the line at that point.

Care should be taken not to let solvents touch a good fly line. Some fly repellents contain solvents which will ruin a line. It is worthwhile to check the labels of any "bug dope" used to be sure it does not contain a substance which might damage the line.

There are many other hazards to long line life. A line may be stepped on and damaged. It may become caught in the reel spool or damaged when scraped across a jagged rock. Lines are expendable. When, in spite of your care, one of your frequent inspections shows a weak spot, although you can splice it without too much trouble, the chances are it will never again be as good as it was. The spare you've been carrying for just an emergency should take its place, and the repaired line should become your temporary spare.

Braided nylon or Dacron backing lines are the most popular, though any fine, strong line will suffice for backing. The type used for bait casting is good. Because of their fine diameter, backing lines take up little space on the reel. They have a strong tendency to float upon the water unless forced under and held there. This makes them easy to pick up and reel in when under light tension. In general, backing is used to maintain contact with a fish when he's beyond normal playing range. In such cases the angler's usual action is to move toward his fish and the quality of floating is a distinct advantage. A line that sinks, especially when a lot of it is out, has a tendency to become fouled with rocks and snags on the bottom, a situation which frequently causes the loss of the fish.

The choice of backing strength depends upon the rest of the angler's tackle, particularly the leader. If the angler is prepared to play his fish gently when his backing line has been drawn out through the guides, he needs backing only a little stronger than his leader point. Where 3- or 4-pound leader points are to be used in low-water summer conditions, 6-pound-test backing is adequate. Where the fisherman may use the line for fishing in heavier water with leaders up to 8-pound-test, a 12-pound-test backing will suffice. Where the angler wants to be prepared for practically any contingency, 15- or 20-pound test line is indicated. The lighter backing lines have only the advantage of taking up a very little less space upon the reel spool and weighing a very little bit less. Unless reel space is at a premium, the stronger backing lines are best.

How much backing line does one need? That depends upon how much space the salmon has to swim in and how far he feels like running. Most salmon can be handled with 100 yards of backing. Yet I recall standing beside Ed Gilligan at the running out of Western Pond when he hooked a strong-minded salmon. The reel sounded a steady scream. The first 100 yards of Ed's backing line were black, the next 50 were white, and the final 50 left the reel with a loud snap. That salmon had 14 miles of flat water to run in and a strong desire to see the far shore. It's wise to carry all the backing your reel will hold. Salmon have been landed even after they had taken out more than 250 yards of line.

How much backing line a reel will hold and how big a reel is required often hinge on the length of the fly used. Fly lines normally run from 90 to a 120 feet in length. They take up most of the reel space. When trying to condense the reel load in order to use minimum reels for ultralight rods, there is a trick of rigging out a new line with the leader attached to the forward end and taking it out to the lawn to see just how far you can cast it. These test casts should be made with the line lying in coils on the ground at your feet. When the ultimate casting distance is reached, cut off the line at the reel seat. In that way, you carry on your reel only the fly line you actually use in casting. To carry any more is a complete waste excepting, of course, in the case of a double-tapered line, where a reversal of the line makes use of the second taper. For every 10 feet of casting line removed, many yards of backing line can be carried. In actual practice, even if the occasional cast were to exceed the length of the fly line carried on the reel, there would be no loss in efficiency, even though the backing line might be drawn out through the guides for a short distance.

Locking loops are the best way of fastening the fly line to the backing. The loop in the backing should be large enough to pass over the reel. The loop on the casting line should be small. By passing the backing loop through the line loop, then over the reel, before drawing it tight, the two lines are locked together. By reversing the process, the line is freed and another line may be put on in its place by the same method. This allows for changing the casting line without unwinding all the backing line with it. This is not possible when backing and casting lines are joined together permanently with a splice.

Another method of attaching fly line to backing, which is usually my choice, is to

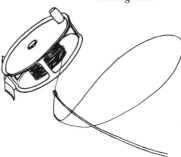

A loop on the casting line.

make a Bimini loop in the backing large enough for the reel to pass through it. The fly line is attached to this loop by a wedge knot. The wedge knot can be clipped close and will slide through the guides easily. This method eliminates the time and trouble required to wrap a line loop and is far superior to a splice when it comes to changing fly lines.

The leader is a finer, more transparent extension of the line designed to go as far as possible in creating for the fish the illusion that an angler's fly is a swimming, floating, or drifting insect, completely independent of the tackle. It is often the secret to the hooking of salmon and is, at the same time, the weakest and most vulnerable link in the chain of tackle with which the angler attempts to subdue him.

The leader material must come as close as possible to invisibility. Old-time leaders were made of horsehair, some of them tapering from a braid of many to a few or, for trout, a single hair at the fine end. Following that, until the early 1940s, silkworm gut, the drawn-out, unspun material which the silkworms create within themselves for the spinning of their cocoons, was used almost exclusively. Then, extruded nylon, which was equally hard to see but which could be produced in endless lengths and was uniform in its strength, came to the market. Whereas silkworm gut was brittle when dry and required soaking before it could be used for fishing, nylon monofilament was just as pliable and strong when dry as when soaked.

Early nylon was as good as gut, and in a short time after its appearance on the market it became much cheaper than gut. Level nylon leaders of any length were knotless, and soon tapered nylon leaders without knots became available. Nylon and similar, almost-transparent substances are continually being improved. They are cheap, easy to carry, and effective.

As with lines, leaders may be either level or tapered. Tapered leaders are more likely to fool the fish and, when coupled with a tapered line, they cast more delicately than the level type. Level leaders, of uniform diameter, are usually used in a diameter and strength which lies somewhere between the strength we'd like and the invisibility we need. If the entire leader length is very fine it is prone to tangle and may be difficult to cast. Any chafing or knotting anywhere along its full length may create a very weak spot. If a heavy level leader is used instead, the section to which the fly is attached becomes more readily visible to the fish and, being stiffer, it detracts from the fly's free-swimming or free-floating appearance. The most suitable level leader is a compromise between casting ease, strength, and invisibility. For Atlantic salmon under normal or favorable water conditions, this calls for a leader in the 10-pound-test bracket between 9 and 12 feet long.

Level leaders are not as effective as tapered leaders. These have the following advantages. The tapered leader is of finest diameter for a short length where the fly is attached, giving maximum invisibility at that point. It builds up in strength as the distance from the fly increases so that only a short section is of minimum strength and subject to breakage at its rated pull (less if defective or weakened in any way). The sections of the leader at a distance from the fish are not so important in fooling him, and the increasing diameters can be tolerated there without loss in effectiveness. By the time the leader reaches the point to which it is attached to the line, it should be nearly the same diameter as the line.

This continuation of the line's taper on into the leader makes for easier casting and smoother flow of line and leader when cast. Any sharp break in taper, whether in line or leader or at the junction of the two, detracts from the smoothness and accuracy with which the fly goes out to the fish. The specific gravity of line and leader are usually similar, both being in the neighborhood of 1.00.

Leader diameters are commonly designated by "X" numbers. A 3X leader has a diameter of .008 inch; a 5X leader has a diameter of .006 inch, a 7X leader has a diameter of .004 inch. The rule is simple. The magic number is 11. The number of thousandths of an inch the leader's diameter plus the X number equals eleven. Subtract the diameter from eleven and you have the X number. Subtract the X number from eleven and you have the leader diameter in thousandths of an inch.

Two main factors must be considered in deciding upon the proper leader. One is length and the other fineness. A 12-foot leader of .012-inch diameter will be just about as effective and stronger than a 6-foot leader of .010. The closer the fly line comes to the fish, the more likely it is to frighten him. Even with tapered leaders, this effect must be considered. If a 4-foot leader is good and a 6-foot leader of the same fineness is better and so on, it follows that the longer the leader is, up to a point, the more chance it has of fooling the fish. It is possible the most perfect rig would be a leader continuing into a line made of uniform, highly transparent material. In practice a leader of over 20 feet is rarely considered necessary.

The balance of increasing length of leader (with its increasing casting difficulty) and fineness (with its danger of breakage) to the fishing conditions is up to the angler. The safest course is to use the longest leader you can cast easily, of a strength you consider adequate for your skill. Reduce its diameter only when conditions indicate that extra length and extra fineness are required. A fine leader in heavy, dirty water is an unnecessary risk.

The leader I like to use tapers in knotless fashion from .025 to 0.12 in 9 feet. To the fine end of it I add varying lengths of level leader material. For high or normal water conditions it will be 3 feet of .012 or .011. As conditions become more difficult, I'll add lengths of finer material, ending up on low, clear pools with perhaps an additional 2 feet of .010 followed by 2 more feet of .009 and a final 6 feet of .008. I rarely go lower or longer, though a .007 point will hold a big fish under perfect conditions. Improved strength in the future may well reduce these diameters.

If, under clear water conditons, a 6-foot leader works to some degree, a 9-foot leader works better and a 12-foot leader a little better still, what is the ultimate leader? The answer, of course, is a line which is made of the same material as the leader and is, in effect, a continuation of the leader. When will we get it? It's here now and I've fished with it. But it has some bugs that still have to be worked out before it is commercially available.

This test line-leader was made of clear nylon, tapering from 6-pound test at the tippet up to .055 inch at the belly and ran at that diameter through the belly for 30 feet before dropping back to a .035 inch running line to match a forward taper fly line. In the tests made by Alain Prefontaine and myself this line seemed to take more fish than the normal line with normal leaders. Now for the bad news.

No nylon has yet been developed which is as soft and pliable as our present fly lines. When wound onto a reel and stored for any length of time it takes on the shape of the reel coils and will not straighten out readily. The only way we could fish with it was to physically stretch the kinks out of it before each fishing period and keep the amount of line needed for casting off the reel while fishing.

These coils of line were stiff and wiry and tended to tangle in the bottom of the canoe or to twist into knots when held in coils while wading. My opinion is that the line-leader, as it presently stands, is more trouble than it's worth in increased rises. But, if the problems can be solved the line-leader will make our present day line and leader combinations obsolete.

In determining the diameter of the leader point, the size and weight of the fly must be taken into consideration. A very small fly calls for a fine leader point while a heavy fly, which would put undue strain on such a fine tippet during the casting, may call for a leader point with twice the cross section. A very small fly won't swim naturally on a stiff leader point, and a heavy fly will break a very fine point because of its inertia and snap at the end of the back casts. When changing flies varying more than four hook sizes, the leader should be changed also. A standard #4 salmon fly shouldn't be used on a leader point of less than .011, and a #10 fly on anything heavier than .010. The leader attached to a #16 fly is much more likely to be noticed by the fish than the same leader going away from a #4.

When the leader is short and the rod long, the junction of line to leader may not be important other than to be sure it is a secure one. When the leader is long enough to have to be drawn partly into the guides during the playing of a salmon, the connection must be smooth as well as strong. This condition is particularly essential for those who, through preference or necessity, must land their own fish.

The simplest knot may well be the wedge knot which, when drawn tight and clipped short, is secure and will pass through even fine guides fairly well.

Locking loops are better. These are made by ravelling a short section at the end and roughening the surface of the line where it is to be joined. The section is then wrapped and varnished and passed through the leader loop. Then, if the point of the leader is passed through the line loop, and the whole leader pulled through and drawn tight, the line and leader will be fastened together by locking loops which will pass freely through the guides. This method, like tieing, permits a quick change of leaders but does not lead to fraying or weakening and constant shortening of the line as the frayed or weakened parts are cut off. The loop must be very small, otherwise the extra concentration of weight at that point will cause extra working and wear at the point. It may also cause a slight splash when it lands on the water or a conspicuous lump more readily visible to the fish.

The splicing of a short section of heavy leader material to the line is a very fine method of joining them. The knots give absolute security, and both sides are carefully wrapped with very fine thread and the wrappings are strengthened with one or two fresh coats of varnish during the season; this union will last for the life of the line. To the short section thus joined to the leader I join the butt of the knotless tapered 9-foot leader mentioned previously, using a standard leader knot.

The most popular line-to-leader connection, and the one I prefer is the nail knot. This is a secure knot with a relatively small weight and diameter. After it has been

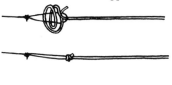

The wedge knot, drawn tight and clipped short.

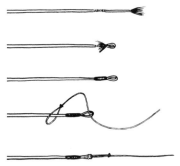

Passing leader through the line loop.

drawn tight and a drop of contact cement covers it, it will strip through the guides with maximum ease.

The surgeon's knot is an excellent one for difficult times. Its holding power and strength are as good as the standard barrel or leader knot and it is very easy to tie, particularly when the light is poor at dusk. Since one end of the piece to be attached must be pulled all the way through the knot twice, it is most valuable for the tying on of tippets.

Nylon and the other present day extruded monofilament leader materials have hard surfaces and are difficult to tie securely. The slipping of knots in nylon has been and continues to be a frequent cause of losing fish. A safe, secure knot should be used in every instance, taking time to tie it well and then drawing it down hard to be sure it is thoroughly set before starting to fish. There are a good many knots suitable for the various fishing purposes. Only one or two of each type will be shown here. Each time a fly is changed cut or break it off to insure new and strong material for attaching the next fly. Leaders are shortened by this process, especially when changes of flies are frequent and when the shortening is serious enough, the forward point of the leader must be renewed.

How strong should the tippet be and how stiff? Strength is one thing and stiffness is another. Visibility is the third factor involved in this decision. The idea is to go as far as you dare in reducing strength for maximum visibility. If you've tried stronger, more visible leaders and had no luck, it may be worth going down as low as 3-pound test at the tippet. Big salmon on this tackle will call for considerable skill. Grilse should be within the range of the average angler, if he's careful. I've taken salmon up to thirty pounds on 4-pound test. In rough or heavy water I may work with 10 to 15-pound test. Where playing conditions are good, 8-pound test should be adequate. Fortunately the need for the longest and finest leaders comes when the rivers are low and at their quietest flow, and playing a fish is easiest.

There is considerable choice within the available nylon monofilaments as to softness and stiffness. Soft leader is fine for tippets although the softer it is the more likely it will be to take on curls and hold them. Stiff mono will follow the cast's flow better, but on the water it will drag a fly across currents soft mono would bend with and follow.

There is a great lack of realization among anglers on just how strong their leaders are and what causes them to break. Every angler should, on occasions, hook his fly to a log or fence and pull hard enough to break it. Most will be amazed at its strength. Leaders break easily under sudden shock. Play your fish carefully when they're wild and may make sudden moves. When they're tired and start their moves slowly, leader pressure can come up to near maximum.

A word about leader materials. There are many new ones on the market. Some are strong in a straight pull and weak at the knots. Some will not knot well with other types. Diameters are growing smaller for a given strength but if the knots are weak there's no real gain. The only solution is to check those you use, for strength, when knotted.

There are times when salmon are not leader shy. Sometimes they'll take a fly tied to a short and heavy leader. There is no sure way to have the strongest possible leader on when one hooks a salmon. One can only try to keep the leader point strength within

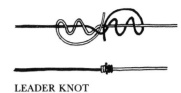

LEADER KNOT

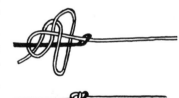

DRY FLY KNOT

WET FLY KNOT

LEADER (ROUGHENED)

LINE (FRAYED & ROUGHENED)

KNOTTED

WRAPPED & VARNISHED

Splicing heavy leader material to the line.

his playing capability and to increase that capability as much as he can. Fine leaders do pay off if only because the finer and softer the leader, the more naturally will the fly swim its way through the varying currents.

Tackle Accessories

In addition to the wet and dry flies which will be covered in the next chapter, there are certain essential or advisable accessories for salmon fishing to be considered. First among these is a net, tailer or gaff.

The gaff, a large, barbless hook mounted on a short staff similar to the handle of a broom, was, for a long time, the commonest instrument for securing and taking ashore a played-out salmon. The sharp steel hook will easily penetrate the flesh of the salmon, and the handle provides a good hold for carrying the heavy, slippery, and often very active fish to safety. The advantage of the gaff is that it is inexpensive. It takes up little space and is easy to carry, often being used as a walking or wading staff.

There are disadvantages, too. The gaff is dangerous to carry. Unless a foolproof hook guard is installed there is always the possibility of the sharp point penetrating one's flesh in the case of a fall. Such accidents have resulted in serious injuries.

Gaffs are not always easy to use. Gaffing a fish takes skill and practice. Often the gaff stroke catches the line or leader and pulls the hook away from its hold in the fish's mouth. Depth of water may be misjudged. The gaff stroke may miss the fish entirely, yet his sudden twisting away in the flow may cause the leader to tangle around the gaff hook or handle. More unfortunate, sometimes the gaff stroke is accurate enough to strike the fish but not to strike him well, resulting in his escaping with an injury which later proves fatal.

The gaff stroke should be across the salmon's back, a swift, sure motion with the hook point down. The point should penetrate the flesh near the backbone just ahead of the dorsal, and as the handle lifts the salmon, he is held by his own weight, helpless in the bend of the hook. A gaff that penetrates the flesh of the belly or is near the tail or hooks into a gill cover is almost certain to let the fish tear free with a terrible wound. A salmon should not be gaffed with the hook under his belly. It takes skill to gaff well and, even at best, it is a harsh and bloody way of securing a beautiful fish.

The gaff should have a spread of at least 3 inches between point and shank in order to get a safe grip on a good salmon. For safety's sake, it should have a good guard, preferably one that locks in place and swings away when in use. A piece of cork pushed down over the point is commonly used, but it may be dislodged quite easily. Handle length should be from 4 to 6 feet, a rugged handle with a good grip. A telescoping metal handle simplifies the carrying of the gaff, but it must be of very sturdy construction to be practical.

The salmon tailer is a type of snare made up of a cable, spring steel bow, and a rigid handle. The spring steel bow, held in a bent position by the cable, forms the snare which is stiff enough to push through the water and hold its shape in a moderate flow. When the fish is tired, this noose is moved up over his tail and drawn against his body anywhere between the dorsal fin and the tail. Any slight pressure against the body of the fish will release the spring from its bend, and it will straighten. This straightening,

This fine hen fish was caught with the author's 6-foot split-bamboo, a White Wulff dry fly, and tailer. This tailer was designed by the author and was manufactured under his patent.

together with a continued drawing movement of the tailer's handle toward the angler, snaps the cable into a tight noose which locks securely in position around the salmon's tail. Thus secured, the fish may be lifted or dragged into a canoe or ashore—or may simply be held in position until the fish is removed for releasing him, uninjured.

Since it is pushed up over the salmon from behind, the tailer does not interfere with the fly or leader, and, if the first attempt is unsuccessful, there is no harm done. Less skill is required to use a tailer than a gaff as the accuracy of placement need not be as great. If the movement of the tailer in placement or in releasing the spring is inaccurate, the fish will neither be injured nor lost. When the noose does tighten on a salmon's tail there is no escape for him. Tailers should be equipped with a loop at the handle which, when wrapped around the wrist of the gripping arm, will insure the tailer is not pulled free by a sudden surge of a still strong and uninjured salmon. Normally the grip of the tailer (or the hand) on the base of a salmon's tail has a paralyzing effect and he ceases to struggle, but this is not inevitably true.

Tailers are safe and light to carry. The spring should telescope into the handle for ease in carrying. The grip should be easy to hold. Such a tailer can be carried safely and conveniently when attached to a loop or snap at the back of the neck of jacket or fishing vest from which it hangs, out of the way but readily available when needed.

A large, long-handled net is an excellent method of landing a salmon. The net should be positioned in the water and the salmon drawn over it by the angler at which time it is lifted, engulfing and securing the fish. The netted fish also suffers no injury and comes ashore unmarred by any wounds. He, too, may be released without injury if that is the wish of the angler and care is taken in his handling. The best procedure is to keep the fish in the water, disengage the fly and then reverse the net without lifting it above the surface.

Nets should be big enough and strong enough for the job. A net of 30-inch diameter is adequate for big fish. All nets big enough for salmon are cumbersome to carry and impractical if the angler must carry his own landing device.

The one remaining piece of equipment, other than clothing and gadgets, are waders or boots. The best wading equipment for the angler who wishes to wade to the limit of his ability with a maximum of safety and comfort are chest-high waders with felt soles. Boot-footed waders are the simplest to put on and take off and eliminate the necessity of outside socks, which are a nuisance to pack and carry when wet. Stocking-

Moving the tailer into position after dark requires skill and good night vision.

foot waders and wading shoes are usually less expensive and permit the replacement of either unit when worn or damaged.

Felt soles are good for the gripping of rock surfaces no matter how hard or smooth. Their failing lies in an inability to hold on mud and slime-coated rocks. The slime fills the pores of the felt and takes away its power to grip. Hob-nailed soles will grip through slime and mud where felt will not, but they fail to grip on hard, smooth rock. Hobnails are likely to damage floors, boat bottoms, etc., and if an angler is careless enough to let a fly line fall underfoot, a hobnail will quickly ruin it for him.

Soles of rubber, whether cleated or smooth, are very slippery on rocky bottom. Rubber soles are much cheaper and longer wearing than felt. Under good wading conditions, over sand and gravel, they are adequate. Where wading is not easy enough to handle with rubber soles, an inexpensive way of providing a better grip for those special occasions is to don felt-bottomed sandals or strap on sets of three chains which lie under the ball of each foot and give the same sort of grip a set of chains gives to automobile tires. There are many new woven fibers like indoor-outdoor carpeting which can be cut to size and glued into position on boot soles with a strong epoxy adhesive.

When the rivers are small or low, or when an angler is only going to leave a boat or canoe to handle his fish in the shallows at the end of the playing, hip-high boots are all he needs. However, if there is an occasional need to wade to waist level it is better to have waders and use them for both deep and shallow wading than to have boots only and have to forgo the best spots when the waters are high.

Some sort of a well-pocketed garment is necessary for the wading fly fisherman. Many years ago in working out the best way to carry all the necessary things above the waterline of waist waders, the author worked out his Tak-L-Pak, a vest which could be worn comfortably over a sleeveless shirt in summer or warm, long-sleeved garments in cold weather. It has become the pattern for most practical, tackle-carrying garments for the wading fly fisherman. The vest has a solid pocket across the back, inside pockets on front, and multiple individual pockets on front and side to make it easy to find any particular fly or article. The large back pocket gives room for a plastic rain jacket, spare reel, etc. All the necessary equipment for the fishing trip, save rod and tailer, may be kept in such a garment at all times—insurance that no vital piece of equipment will be left behind.

The gadgets a fisherman carries are often the result of personal needs. Things one man considers essential may be merely excess baggage to another. The following is a listing of the things I carry in my fishing vest, which may serve as a guide for those who are uncertain as to what's worth carrying.

Insect repellent. Liquid repellent is probably still the most effective although some of the stick types are reported to work very well. I carry liquid repellent in a refillable metal or plastic container with dispenser end. Glass bottles always mean the possibility of breakage and the presence of sharp cutting edges.

Rain jacket. A short rain jacket which, when worn over waders, will give the wearer complete rain protection is worth the small space it takes up. Jackets made of lightweight plastic material are compact and completely impervious to rain.

Utility knife. A knife which includes a screwdriver, can opener, file, leather punch, as well as a normal blade is useful in emergencies.

Small pliers. Pliers are handy for many things. They can be used to bend down the barbs and make hooks barbless and to take hooks out of fish, even out of people.

Leather thong. A 3-foot length of leather thong will serve to carry a salmon when necessary. A salmon's gills will break under his weight and one cannot be carried far with a hand grip on the gills. A salmon's tail is strong, and it is possible to hold him up by it for a short time, but the hand soon grows tired. When carrying salmon for any distance, a thong tied around his tail is better. It can be tied to the middle of a short, stout stick at a convenient distance to give a carrying grip, or it can be tied both at the tail and around the head at the gills for an easy carry.

Salt. A small container of salt comes in handy when there's a sudden desire to add a bit of broiled trout or salmon to perk up a lunch.

Scotch Electrical tape. This plastic tape will serve to mend small leaks in plastic waders, to wrap on damaged guides, to secure an uncertain reel in its seat, and for any number of similar emergencies.

Scissors. A pair of small but sturdy scissors, which I find easier to use in trimming flies and snipping off the ends of leader knots than a fingernail clipper, should be included.

Wader patching material. A large tear or rip in wader or jacket calls for this type of patch.

Also necessary are: a hook hone, which is the best insurance against missed rises; a thermometer for checking water and air temperatures; spare reel and line leaders, flies, line and fly grease, and sunglasses.

5

The Flies

The key to salmon fishing is that small device whereby a distant fish is tricked into attaching himself to the tackle. Until the salmon takes the fly he is independent and aloof. Once hooked he is trapped like a great insect in a spider's web from which he may break free and escape or, at the end of a struggle in which his strength and speed have been thwarted, be subdued and consumed or released.

The fly then, is a device to conjure with. The perfect fly is to an angler as his potions are to a witch doctor. The angler guards them jealously, handles them with care and reverence, and casts them out in the same mixture of faith and cunning the heathen sorcerer uses to destroy an enemy or make it rain.

Wet Flies

In the year 1845 a salmon angler on a voyage to Norway was touched with sudden inspiration. He tied a new fly. Into it he put, so the record shows, some yellow and some black silk floss and feather sections or vanes from no less than eighteen different birds—to wit: golden pheasant from China, guinea hen from Madagasgar, teal, swan, barred summer duck, mallard, game cock and blue chatterer from nearby European sources, black ostrich and bustard from Africa, peacock and peahen from Ceylon, turkey from North America, Indian crow, jungle cock and florikan from India, and toucan and macaw from the Central American jungles. All these things he cunningly contrived with fine silk thread on a small hook of barbed steel into a new pattern which today still bears his name. No more reverent tribute to its effectiveness could be found than the reply of an old, experienced guide to a query as to what flies would take salmon on his river. He said, "It doesn't matter much what sort of fly you use here, sir, as long as its a Jock Scott."

Many thousands of variations and patterns of salmon flies have been tied and tried at one time or another. Small differences, such as replacing half a dozen blue fibers with the same number in green, or changing the ribbing wire from silver to gold, are often held to make the difference between a salmon captured and a fishless day. No human knows just how important these small variations actually are to the salmon, but it is certain they are thoroughly appreciated by most salmon anglers.

A Jock Scott, perfectly tied, is a salmon fisherman's dream. So is a Mar Lodge, a Black Dose, and a Silver Wilkinson. In them one may find feathers from exotic birds nestling together over the sheen of American tinsel on a stout British hook. With a painstaking care that may not long survive in this world of machine-made products, each hook is carefully dressed by hand with fine waxed thread and fashioned into a precise copy of the original. Some patterns are still made as listed by their originators; others have been embellished over the years from flies whose beginnings have been lost in antiquity.

Too simple a fly would hardly command a good price. Salmon fishermen have been able to afford the best available, and the canny Scottish fly tyers have been prepared to sell it to them. A fly as simple as a Silver Blue, which consists only of a pair of matched mallard or teal feathers for wings, topped with a pheasant crest feather, a tinsel body, and a flare of blue hackle, looks out of place in the average salmon-fly display. Too plain and hardly worth the price! A fly tyer loves to sell such flies. Easy to tie, they command the same price as do those that are complex and difficult.

The original salmon wet flies may have had some basis of imitation, but it seems doubtful. As a whole they are poor imitations of either the insect or small fish life of the stream. More likely, rather, that they were made as an individual expression of a fly-tying angler. Some may even have been concocted in desperation due to the failure of those at hand to lure the fish. Throughout the years, there have evolved patterns featuring every color or combination in the rainbow. Want a basically black and yellow fly? Try a Jock Scott or a Teagle Bee. One that's strongly red? A Durham Ranger. One that's dark? A Black Dago. A Light one? A Lady Amherst.

How do the salmon look at them? Are the fish reminded of a long forgotten but delicious bug? Do they compare the drifting fly with the living stone-fly nymph that just went swimming by? Do they note the neatness of the tying and how perfectly the feather fibers of some birds that lived and died on separate continents are married together as if a single bird produced them on a single feather? There are anglers who will insist that dyed feathers will not serve well in a salmon fly. Such imitations, they maintain, will not fool the fish.

It is pertinent to ask by what stretch of the imagination one can feel that a salmon, whose worldwide terrestrial experience is nonexistent, could possibly be expected to tell whether a bit of feather in a fly came from a rare bird of India and was natural, or was dyed and came originally from a chicken or a duck that was raised and slaughtered in New Jersey? Perhaps a fisherman can tell the difference, but it does not follow that a salmon, even if he could, would give a damn. If a salmon had any inkling the fly was made up of feathers at all he would most certainly spurn it.

Regardless of what the anglers think, there's no question but that the old, tried-and-true patterns have their effectiveness. They may have evolved from an irrational supposition in the first place, and those with dyed feathers may not catch salmon as well for some fishermen as those blended of the real things, but they do catch fish. No salmon fisherman should be without a few and, perhaps, quite a few of the old standbys. A list of some of the preferred patterns follows:

Jock Scott, Silver Grey, Black Dose, Dusty Miller, Thunder and Lightning, Mar Lodge, Silver Doctor, Green Highlander, Black Doctor, Blue Charm, Durham Ranger, and Silver Wilkinson.

The choosing of the right fly gives pause to many a salmon angler. Friends, books, and tourist booklets all offer lists of popular patterns. Such lists have their value and each fly listed will have its virtues. Usually there is one among them better by far than all the others. It is the particular fly in which the angler himself places the greatest faith. Especially when the angler may get only one or two rises for a full day's fishing will he find it difficult to fish properly, hour after hour, with a pattern about whose effectiveness he is in doubt.

NEW

The standard salmon patterns, created long ago and thoroughly tested over the intervening years, are tokens as precious as memories, to collect and dream over through the long winter. But let a salmon once close his massive jaws tightly upon this work of art and then be captured and the fly has changed. For every wisp of feather out of place, for every bit of raggedness marring the sleek, trim beauty of the unused fly, there has been added a new memory and mark of success. And, when a fly has lured a dozen salmon to the shore, the ragged wisps of feather and the shiny glints where wear has uncovered the raw metal of the hook are mute testimonials to its magic powers. These, then, are the flies salmon anglers cling to and save for those dark days when nothing else avails. "Whenever I give a fly away," as one old, wise angler remarked, "it's always a new one."

OLD

It is reasonable to wonder, then, if it would not be better to start out with the ragged flies we find so effective or, even better, to make our new ones with a look of studied carelessness. In essence, this is being done. New patterns, new materials, combined by amateur fly makers who have neither the skill nor the patience to tie them in the time-honored tradition, have reached the salmon rivers and matched catches with the old and storied flies. Trout fishermen, wandering afield to the salmon rivers, pinning their faith on favorite trout patterns, have been well rewarded. To say the standard patterns of salmon flies are dropping out of favor would be wrong, but to say they are essential to maximum success would, I believe, be just as much in error.

Flies, new and old.

The casual fly tyer, lacking the professional's worldwide selection of materials, has had to improvise, and so created many new and effective patterns. Many, like myself, have, in their travels, taught others the way of making flies. These newcomers to the fly tyer's art soon run out of the materials an itinerant fishing fly tyer can spare for them and start experimenting. In Corner Brook, near Newfoundland's Humber, I fished long ago with Ted Bugden and Max Rabbits. Ted was an experienced and an excellent fisherman, and Max was new at the sport. I taught them both how flies were made. Max was especially adept with his fingers and almost immediately started turning out professional-looking flies. Ted's flies were quickly but sturdily made. He soon ran through his gift materials and fell back on colored yarns and some coarse bristles from a moose's hide. His flies lacked finish, but they did catch fish, more fish, as it happened, than did Max's careful copies.

Flies with wings of bucktail, squirrel hair, moose hair, caribou, and elk hair are quite effective for salmon. Hair flies can never have the svelte look of precision so essential to the conventional salmon fly. The hair, being stiffer, doesn't arrange itself with the neatness of feathers. Because of the thickness of the hair fibers at the butt ends, the heads of the hair flies can never be as trim and neat as those of feathered construction. The success of the hair flies is a fair indication that these details are not necessarily important to a salmon.

Within the ranks of those who limit themselves to flies patterned in the conventional manner, there are those who believe a wide variety of patterns is not necessary. The old guide's statement that any fly would do as long as it was a Jock Scott contains an element of humor but, perhaps, also an element of truth. When we find one of the most able and best known of modern salmon anglers, A. H. E. Wood of Glassel, Scotland, who, during his years of fishing, captured thousands of salmon, limiting himself to only three flies, it is a matter for most serious consideration.

Wood's three flies were among the simplest of patterns, the Blue Charm, Silver Blue, and March Brown. In describing his greased-line method of fishing in the Lonsdale Library edition of *Salmon Fishing* he states, "I use only three patterns now. Blue Charm and Silver Blue are my stock, simply on the principle that one is more or less black and the other white and so give *me* a choice. But some five years ago, a friend, seeing my box and hearing I did not think colour mattered at all, offered to bet that I would not use a March Brown for the rest of the season to the exclusion of any other pattern. I took his bet, on the condition that I could use any size I wanted. I did not, on any occasion, find the change of pattern made the smallest difference. I got my share and more, of the fish caught. Since then, the March Brown has been added to my collection and forms a third pattern." There can be little doubt but that the presentation of the fly is a major factor in the taking of a salmon, and that the importance of a pattern is often overemphasized.

A streamer fly.

It has come as a surprise in many quarters that streamer flies, which are designed as minnow imitations, can sometimes be quite effective for salmon. Bob Reedy, an American Army officer stationed in Newfoundland early in the Second World War, started fishing with streamers for salmon on the Trepassy River for lack of any traditional salmon flies at the time. He caught more salmon in that tumbling, deep-pooled river on his streamers than any other angler caught that year.

Long ago on the St. Mary's River in Nova Scotia, I cast out a long white streamer on a #1 hook and took a salmon on a day when all my other offerings had failed to draw a rise. One fall on the Miramichi, Perley Palmer, a respected old-time guide of those waters, slipped a #2 Mickey Finn into my hands with the words, "This is an awfully good fly, and it will take them sometimes when nothing else seems to." He was right. It took two salmon in short order.

Still, in the overall picture, streamer flies are not very effective for Atlantic salmon. They may take an occasional fish, and they may work when nothing else seems to attract the fish, but they're a sort of last resort and in few waters will they produce salmon in comparison with the more conventional wet flies. Streamers have been tried out extensively. The consensus is they're good for special occasions; poor producers for steady usage.

Within the experience of most salmon anglers, there is a time when a change of fly pattern has resulted in the taking of a fish after a period of inaction. Often the continued use of the new fly produced additional rises or captures. Sometimes tests are made and two different flies fished for alternating, equal periods and the results favor one fly or another. Such tests are rarely conclusive.

For instance, when an angler says, "I tried everything, but the only fly they would rise to was a #16 Bawdy Babe," it is wise to consider these things: Exactly how many flies did he try? Exactly how long did he try them? It is obviously impossible to give each of the hundreds of available patterns in a dozen different sizes, a fair trial in a solid week of fishing, let alone in one afternoon. A pattern fished at high noon in brightest sun does not have the same trial as another fished two hours later under a solid overcast, nor a third fishing in the dusk of evening in a rain.

What constitutes the "trial" of a fly, one cast or a dozen or a hundred? Often a persistent fisherman will take a particular salmon on, let us say, the hundredth cast with the same fly. Had he been changing flies every ten casts it might still have been the hundredth cast which proved effective. No two casts are identical, and no two bits of water. To be qualified, a test of the efficiency of two patterns should be made over exactly the same water and at the same time, as closely as possible.

If it is possible to make such a test, it might be done in this way: a cast to a good salmon lie should be made with one fly and immediately followed with an identical cast with the second fly. By using two outfits, identical in every way except for the fly, a duplicate cast should be made with the other, not alternating casts as one moves through a pool, but identical casts, alternating to give first one fly and then the other the first cast to the new water for, normally, the first fly that comes to a salmon has the advantage.

It would be necessary to take several fish in each comparison of flies to be sure circumstances were not dictating the preference, instead of actual attractiveness of the fly to the fish. By the time the second or third fish was taken, the conditions might well be changed. Even with any decisive test, limited to only two patterns, the hours involved would mount up. It is easy to see that a thorough testing of as few as a dozen patterns in only three or four sizes would mean the work of days, perhaps weeks, rather than hours.

When someone starts out with "I tried everything but—" you may safely discount the statement to follow by 99 percent, unless it is, "I couldn't take one." Suppose, for instance, when Perley Palmer handed me the Mickey Finn on that cold and windy fall afternoon on the Miramichi, I had instead put on a large Red Sandy, a conventional salmon pattern which would generally match the trout streamer in size and coloration. The same two fish might have taken it, and perhaps even a third and larger fish might have come to that fly. As it happens, I did not have such a pattern in so large a size. To carry a full line of patterns and sizes is beyond both the capabilities and pocketbooks of most anglers.

How important, then, is pattern to a salmon fisherman? Its greatest importance is in his confidence. His faith in it gives it a fair trial. When an angler is defeated in his efforts and is wildly trying his last resorts, he isn't likely to give them the same careful fishing he gave the flies he had faith in when his hopes of good results were at their peak.

Scientists agree that fish detect color. It seems reasonable that color should have a degree of importance to them. Even the most minor effect is important if it means the difference between catching a salmon and failing to take one. Neither this writing nor any other is likely to give a full solution. The thing of greatest value to the angler is a faith that salmon can be taken on certain flies of certain colors—and an open mind as to whether or not certain *other* flies might not do as well, or perhaps better.

A salmon's notion to rise to the fly is an intangible thing. Suppose an angler examining a low, clear pool counts eighteen salmon in it. Suppose, too, he raises and catches one and only one during an entire day of fishing. One of his flies, therefore, must have been effective. It worked, though, on only one salmon. If it had been completely effective on all salmon, he should have been able to catch or at least raise every salmon in the pool. Let us assume a second fly produced a second fish. One of the seventeen found it satisfactory, but the others at that time did not. More often than not, anglers taking several fish in a day take them on different flies. The obvious inference is that salmon have individual tastes, that what pleases or excites one will not necessarily stir another, that salmon flies may be designed to interest *some* salmon, not all salmon. A realization of this is an admission that the choice of flies can never be precise and rigid, that it must always be a matter of compromise and experience. The proper choice of flies for salmon is not a science but something more subtle, like an art.

Peter McElligott, friend and fine salmon fisherman, says he fishes differently for male and female salmon. He fishes the Margaree, late in the season, therefore his may be a special case. With spawning just around the corner Peter feels that the males become territorial and are resentful of anything that comes within their chosen domains. As a result, for the males he uses fair-sized or large flies and moves them swiftly through the area he believes a male has staked out.

It takes a good eye to tell a male from a female salmon, particularly in the early season. Distinguishing the slightly larger head size or heavier lower jaw as a fish lies in a pool, or even when he jumps is something that few can bet on. Later in the season, when the kipe grows and the general shape of the male becomes deeper and more slab sided, a knowing angler who gets a good look at a fish can make a good guess at its sex. In rivers like the Miramichi there's a good chance that a grilse will be a male, but in many rivers that have a run made up almost entirely of grilse the ratio has to run about fifty-fifty. For all but a few anglers it will be next to impossible to determine the sex of the salmon they fish for before they are hooked or caught.

Peter uses much smaller flies, usually #10s and #12s for the females and he fishes them at normal speeds, with a conventional swing. He finds that while males are given to frequent movement and to resting at various places within their selected sphere, the females tend to choose a good lie and stick with it, just as most salmon do most of the time.

One would expect the females to be a better judge of a spawning area and more likely to make any territorial selection. The big females may have one or more suitors, including grilse and even parr, and for her to move to suit a suitor doesn't seem reasonable. During the angling season these fish are not yet engaged in spawning and have not yet come to the redds where they will join up to spawn. Perhaps the males become territorial on a temporary basis before the actual spawning takes place.

Peter tells of an instance where there were three males in a pool. All the males were caught before the female could be taken. There may be, he suggests, a protective measure to the territoriality as fall approaches.

How much territoriality exists in males I do not know and can only guess but it does open up an interesting line of thinking. McElligott's experiences indicate to most of us that, in late season especially, we should cover the field and fish both small flies normally and large flies fast. It will be interesting to note which sex we catch on each method and if the percentages change between early season and late.

Of more importance to most anglers is the choice of flies to take large salmon as compared to grilse. Looking back over a great many years I can say with certainly that my most effective fly for big fish is the Surface Stone fly which is somewhat similar, when fished dry, to the more recent Bomber and, when fished wet, to the Muddler.

Many a time I've fished over a group of salmon, made up predominantly of grilse, and taken one of the big fish rather than a grilse on that fly. My reasoning is that the stone fly has a stronger imprint on the salmon's mind as a parr than other insects do and is therefore more likely to trigger a response in a big fish which has had a longer sea period to forget his stream preferences than the grilse have.

It has been my experience that with wet flies the drab patterns are more likely to take big salmon than the bright, flashy flies like the Silver Doctor. I do not consciously fish my flies differently for big salmon than for small ones. There may be something in a certain speed or swing of wet-fly or a certain length of dry-fly drift that is particularly appealing to big salmon but, if so, I have yet to determine it. It is something a fisherman can amuse himself with and keep records on and, one day, we may know more about this part of salmon fishing than we do now.

When fishing dry I do like to work over big fish with a big fly like a #4 White Wulff. Here, again, it may be that it takes something larger to trigger the rise response in a salmon that has been at sea for two years or longer than it does for the one-year-sea-feeding fish. I find the Skater one of my better flies to interest big fish. That may be, too, that the extra excitement of its motion may trigger a response from the big fish that are longer away from parr feeding.

If, on only slight evidence, we begin to fish one way more than or exclusive of all others we will miss out on a lot of fish that might have been more receptive to a different presentation. Only an impartial testing will give us reliable results. This is particularly true when an angler fishes several different rivers. Each river is different and so are its salmon.

Within the maze of personal preferences surrounding the selection of salmon flies, certain favorings of the salmon have been catalogued and noted. These are the tenets we go by, the guidelines by which we choose. They are real, they are solid—but they are far from complete. Originally, all salmon taken on flies by anglers were caught on wet or sinking flies. There were no others. The advent of the dry fly did not change wet-fly fishing but added a new method. Greased-line fishing, the "hitch," and the "Patent" methods opened new avenues for the wet fly. New types of dry fly are still being developed. We now know more than ever about the types of fly a salmon will take. It would be foolish to think we know all there is to know, or become convinced that a certain fly or type of fly *will not* take salmon if it falls within reasonable size limits. As certainly as one tries to limit the possible actions of the salmon with regard to a fly, just as surely will that individual be confounded.

Typical of this was an incident on the Ecum Secum River of Nova Scotia. The water was low and clear, the fish were listless. The small group that had been fishing the waters had become listless, too, and not a fish had been raised or taken for over a week. A lad from one of the nearby houses, not yet in his teens, came down to the bridge overlooking one of the best salmon lies. With a flourish he whapped a ridiculous creation of his own down on the water over the fish. The "fly" was composed of two white goose feathers wrapped with twine to the shank of a small cod hook about 4/0 in size. One of the nearby fishermen clapped his hand to his forehead in dismay at this disturbing of the pool. However, no sooner had the fly landed and before the rings of the splash had spread a foot-wide circle than a salmon rose, was hooked, made a beautiful leap, and tore free on a run up toward the deeper water.

Few fishermen are broad enough in their thinking as to the range of flies that can interest a salmon. What is not tried cannot be denied. The angler who is afraid to appear ridiculous by using a fly or pattern which is out of the ordinary will, now and then, fail to catch salmon that could have been caught.

Most anglers will agree that bright, colorful patterns are most effective when the salmon are newly in from the sea and that the brightest, most unusually colored patterns are less effective than the dull, drab ones after the fish have spent weeks or months in the streams. It may be when the fish arrive they have forgotten how drab most of the nymphs and insects of their streams really are. After they have been back a while and have watched these insects swimming in the waters around them, their judgment is a more sober and realistic one. At any rate, as a general rule, the gay patterns are for the bright, new fish and the staid patterns for those who have settled again into river living.

Thus, the Silver Doctor is considered a better fly for early fishing while a Blue Charm is generally accepted as one of the better flies for late fishing. It may be that the amount of silver or gold on a fly in the form of tinsel has an impact in this sense, too. Silvery flies are better early and dull ones better late. There are some very successful anglers who tie their flies and limit themselves to simplified patterns in which the main variations are shadings of light and dark and amounts of tinsel rather than of color. A dark fly, a light fly, and a silvery fly thus are able to cover, in a general fashion, the fisherman's basic needs. Embellishments beyond these may not be essential, but they add variety and interest to the fishing and, in the opinion of most anglers, increase the catch. The black and yellow combination basic to the Jock Scott and Teagle Bee and others is a very good one. The Durham Ranger and Wilkinson feature red and blue. The Mar Lodge, Silver Grey, and Dusty Miller are basically silver and grey. Thunder and Lightning and Fiery Brown are dark brown and orange. The Kossaboom and Green Highlander are basically green.

From those who tie their own flies and tie for the salmon's attention rather than for the judgment of other anglers, comes this valuable advice. Make flies wispier and slimmer, with the feathers, hair, or fibers lying close to the shank and make the fly, in general, round. But, since all rules pertaining to salmon flies seem made but to be broken, do not make *all* of your flies of any single characteristic shape lest you lose the advantage of offering a stubborn fish something in the way of variation.

The hook itself becomes an important factor in the overall "look" of a conventional salmon fly. The bend of the hook and the distinctive barbed point extending behind and below the fly itself give *all* salmon flies a somewhat similar look. In the belief that this shape may not be the most attractive one to all salmon, salmon flies are sometimes tied upon an eyed shaft behind which a very small double hook is trailed. In this way a #14 double may be used on an arrangement of material which would normally be balanced on a #2 hook, for example. Small hooks when well set in a fish's jaw and, in particular, at the corner of the mouth have extremely good holding power. The use of small doubles and the breakaway from the conventional overall shape has an

Place the hook behind the fly.

STANDARD

LOW WATER

Different waters need different flies.

advantage, perhaps, particularly on hard fished waters. The flies of this type would be better if treble hooks were permitted, as the hooking power of the very small doubles is questioned by many. So far these flies have not been widely used on the western side of the Atlantic.

Rivers in flood call for large flies since, on the initial runoff of water from a parched land, the angler's lure must compete for the salmon's attention with leaves, sticks, even whole tree trunks sometimes swept downstream by the main current. When pulp logs are being driven down a river, even though they may be widely separated, they will cause the salmon's interest to swing to larger flies than normal. Just how much larger is often surprising. On a New Brunswick river where small flies are the fashion, I have taken grilse during a pulp drive in moderately low water which was clear and otherwise free from debris, on 3/0 flies when none of the smaller flies of my own or of my companions drew a rise.

Large flies can be seen farther in dark or roily water, and the heavier hook of the large fly will cause it to swim deeper and closer to the salmon which lie much nearer the streambed than the surface. The angler who can dig a stray 3/0 or 4/0 fly out of his kit at the time of a sudden flood may be the only angler to take salmon on a river normally calling for flies of #6 and #8.

Large and heavy waters usually call for larger flies than the smaller, quieter streams. The great mainland salmon rivers of Quebec and New Brunswick sometimes demand flies that would seem monstrous to the small and intimate streams of Newfoundland. Before setting forth for new waters, the wise angler consults someone who has fished his prospective river or, at least, the general area with regard to fly patterns and sizes.

When the rivers are low and the current in them has almost disappeared, the smallest of wet flies are in order. Then the angler whose kit contains only the proper flies for normal water finds himself in an almost hopeless position. He is still slightly better off than the angler who lacks the large flies for high waters, for he can trim down his smallest wet flies until little remains of them but the bare hook and a bit of fuzz. Even bare hooks with painted or tinselled shanks are used by some anglers and, in rare cases, ordinary black or bronzed hooks in the natural state have taken salmon. This trimming down of flies proved effective enough to cause the development of a special type of wet fly, the *low-water* wet fly.

The low-water fly is really a small fly tied on a large hook. It presents a small bulk to the fish, yet holds him with all the power of a larger fly. In order to make these flies have a more balanced appearance, they are tied on hooks of finer wire and usually of a slightly longer shank than the standard hook of the same number size. The advantages of the long, fine-wire hook are twofold: they obtain greater hooking and holding power with the same weight, and they hook a larger percentage of "short-risers," since the point of the hook trails farther behind the body of the fly. These low-water flies give an advantage of two or three hook sizes over the regular patterns. Their real advantage begins at the point where the standard hook becomes too small to be fully trusted to hold a large salmon. The #4 low-water fly will give less of feathers and tinsel with practically the same holding power as the standard #4 fly. From there on down the line the advantage in hooking and holding lies with the low-water series. The holding power of a #4 hook is considerable, regardless of type, but when it comes to a

#12 standard fly which can, instead, be tied on a #9 hook the difference in holding power becomes extremely important. In the very small sizes the low-water-type fly offers the greatest advantage.

Low-water patterns, as well as being shortened and condensed, are usually simpler than their standard counterparts. They are slim of body, light of feathers, and wispy of hackle. The dressy "married" feather vanes are often missing, and wings are made up of but single feather layers on each side, not several. They are flies in essence, simple, inexpensive, and extremely effective. Where salmon prefer flies in the #4 to #8 range or smaller, the low-water types are a logical choice for all but extremely high-water fishing.

Salmon flies are available in either single or double hooks, the latter having a common eye, parallel shanks, and the two bends set with an angle of approximately 60 degrees between them. Double hooks are more likely to hold their upright position when fished, since they have twice the weight in two bent and barbed points to keel them. When solidly set they have twice the gripping power in the flesh of a fish.

Yet there is considerable difference of opinion on the relative merits of each form. It takes twice the pull to set a double hook into tough flesh, a distinct disadvantage when leader points are fine. The double hook is heavier, too, for the same feather-and-tinsel bulk which makes it more difficult to cast and more likely to cause wear at the knot where it is fastened to the leader. The sudden changes of direction occurring in fly casting make the point of attachment of the fly a vulnerable spot. The heavier the fly, the more vulnerable that spot becomes. Furthermore, the double hook is readily felt by the salmon when he takes it into his mouth, and he immediately ejects it. A single hook, in contrast, will lie flat upon his tongue, and salmon will usually hang on to a single-hook fly until the light tension of the tightening line starts the point digging into the flesh. Single-hook flies are lighter and may be cast with greater ease, landing with less splash.

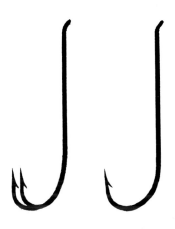

Double and single hooks.

The double hook's holding power which at first glance is so apparent may be more than nullified by its tendency to shift in its setting under pressure from several angles. It is possible for one of the paired hooks to form a fulcrum on which a side pull by fish or angler exerts a great force upon the other. By changing the pull back and forth from side to side, the fly may work free.

Double-hook flies may have an advantage if they are to be used with the Portland Creek hitch and skimmed over the surface. The paired hooks help hold the skimming fly upright and in that position may be fished from either side with equal effectiveness. The hitch on a single hook must be set for one side or the other.

Double-hook flies are more expensive and more bulky. Many more single-hook flies can be carried in the same space. Because of these and perhaps other advantages, the single hook is a general favorite. In the eyes of most salmon fishermen, the hooking and holding power of the single hook is at least the equal of the paired barbs.

The hook is unquestionably the most important part of the fly. If it fails the salmon is lost, and all the effort that went into the making of the fly and the working out of the design have come to no avail. Exactness of reproduction to pattern may come next in value. The feeling that a certain, very precise combination of materials will catch a salmon and that any variation from that pattern makes the fly less effective causes most buyers to inspect their purchases with especial care. Actually, renditions of a Jock Scott will vary far more than interpretations of Beethoven's Third under different maestros.

The angler who wants the exact fly, order after order, must stick to the same fly maker or to a limited few who have no need to substitute for any of the required materials and always tie in the same manner. Nowadays there is a general similarity rather than identicality in flies of the same pattern from different makers.

In selecting flies, the first thing to look at is the hook. A well-designed salmon hook is the perfection of the hook maker's art. The best grade of salmon hooks are japanned black and they have return eyes in which both ends of the loop of steel are covered by the wrapping of the head. This leaves no possibility for a fine leader to escape through the failure of an ordinary eye to be completely closed. The hook's shape will depend upon the design or classification the manufacturer of the fly chooses to use, but the preference lies with a hook of the general shape and silhouette shown in the illustrations.

Short- or standard-shanked hooks are usually good holding hooks. When the shanks are very long they give an extended leverage on the embedded point when the angle of the pull on the fish is at variance with the pull from which the hook was set. Any working back and forth of the hook point and barb enlarges the hole into which it was driven at the strike and will loosen its hold.

Heavy hooks will make a fly travel a little deeper and sink more readily. Very light hooks may sacrifice strength and should always be of the very highest quality. It is worth remembering that fine-wire hooks will cut through flesh under pressure. Though a hook may have a wide bend, if the wire is very fine, it may hold no better than a hook of heavier wire several sizes smaller. On the best quality salmon hooks, the diameter of the wire at the bend is increased above that of the shank because of the possibility that pressure on the hook at that point may cause it to cut. This increase is for added bearing area and not for greater strength at that point.

Although the hook is recognized as one of the most important parts of the angler's tackle, it is often taken for granted because of the excellent quality and uniformity of modern hooks. The new hook can be depended upon to be perfect, but hooks can easily be dulled. It is a primary point to keep hooks sharp. A touch of the hone now and then is good policy. Dull hooks will slide over tough flesh without digging in. Hooks can never be too sharp.

The workmanship in the fly determines how well it will hold its shape and how long it will last. Flies of a reputable maker can be depended upon to be sound, except in rare instances beyond his control. There is no better check of quality of a fly than the integrity of the maker. It is impossible to thoroughly test a fly without using it.

Trout patterns are often effective for salmon. Being smaller than salmon flies they are most likely to be used when the waters are low and when the salmon have been in the rivers for some time. In general, the more staid patterns like the Dark Cahill, Cowdung, Black Gnat, Blue Quill, and Quill Gordon are the most favored. Paradoxically the Royal Wulff, a bright and colorful fly, is one of the most effective of the trout flies for salmon. A box of trout flies in a salmon fisherman's outfit extends greatly the variety of his small-fly coverage and is well worth the space it takes when the waters fall to low, low summer levels. Be certain, however, the hooks are of fine quality before using them. You can test them for softness by trying to bend them. If they bend readily don't use them.

Trout flies normally have the eyes of the hooks turned down while salmon fly hooks are turned up. Whether the eye is up or down has no real effect on the action or

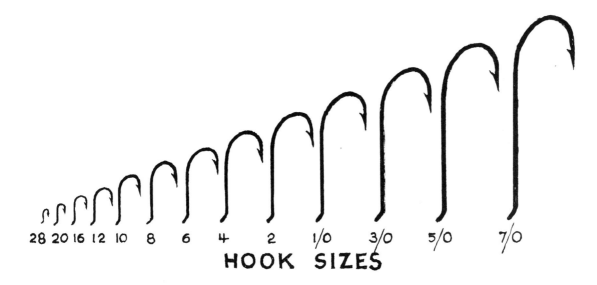

HOOK SIZES

28 20 16 12 10 8 6 4 2 1/0 3/0 5/0 7/0

effectiveness of a fly if it is properly knotted to the leader. The offset in each case, regardless of the direction, is for the purpose of giving the fisherman a straight pull from leader to the axis of the shank of the hook. The wet-fly knot should carry through the offset eye and be made around the shank. With the dry fly, which floats freely, this is not important. The manufacturers usually expend more care and put their very best materials into salmon hooks, and turned-up-eye hooks are almost always of the very best quality. A good trout hook is perfectly adequate for salmon, but a poor one will break or bend where a salmon hook would hold.

Some European anglers, who fish where the rules permit the use of treble hooks, tied their materials on tubes to replace the conspicuous down-hanging single- or double-hook bend with the treble's cluster of small hooks and so give a different shape and character to the fly. I found other uses and advantages for the tube while still using the single hooks preferred on this side of the Atlantic. I found I could increase or decrease the size and shape of my fly by adding segments or changing their order. I could use short-shank hooks on a long snell or terminal tippet. This arrangement could give me minimum hook weight for dry flies or skaters, particularly with skaters where I could double the floating characteristics by adding a second tube segment. With wet flies I could change the type or size of hook by changing one snelled tippet for another, sliding the fly off one and onto another and re-tying the blood knot. This widens the scope of the flies the angler carries.

The Muddler, invented by Don Gapen as a trout fly, has become one of the more successful trout-to-salmon innovations. It is a more or less typical wet fly with the added twist of a clipped-hair collar just behind the eye of the fly. This gives it an unusual shape and, on a retrieve, may even put a small air bubble behind the collar to change further the appearance of the fly. Muddlers will skim at speeds where a typical wet fly of similar size and shape would swim under the surface. Whatever its charm, the Muddler, which is a category of flies rather than a single pattern, has found a place in the hearts of many salmon anglers.

Imitations of the nymph form of the stream insects are effective for salmon but are not often available in tackle shops. Were salmon avidly interested in food, it seems

The author took this 27-pound Moisie River salmon on a #16 single-hook Black Bear wet fly in 38 minutes flat.

Stone fly nymph.

certain such common nymphs as those of the stone fly would form a large part of their diet, since they make up a large part of the available food in any salmon stream. It is surprising that those anglers who believe salmon are serious feeders do not carry in their fly boxes many exact imitation of the nymphs common to the waters they fish. Logic would suggest the nymph imitations as superior to the abstract fly pattern, just as it is for the wariest of trout. If the food element were a foremost factor in the salmon's rise, nymphs and streamers should be best and conventional wet flies way down on the list.

Not many salmon anglers have ever used nymphs. Having tried a good many nymphs for many hours, it was my finding that nymphs would take salmon about as well but no better than the simple forms of salmon flies I most often use. Rubber or plastic replicas of nymphs which were quite accurate in shape and form were less effective than less accurate imitations made of feathers or hair or other soft materials which could give a greater degree of "leg" movement as they drifted through the water. In general, I do not believe nymphs are as good as wet flies, although in some cases where the water was almost still and the nymph was fished deep and very slowly, they showed a definitely better return than wet flies.

The field of nymph fishing for salmon is one in which very little work has been done. It holds considerable possibility for development. I confess to neglecting it in preference to extensive experimentation in the dry-fly field. Dry flies are normally most effective at the time nymphs could be expected to be most valuable, when the water is low and the flow is slow. Salmon-fly patterns do not look like nymphs. Nymph patterns may not only prove better than flies for salmon under some conditions, but they may throw new light on the unending controversy as to whether salmon feed in fresh water and on what and why.

The writer has experimented widely with flies made up with plastic bodies and holds a patent on the basic method of embedding fibers for their manufacture. While tied flies will come unwound, plastic flies can be damaged only by severe blows or extreme heat. With a plastic body, fibers need not always be wound around the shank but can be applied in almost any quantity in any direction. Such flies can be made by assembly-line methods, and it may eventually be possible to make them by machine. In this era of changing methods and reduction of time-consuming handwork, the fly tyer's art holds a precarious position.

Dry Flies

Wet-fly fishing is hundreds of years old. Dry-fly fishing for salmon is the product of this century, and its real impetus has come within the past twenty-five years. Prior to 1933, not one hour of dry-fly fishing was practiced for 100 of conventional wet-fly fishing.

In the early thirties, it was unusual to meet another dry-fly angler, and it was quite common when moving to a new river to find guides and fishermen who had never seen a dry fly fished and who were frankly doubtful that a floating fly would have any attraction for "their" salmon. As late as 1946, when I opened a fishing camp on Portland Creek in Newfoundland, none of these guides there had ever seen a dry fly fished and, as far as they knew, no one else had ever fished dry fly there. How effective the dry fly is may be judged by the comparative take on a river like the nearby River of

Ponds, where, during a recent season, there were nearly twice as many salmon taken on the dry fly as on the sunken fly.

The dry fly, however, is not always as effective as the wet fly, and in certain waters seems to have very little allure for the salmon. In general, the darker and more peat-stained the water, the less effective the dry fly is. Conversely, the clear streams and the low-water periods, when the brown streams are clearest, are best for dry-fly fishing.

As the name implies, the dry fly floats upon the surface instead of sinking under it. Therefore it must be lighter in weight than the wet fly or it must contain materials that will give it flotation. That quality is normally achieved, not by the use of cork or other self-buoyant materials, but by fibers which will ride above the water on its surface tension. Many small fibers are combined in order that the total lift will be great enough to hold up the fly's weight.

An ordinary steel sewing needle placed carefully upon the surface of smooth water will float. When the surface tension of the water is broken, or if the needle is dropped from a height, it will sink, being heavier than water. A dry fly floats upon the water as the steel needle does.

A dry fly floats upon fine fibers and a water-repellent coating which, if worn off or for any reason dissipated, takes away from the fly its ability to ride the surface. Without waterproofing, neither wool, nor silk, nor tinsel, nor hook, nor feather would come to the top after immersion in turbulent water. In order to create or maintain this waterproofing a film of oil or wax is spread over the filaments upon which the dry fly rests. A solution of parrafin dissolved to saturation in gasoline is adequate. Special silicone solutions are available, and their manufacturers claim longer life for them.

A very soft line grease may be applied easily to the ends of the fibers with the fingers. Albolene, a petroleum grease with a very low melting point, will serve. Specially prepared greases like "Mucilin" are convenient and effective. Almost any grease suitable for floating a line will do for flies, too. Liquid floatants are easy to apply and quickly coat all surfaces with little deranging of the fibers. Liquids are more difficult to carry than greases and are subject to loss through spilling or leaks or breakage of the bottle or container. Application of liquid is made by dipping the entire fly into the solution or by spraying from a pressure can. A fly should be completely dry when the first application is made. A thoroughly water-soaked fly will not accept waterproofing.

Snapping the fly through the air on a swift cast or on several false casts will throw off any excess water, as long as the waterproof coating is still effective. If a fly fails to float as it should and it is not yet water-soaked, a renewal of the waterproofing may remedy the situation, but the chances are the fly will not float quite as well as it did originally. If a fly waterlogs, it should be set aside where it can dry out and replaced with another completely dry and freshly greased one.

Dry flies usually depend for the main part of their flotation on the "hackle," a ring of feather vanes radiating from the shaft of the hook. This "wheel" of fibers is created by winding the stems of one, two, or several suitable feathers around the shank of the hook a short distance behind the eye. The most common feathers for hackles are those of the rooster or game cock which have fine, stiff vanes. These fibers are considered to represent the legs and sometimes the wings of the insect the fly imitates, but normally the amount of "hackle" required is bulkier than an insect's leg would be. The ends of the hackle fibers must taper to a fine, soft point which will bend under the weight of the fly and give each one a considerable bearing surface on the water. If the fibers are stiff right to the end, their points will penetrate the surface film and lose the ability to hold up the fly.

Some fly bodies have a low specific gravity and will float of themselves but, without being very large, they could not by themselves hold up the weight of the metal hook. Most bodies, like the wool that absorbs water or the tinsel wrappings, detract from rather than contribute to the buoyancy of the fly. A plastic body, which is just about the same density as water, is a good one simply because it does not absorb water or weigh enough to drag down a fly.

The tail of the fly, in most cases, stretches out upon the water's surface and helps it to float. The heavy part of the hook is toward the tail, and good strong fibers in the tail section are a boon to any dry fly. The wings in an erect position do not touch the water or aid in holding the fly up, but wings in the horizontal or spent-wing position may be a major factor in keeping a fly afloat.

A special type of conventional dry fly is the "gyro," or "aero," fly. In this case a metal stub projects from the hook's shank at the point at which the hackles would

Gyro hook and fly.

Fishers four: Alex Rogan, guide Arthur Perry, Lee Wulff, and H. G. Tapply admire a 15-pound salmon . . . caught on this #16 spider.

normally be wound. The hook is a little heavier because of the extra metal. By winding the hackle feathers around this metal stub, the axis of the hackle "wheel" is changed by 90 degrees and lies flat upon the surface when it floats. This is a better imitation of legs radiating from an insect's thorax, though neither can be claimed to be a particularly good one. These flies have been a little more expensive, but that would hardly seem to be the reason why they have not become more popular. Apparently there is not enough difference between them and the conventional fly to the fish's mind to make them any more effective.

The conventional dry fly, as described and pictured, makes up the majority of the flies now in use in surface fishing. A second important type is either the bi-visible or the Palmer-tied fly, and a third is either the spider or the skater. When a hackle is Palmer-tied, the stem of the feather is twisted down the shank in wide spirals from head to tail of the fly.

The bi-visible, as originally designed by Edward R. Hewitt, was made up of one white or light-colored hackle, wound round the shank right behind the eye, and several others of the desired color between it and the bend of the hook. The white facing on the front of the fly was for better visibility, while the bulk of the fly was made up in the color designed to attract the fish. The name has now become widely used to refer to any fly made up of hackles wound around the shank's length.

The spider is a type of dry fly in which the hackle vanes are very much longer than those of a normal dry fly or bi-visible. Only a comparatively few turns of hackle are used and the result is a light, spidery type of floating fly. These flies offer the least solid silhouette to the fish below them. They are always tied on very small hooks. The #16 hook is the commonest for spiders, though with extra large hackle feathers, a hook as large as a #12 or in rare cases a #10 can be satisfactorily floated. A tail is added to keep the spider floating in a normal position, and a small, light-colored feather tip may be tied to the shank to make the fly more readily visible to the angler at a distance.

Skaters are like spiders, though more heavily dressed, but they lack tails. Although otherwise similar in shape to the spider, they ride with the wheel of hackle vanes flat to the water instead of perpendicular to it. They are designed with a high floating power for skittering across the surface, whereas the conventional use of the dry fly calls for it to float freely with the current, entirely free from any drag or pull of the line.

Probably the most widely used dry-fly patterns for salmon are the Grey Wulff, Royal Wulff, and White Wulff, designed by the writer in 1929. Although originally designed for trout as a general imitation of the larger mayflies, they were also an immediate success for salmon. They incorporated animal hair (bucktail) for the first time in wings and as tail for a dry fly, giving these patterns extra toughness and durability and finer floating qualities than feather fibers had been able to supply. They floated a heavier body than the other dry flies of that time and were more representative of a class of insect not then well represented. They captured the "look" of an insect which seems to be the basis of the salmon's rise.

The original three patterns were extended to include a Brown Wulff, Black Wulff, Grizzly Wulff, and Blonde Wulff in order to give the same durability and high floating quality to a variety of color combinations. Using the same hair wing and hair tail, various body combinations were developed. The late Kenneth Lockwood changed the blue-grey Angora body of the Grey Wulff for one of clipped, wound bucktail and it became the Irresistible. The use of hairs to help float a dry fly and give extra durability is becoming increasingly widespread. Hair enables dry flies of heavier bodies and unusual shapes to stay on the surface.

Hair-Wing Salmon Flies

By the turn of the century the Atlantic salmon fly had become the most complicated, the most artfully constructed, and the most expensive fly in the world. Britain, where fly tying reached its artistic zenith, ruled the seas and British ships brought back from all corners of the globe the most exciting feathers to be found. British fly tiers flourished in their trade, making their flies ever more magnificent, at times by using dozens of exotic feathers in a single pattern.

At that time anglers as a group believed that a fly which conformed rigidly to the standard of a pattern such as the time-tested Jock Scott would draw rises, while one that varied even slightly from the norm would fail to draw fish. Most salmon fishermen of the day were well up on the social ladder. They used long rods and equipment special to their fish, and they were as fussy about their flies as a society matron about her dinner table settings or the style of her dress. Those were the days before trout tackle was accepted as adequate to conquer salmon and before the hordes of erstwhile trout fishermen crowded the public salmon waters of the New World.

This new type of angler was often short of cash and had to make do with cheaper flies and tackle. He questioned the need for feathers from distant continents, plucked from birds that, after all, no salmon had ever seen. New laws for the protection of wildlife made many of the feathers once considered essential almost impossible to obtain. The more durable and readily available animal hair was substituted for the fancier feathered wings, and the users claimed that these new flies were more effective than the old standbys.

Will a Dusty Miller or a Silver Grey with hair wings catch as many salmon as one of the old-time varieties? My feeling is that it will, and yet when the fish are dour I never fail to dig out one of those old treasured works of art; and often enough the salmon tell me that they, too, still love them. There's a movement or "life" to a hair wing as it drifts through the water that the carefully married feathered wings do not have, but those old-line feather marriages have a special sophistication that can charm a salmon. If you can manage to come by some of the perfectly tied old patterns, they may bring an added pleasure to your casts, take you a little deeper into the history and mystery of salmon angling, and, perhaps, bring to your steel a fish or two that has refused your simplified or hair-winged fly.

One such fly has a single long wing tied at the head that extends down the back. These flies may be short and stubby, or long and slender, like a streamer. They may float low or high on the water, and the animal hair has enough floating power to hold up the entire fly when properly designed.

Dry flies fall into other unusual shapes which may receive passing mention. One of these is the plastic-bodied Surface Stone fly with which I have drawn up many very difficult fish. The Bomber, a fly with a cigar-shaped body of clipped bucktail and a palmer-type hackle that floats like the Surface Stone fly in the surface film has become, too, a most successful dry fly. The spent-wing type with hair wings is another. This field of varying dry fly shapes is now in the era of serious development, and in all probability, the presently available dry-fly patterns form only a small part of what will one day be considered a normal dry-fly coverage. Whiskers, a pattern developed on the Miramichi, has a squirrel-tail head and tail piece and flattened hackles along the shank. It is designed to skip like a skater.

Few dry-fly fishermen carry many different patterns, and there are not many different patterns available to carry. Contrast this with the wet-fly patterns which run to many hundreds. When dry flies have been fished for two or three hundred years, there will probably be just as many dry-fly patterns as there are wet-fly patterns now.

The simple fact that British salmon anglers have been so slow to realize the effectiveness of the dry fly and have not used this method to any extent has caused them to lag behind in the development of this field. Few large dry flies suitable for salmon are available from British sources from which most of our best wet flies have been drawn. Due to the dearth of dry-fly patterns designed for salmon, many anglers have, instead, used extra large trout patterns or used their trout flies in the same sizes they use for trout. This gives a great variety of patterns but limits the size. To most salmon anglers, the pattern of the dry fly hasn't become very important. For every dry-fly pattern they carry, they have a dozen wet ones.

Dry-fly fishing is to many (and the writer is among them,) a more exciting type of fishing than catching the same fish with a sunken fly. Having fished for so many years with so much interest in this particular phase of salmon fishing, it may be worthwhile to describe some of the basic flies, many of them special patterns of my own, on which I depend in the taking of salmon on the dry fly.

Originally I could depend upon my Wulffs to let me put something that was new and unusual yet effective over the salmon. I used hair-wing floaters quite consistently. Gradually, those patterns became increasingly popular, and, wherever much dry-fly fishing was practiced, they were used. When I undertook to establish a salmon fishing camp, it automatically left for me the waters everyone else had passed by or had already fished over to a considerable degree. With competent anglers and good guides working with my erstwhile floating favorites over the fish, I felt the need for something new and quite different if I was to have signal success in my fishing. So I extended my range. The easiest and most important way was in shape rather than in color. The limited dry-fly shapes left plenty of room for experiment.

The area in which I hoped to extend the range of patterns was that of the low-floating, or half-sunken, dry fly, a type studiously avoided by almost everyone else because they are so difficult to float and to use. By removing the hackles from a conventional Wulff fly and spreading the wings to a horizontal position, I created a good, low-floating pattern. It is very hard to see, as nothing shows above the water, though its visibility to the fish is not impaired. Hard to float and hard to see, it is a good imitation of the hatched-out insects that fall to the water in the spent stage or at any other time and are captured in its grip. It may be that when salmon are seen to rise to the surface yet do not take anything visible to the angler, they are taking this type of insect.

The low-floating, single-winged fly offered another productive field to work in. A long plastic body molded on a small streamer hook gave me a good start. It soaked up no water, was light and easy to cast. I began with wings laid down the back shorter than the body but soon lengthened them to a point beyond it as more typical of the true insect form. For heavy water, a heavy wing and hackle at the throat was needed to keep the fly afloat. On smooth waters, a fairly light wing of bucktail or bear hair was all that was required. Crinkly hair, typical of bear hair or of bucktail, taken from near the end of the tail, gives fine flotation. Straighter, thicker hairs make a bulkier fly but do not float it as well. A vertical extension of the plastic body near the head let me tie the hackle on in the gyro, or parachute, fashion.

This was a secret weapon, a fly to charm salmon with. Whether in rapids or a pool, it rides with the hair spread flat upon the water, like the long, floating platform of the real insect's wings. The yellow body hangs down, completely submerged in the water. I called it a Surface Stone fly.

It is not an easy fly to float. At the start, I found that if it dropped as much as a foot to the water at the end of the cast, it would sink. I ended up using a side cast, keeping the line low as the cast drove the fly out over the water to the intended point of landing. At the finish, I'd let it slide onto the surface with a bounce or two, then come to rest.

For more than thirty years, these two flies and variations of them have been among my standbys. Other anglers have seen and noticed them, but often, even when I've given them away, they've seen little service. They're hard to use and demand considerable skill of a caster. Some fishermen, finding the fly didn't float well, thought it was a gag and that I'd given them a cull I didn't want. Others thought it was a red herring to draw attention away from some other secret fly I used which was the real killer. Still others fished them wet which is another story.

While doodling on a pad at a meeting of the International Salmon Council a few years ago it occurred to me that a hackle, looped around to form a fly's wing, would give it a good moth-wing shape when lying flat on the water; also, it would move well because of the springiness of the hackle stem and be very durable. Add these effects to a clipped-hair floating body and you have a very natural-looking fly to which salmon have responded well on a number of occasions. The looped hackles can be single or doubled for greater floating capability.

The dry-fly patterns mentioned and illustrated offer a wide coverage by today's standards. Even though far less varied than wet-fly patterns, a wise choice from among them should be effective. Here is a list of recommended available dry-fly patterns:

	In Sizes
Bi-visibles (brown, grey, ginger)	4, 6, 8, 10
Spiders or skaters (brown, grey, black)	16, 14
R. F. McDougall	6, 8
White Wulff, Grey Wulff, Royal Wulff	4, 6, 8, 10
Quill Gordon	8, 10, 12
Black Gnat	8, 10
Bomber	4, 8

6

Where Salmon Lie

almon enter the rivers through the tidal pools where the level of the salt water is reached. During the time of the heaviest runs of fish, following the spring freshets, the water in these tidal pools is completely fresh and the influence of the river's flow extends far out to sea. The salmon will then be working through these low pools just as they do in the other pools farther up and may be fished for in the same way. But when the rivers are very low the current in them dwindles almost to nothing and may even change the direction of its flow with the rise and fall of the sea. Then tidal pools often become brackish because the quantity of fresh water coming down is not great enough to keep the salt water swept from the pool.

There are two sets of conditions under which the fishing in the tidal pools may be the best in the whole length of the rivers. The first of these occurs when the salmon are just beginning to arrive and the water in the stream itself is too cold for the salmon's comfort. The temperature of the river water seems to be the factor governing the time of first entrance for the salmon in the spring. Where two rivers enter the sea only a few miles apart there may be a month's difference in time of the salmon's first entry into each river. Usually shallow rivers with a quick runoff and a sunny drainage slope warm up far ahead of those rivers that flow through lakes and deep channels that help them to retain the cold. The colder rivers get their fish later but since they warm up more slowly they have good fishing later in the season than the early rivers. Thus, while they wait for the river water to reach the proper entrance temperature, many salmon may move in and out of the brackish pools with the tide's flow. Again, when the river is too hot or too low for the salmon to make the run, they will hang on in the cooler, deeper brackish water influenced by the tides while they wait for a rain to swell the stream. When either of these two sets of conditions exists the anglers concentrating on the tidal pools should be most successful.

For the most part the salmon in tidal waters will choose as resting places those spots where the flow of water is concentrated in narrow channels or where it spreads evenly over a gravelly stretch of bottom. The fish will head into the flow, facing outward on a strong incoming tide and face upstream when the stream-flow is the stronger factor. When neither tide nor stream-flow is strong enough to move the water the salmon tend to school up and cruise around the pools, often drifting along with only their tail tips showing above water or rippling the surface with a slow V-shaped wake. During very warm stream-water conditions the salmon may work up to completely fresh water at the head of the tidal influence on one day or one tide and drop back to the completely salt water of the bay for the next.

Salmon in the tidal pools have expended none of their energy in the arduous spawning journey and are usually at the peak of their physical fitness, ready to offer the angler the full show of their stored-up strength. More than that, they have the advantage of the larger space the tidal pools normally afford for their long runs and spectacular leaping. And so, although the tidal pools may be almost barren of salmon at one time and bright with their leaping a few hours later, these waters should not be overlooked by the angler who finds fishing on the rest of the river unproductive.

In the river proper, salmon will be found lying in the same resting spots year after year, barring a change in the streambed or the flow of the river itself at that point. These positions vary with the rivers, and in seemingly identical pools in separate rivers one pool may hold fish while the other is barren. The eye of man does not see things as the salmon does, and often, for no determinable reason, one pool holds salmon while another of seeming equality, equally well situated, does not. There can be no hard and

A salmon resting in slow water.

fast rule for locating all the resting places for salmon in a given river save by actual experience, but there are certain general habits that give the angler a key to most salmon positions even in a river with which he is totally unfamiliar.

Unlike the trout the salmon does not seek a hideaway for his safety but looks instead to the open water. To some the salmon may appear to be either fearless or stupid when he first enters the stream since at that time the angler may walk almost up to his quarry before the salmon turns leisurely and swims away. However, the angler will find that he can only approach closely from the shallow side. Let him come toward the fish from the deep side, barring the salmon from the deep water on which he is counting for his safety, and the fish will be off like a shot. In deep, open water the salmon can outswim his enemies, and in its depth he finds protection from the eagles and ospreys that might drop down on him from the skies. His amazing speed gives him his safety and he dislikes any position that prevents the full use of this safeguard. The best trout water, protected by overhanging bushes and cut banks, is rarely, if ever, attractive to salmon who can think of such a spot only as a trap in which they may be cornered by an otter or a seal.

As he works his way farther and farther up the river, the salmon becomes increasingly wary and more reaccustomed to the narrow confines of his old home. He lies out on the shallow bars less and less, seeking instead the protection of the deeper water or the swirling currents that will hide him from view. His color, too, blends in more fully with the rocks or sand over which he lies.

The salmon, restless and impatient, seek positions where the soothing flow of the current lulls this restlessness without being too much of a tax on their precious store of energy. The slow flow over gravel bars, the steady runs near the tails of the pools where they neck down and spill, the sharp drops in the stream bed where the pools first find their depth, the steady flow against a curving bank, or the swirling water behind a ledge of rock, these are the places salmon seek. Even there their restlessness sometimes overflows and they make a vibrant leap into the air and perhaps follow it with a tour of the pool before returning to their resting spots.

Salmon in the stiller pools, lacking the soothing flow of water, seem to be constantly on the move. Often they take the same course around a pool, as regular as clockwork, as they wait, wait, wait for the rains and heavy freshets that will allow them to progress on up the river to their rendezvous with reproduction in the fall.

The speed of salmon travelling up a given river may vary a good deal depending on the water conditions and the ultimate destination of the fish. Those salmon spawning in the lower reaches of the rivers can afford to travel slowly and usually do. They may reach their spawning pools a day or two after entering the river and spend months in the same pool before spawning. Some of the first fish to enter the river usually take all summer to reach the headwaters, while the salmon entering the river in September may travel the same distance in a few days. Late in the season salmon that have become blackened by a long stay in fresh water will often be found lying side by side with a bright newcomer still spangled with sea-lice.

One circumstance attending the first fish to enter the rivers is unusual and interesting. In many rivers, the first fish to be caught by an angler will be far upstream rather than near the tidehead. Obviously, the upstream fish have to pass through the lower section of the river, but they are rarely caught there. Why should the first fish to enter race through the river, covering in a few days a distance the later-arriving fish will take weeks, and more, to equal?

The first fish for many years was taken about 30 miles upstream on the Margaree. On the Humber, the first salmon will usually be taken at the falls 60 miles upstream from the bay, while the fish for the lower 8-mile stretch of water from Tidehead to Deer Lake will not settle into their lies until July is almost spent. At Portland Creek, the first run of fish will settle into a feeder stream above the big lake from two to three weeks before fish are usually caught in the main river below the lake through which they all had to pass.

The first run is usually made up of maiden fish of two or three years, depending on the river. About ten days later on, the grilse and some of the larger fish, often previous spawners, will sweep in from the sea. Occasional scatterings of fish will follow in some rivers where the waters run well all summer. Among them will be small salmon entering in early August slightly larger and more mature than the grilse that gave up sea feeding a month earlier, late arrivals delayed along the way. The late spring or early summer runs usually make up the great bulk of salmon coming into a river. Some rivers, however, perhaps because the sea nets almost completely destroy the early fish, have heavy runs in the fall after the nets are lifted. The Maragaree, which, in the memory of men I fished with, had its heavy run of salmon in the spring, now has the great preponderance of its salmon enter the river after September first.

Salmon resting in pools may lie directly on the streambed with their weight being carried by their pectoral and pelvic fins, relaxed, yet poised for instant flight. They may hover easily in midwater, expending a minimum of effort to hold their positions. Often a rock or ledge will give them an eddy in which they can have water flowing past them in different directions on either side by taking up a position at the exact break of the current.

As they come in from the sea the salmons' backs are dark blue and their sides and bellies are iridescent silver. A scattering of black spots is superimposed on both the silver of the sides and the blue of the back. Seen in the water they show a bluish tone that is the mark of a fresh-run fish. With their lengthening time in the rivers the blue fades into a gray matching more closely the bed of the river. While those in clear streams hold more to the neutral gray, fish in rivers of brownish water take on a reddish tinge.

The dark section of the salmon's back spreads downward until only the belly is silvery white. The spots enlarge and become more prominent, giving the fish a mottled appearance as the spawning period draws near. All these things make salmon difficult to see—perhaps the best way to spot them is on a bright day by the solid black shadow the sun makes on the streambed.

A salmon does not always look like a salmon. Sometimes all one sees is the opening and closing white slits of his mouth, or the white of the mouth and a small light patch on his tail about a salmon's length apart. From above, his solid shadow under a high-hanging sun is easily spotted, but when seen from the angler's usual low level, his shadow spreads out upon the rocky stream bed into a queer, unsalmonlike shape.

When there are not many salmon in a river it is the course of wisdom to be certain, whenever possible, that the fly is passing near a fish. When the sun is in a

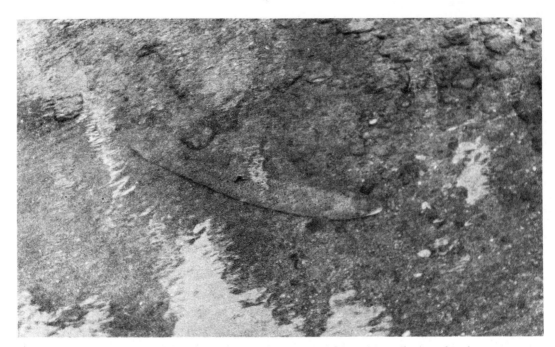

Salmon returning to their native river to spawn revert to a camouflage coloring that matches their new environment and causes them to fade well into their shadowed lies.

favorable position it is often possible to see whether or not there are fish in a particular pool and where they lie. It pays to gather information like this at the proper time so that for the rest of the day or even longer when fish are not on the move, the angler can know a few spots where he is certain to be covering fish.

There is a classic story of the old-time salmon fisherman who came along and rested on a high bank to watch a novice casting diligently over a salmon pool. Time after time the beginner worked the water from head to foot without a rise from a salmon. After his fifth trip down through the pool, he gave up and puffed his way up the sandy bank to sit down on its crest of sod beside the watcher. "You try it now," he said, "I'll be darned if I can catch them."

"Of course you can't," replied the old-timer, "there aren't any there."

From that point of vantage, every rock, every patch of sand on the bottom of the entire pool lay exposed before his eyes. The older man quietly pointed out that not a single salmon rested in it anywhere and continued, "You were enjoying it so much I didn't want to spoil your sport."

Local guides can be counted on to know where salmon should lie, but good guides or even poor guides are not always available, and when the angler finds himself on a new river, alone, there is still no reason why he shouldn't come fairly close to locating good places to fish. His best bet is to concentrate on the pools, for they are almost certain to contain the majority of salmon in the river. He may well leave the shallows or ripples to those who know the stream. The pockets and shallows do contain salmon, but there is much blank water of this type and the stranger's chances of finding the few good spots are slim.

The reasons for choosing the pools is shown graphically by these illustrations which show how the *same* river may look before and after a heavy rain. The dry, hot, stone-studded riverbed bears mute testimony to the salmon's wisdom in avoiding a place that may be secure today but almost dry next week. A very shallow pool or a small, deep pocket surrounded by a long stretch of shallow riffles may become a dangerous position for a big fish when the water has dropped a foot or more. The

ABOVE: The Garia River in Newfoundland swells to full flow during the spring, becoming an easy pathway for salmon in their runs upriver. BELOW: By contrast, the water may be very low on the Garia by early July.

salmon, running his river in high water, selects as resting places those spots that will still be safe when the river resumes normal flow or even falls under drought conditions.

The deep pools, and particularly those pools that are just at the head of a long stretch of swift and shallow water, are the surest to contain fish. Salmon always seem to hang up in pools that mark the end of a long, tough swim, and the very deep ones offer them a good measure of protection from their natural enemies. These are the sure pools for finding salmon although they may not be the easiest from which to take them. Ordinarily, salmon rise more quickly in the shallower pools where the water is swifter, perhaps because the fly is not so far above them and consequently much easier to see and reach.

Where there are two nearby pools of similar makeup many salmon may lie in one and few in the other. Perhaps the salmon have just come through a long stretch of rough water and are resting in the first of the two pools, a very few stopping in the second. If the long, rough shallow or otherwise difficult stretch were above the two pools, it is more likely the fish would rest in the upper pool, waiting there until conditions were suitable for further progress.

Where the water sweeps uniformly over a smooth bottom salmon may lie anywhere. They do not like to rest in a steady flow for there is really no "rest" for them there. Unless there is an eddy caused by a depression, snag, or rock in which they can relax, they must be swimming constantly, using up their stored energy which they must so husband that it will carry them to their spawning ground, through the spawning, and in the case of many, back to the sea again.

Photographs of the smaller rivers are used to illustrate the positions favored by the salmon since they show the water with a great degree of intimacy. The actual choice of positions is almost identical whether in large rivers or small. But in the large rivers fish may lie in a certain section of a pool because of a local condition, a sort of pool within a pool, and so confuse the angler as to the reason for this choice.

Depth of water and river location enter into the choice of salmon pools to fish. An angler can usually take more fish from a shallow pool than from a deep one that may hold more salmon. I remember such a case on the Conne River of Newfoundland's south coast. Not far up from the mouth we found a long deep pool holding many salmon. It lay just above a long stretch of rough and shallow water, which made it a logical resting place for the salmon and, indeed, it held a great many fish. Although we fished it hard we only caught one salmon.

A hundred yards above that pool was a small pocket of deeper water between two large rocks. In it the most restless salmon, those that were ready to run the next long stretch of pool-less river, were waiting for darkness or a rise of water. There could only have been one salmon in the pocket to every ten in the pool but from that small spot we caught three fish. Both a salmon's restlessness and the water depth have an effect on his willingness to rise.

A long, deep, slow pool can be difficult to fish, especially if the water is peat-stained and dark. It is almost impossible to see resting fish in such water. One knows they are there and if one can get a sense of the shape of the streambed it is possible to estimate the lies. The first spot to look for, as always in pools, is the place where the stream speed slows down to one in which a salmon in a full or partial eddy can lie without much effort. After that, salmon will lie where the bottom drops off or lifts to create a safe and comfortable eddy. A big submerged boulder, a ledge of rock, sometimes even a slight variation in an otherwise smooth bottom will draw fish in to rest.

A salmon coming into a pool on his upstream run may cover the pool with a number of exploratory circuits and pick the most comfortable lie available. Another, wearier from a rough stream climb, may simply drop into the first suitable resting place. A third, coming into the pool and seeing a salmon or two resting, may simply slip in beside them, knowing that they've chosen a comfortable place. With the long, deep pools, experience is the best way to learn and usually one must depend on a guide unless he can cover the pool by wading or in a canoe and actually see the bottom and then have the knowledge to translate the contours into resting places. If he can drift a pool and see the salmon he will know where to cast his flies . . . as long as the water doesn't change its level very much.

Whether the water is shallow or deep most salmon tend to lie near the bottom. The eddies there are steadier, more certain in their flow. The fish are always harder to bring up from the depths and the best fishing spots may be at the shallows near the head or tail or at some spot in a long deep flow where a ridge in the stream bed shallows the water and lets the salmon lie closer to the surface and thus to the fisherman's fly.

The photograph below, taken from the air of the Bluie branch of the upper River of Ponds, Newfoundland, shows the preferred lies of the salmon in a stretch of river between two lakes. Salmon prefer the outlets of lakes, all other conditions being equal, but in this case the outlet comes quickly from deep water to stream flow and many more salmon lie at the inlet of the lower lake where the flow into the still water is slower and the deepening of the stream bed more gradual. Salmon lie just below the first widening of the stream where the water slows down. Salmon lying there have ready access to the deep water of the entire lake. At the lowest spot, between the island and the true right bank the water is a little deeper and there's even better deep water access. That is the best spot of all.

This photo indicates the main salmon lies at Western Bluie pool on the River of Ponds.

The photograph on this page shows a typical small river pool. The salmon tend to lie where the water deepens enough and slows down enough to give safety and a comfortable eddy to lie in. From there on downstream to the speeding-up water of the tail a salmon may lie wherever there is depth for safety and an eddy for comfort. In such small rivers the depth of water and the comparative safety are most important. A salmon will sacrifice a little in comfort to be sure the water he lies in or has access to is adequate for protection or escape.

Small river pools which can be fished from either side are fished best if fished first from the preferred side but also with the fly's swim reversed. One side, usually the one toward the beach or the shallow side, offers the best fishing but just because the salmon, especially if he's reluctant, has seen your wet flies in the preferred swing and refused them doesn't mean that he won't respond to a cast from the other side. It's good policy, on many pools, to try the other bank after a suitable resting of the fish.

As rivers grow larger and deeper they contain many more suitable lies for salmon to rest in. The larger the rivers the more difficult it is to spot precisely the places where salmon will choose to lie. The deep, slow moving rivers are the hardest of all. It is

Salmon prefer to lie in deep water with a flow strong enough to create eddies as it moves over the rocky bottom.

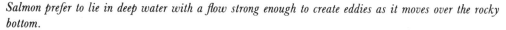

practically impossible to tell where the deep spots and drop offs are. However, the salmon angler has an ally in the wind. Where the water is fairly smooth the wind will develop waves over the entire surface pool. If there is a deep spot in an otherwise relatively uniform flow the waves over that spot will be distinctly deeper than over the shallower water. This "wave" method of finding the drop off can be very valuable at pools that are flowing into a lake or into the sea. Waves on the lake will be rapidly diminished when they hit a sudden shallowing of the bottom and that shallowing usually marks the farthest downstream place that salmon will take up lies. Beyond that drop off they'll usually cruise rather than settle into relative immobility.

Because the surroundings, tackle, and general methods are so similar, the trout fisherman starting with salmon often falls into the error of thinking he should fish the water as if for trout, which is just about the poorest way to do it. The frustration which may follow can drive these normally competent anglers to the wildest extremes. I have seen rods broken in anger, trips cancelled midway in a sudden fury, and longtime friendships rent asunder because a beginner at fly-fishing caught more salmon than one of these fly-rod veterans.

I was caught once, long ago, in the thinking-trout instead of thinking-salmon trap myself. The river was lower than it had been in many years. My fishing companion, who had been lagging behind my catches in his usual manner, for he fished nowhere near as diligently as I, suddenly began catching two salmon to my one. A few days of this drove me to fishing harder and longer than ever. At the end of a week I was still stymied and puzzled.

The water was hard-fished, and each pool was worked at least once daily and sometimes both in the morning and in the afternoon. The secret of his catches was that he had discovered salmon lying at the very lip of several pools where the water at the point of spilling over was less than a foot deep. Sizeable trout would rarely have lain in such a spot and it was ridiculous to the trout-fishing mind that these large salmon would choose to lie in the very shallowest water of the pool. One of the axioms of salmon fishing applied there: "The shallower the water in which salmon lie, the more likely they are to rise; the deeper it is, the more difficult to bring them up to the fly."

My companion had made a practice of starting his casting a long way back from the water, just barely reaching the narrow outlet of the pools with a long cast, without frightening the fish. When a salmon took the fly he would rush up to the water's edge to play him. The rest of us were getting too close to the pools before starting to fish, thus scaring the salmon back into the depths where they were much harder to catch.

The very situation that creates a good salmon lie is subject to change. These fish seek out eddies where they can rest and yet have the slight flow or turbulence to soothe their restlessness while they wait. Where the normal pool level provides such a spot an additional inch or two of water may increase the flow enough to make holding that position too serious a drain on their unrenewable supply of strength—or it may even reverse the flow completely in a certain eddy.

As the water rises and the flow entering a pool grows stronger, the fish usually drop back toward the center of the pool, following a certain preferred water speed. As the stream level falls again they will shift back toward their original positions. And if it drops even lower than before they will keep on edging up closer to the point where the diminishing flow pours into the pool.

Another preferred lie is near the tails of the pools where the still-smooth water readies for the rapids. Frequently they choose shallow water and lie very close to the bank or near prominent boulders. There, with their tails waving slowly at the quickening pulse of the run behind them, they are headed upstream toward the safety of the wide and open waters. As the river rises, these salmon tend to move farther up into the pool, but if the water drops to an even lower level, they move back closer and closer to the lip over which the pool empties.

When the rivers rise well above normal, there is a satisfactory depth and space for salmon through a greater part of their length, and the fish become much more difficult to locate. With such a wide choice of resting places to cover, it takes a lot more fishing to reach a given number of salmon with a fly and, because there is little certainty about which of the hundreds of available places they will rest in, the element of luck is at its peak.

In the real floods the usual pools are filled with rushing water through which the salmon might travel if the urge were upon them to run the river, but which no longer affords them any place to rest. In seeking a good place to lie they may follow a river right out of its banks. I recall once hooking a salmon while I was sitting on a pole fence and fishing a flooded pasture completely out of the regular riverbed upon which I had turned my back.

That taught me, as no other single incident, that a salmon pool is a little patch of water of certain qualifications which, though it is usually well established during normal flow, may at some time be found in almost any spot in the river. My salmon from the field had enough water to cover him in a gentle flow situated in a broad reach of water where he felt assured of safety.

Lakes must always be considered as giant pools. The fish congregate at the head and tail where the flow of water is greatest. At the inlet, the fish will work into shallow water to rest and wait for their time to proceed farther up toward the spawning grounds. The outlet of such lakes is normally a prime salmon fishing point. The fish have the nearby depth of the lake for safety and comfort but drop back periodically into the faster flow of the river. Sometimes such a pool may harbor very few fish at one hour of the day and a great many at another. The fish will move in and out of the pool as they do in tidal waters. At evening the salmon normally drift farther back into the current and become more active in their movements. At that time they take the fly better.

Salmon lies can be created. In some places large boulders have been hauled out onto the winter ice where, when thaw came, they would settle to the riverbed in water that flowed fairly steadily and in sufficient depth over a smooth river bottom. Often good lies are created in this fashion. The water was right for the salmon to lie in, and the placing of a boulder in such a generally acceptable location drew salmon to the eddy forming behind it. No greater number of fish may have rested in that pool but it concentrated those that did into one place, or, if several rocks were dropped, into several places. The chances are the salmon might have chosen to lie in the same area even if the rocks had not been put there, but once there, the guides had a mark to shoot at and knew where to find the fish.

Wing dams which form an eddy and tend to scour out the bottom where the wing extends, if placed in suitable water, will tend to draw salmon. The selection of suitable water is difficult and any "making" of salmon pools is a gamble. The best opportunities to create pools are at the inlets or outlets of a lake or pond in a salmon river where no suitable natural lies for salmon exist.

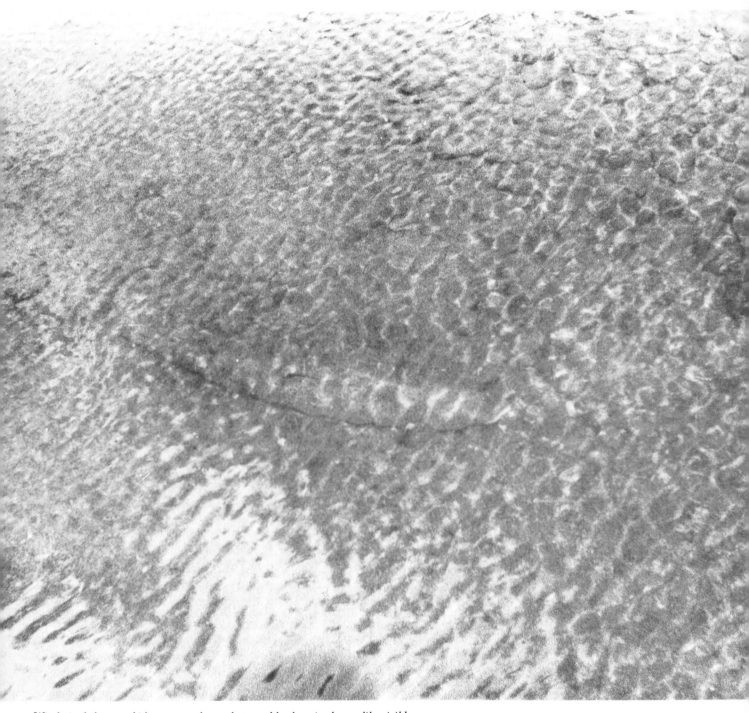

Wind-rippled water hides many salmon that would otherwise be readily visible.

Any changing of a salmon river has other effects. A change in the flow to favor one spot may harm another. The judgment required to improve a river is great and the reaction of the fish so baffling at times that it is wisest to let Nature make the pools, and for the angler to take them as they come. Those who wish to play God with a salmon river may need His help to get the river back into as good a shape as it was when they started.

7

Casting

Fly casting calls for the sending of a fly of very little weight to a distant point by means of a fairly heavy line which is worked out through the guides of a rather long and delicate rod. As the caster brings the rod back and forth in a coordinated action the line is switched back and forth, too. Line freed from the reel can be worked out through the guides during the casting process to extend the distance the fly will travel or it can be taken in through the guides to shorten the distance the fly can go before the limit of travel is reached. Assuming the reader has a basic knowledge of fly casting there are some types of casting and casting problems which, if covered here, may better enable the fisherman to cover the water or to make a favorable presentation of the fly to the salmon.

The usual practice in casting is to aim at a spot a foot or so above the surface of the water and cast to it. The rod goes forward on the final cast of the series, the line straightens out to complete the cast, and line, leader, and fly fall to the water. They will fall in that order unless the rod is long and the cast is short. At the completion of the casting action they should all be more or less stretched out straight in front of the angler. Then they fall. The line is heavier than leader and fly so it falls fastest and hits the water first. The leader at its butt end usually hits next. If the fly is a light dry fly with little weight and a lot of air resistance it will settle slowly and be the last thing to touch the water. If the fly is a heavy one it may splash in as soon as or before the heavy end of the leader.

A high back cast leads to good forecasts. Keeping the line high in the air behind the caster is a major factor in good casting. It lends the power of gravity for the forward drive; it helps lift the fly and leader above any obstacles behind the fisherman. A high back cast can be achieved by a definite lifting up of the line in the casting motion and by halting or slowing down the rod's swing a little bit earlier than normal. The surest check on the back cast when it is touching leaves, grass, or other obstructions is to turn and watch it. If the caster turns to watch his back casts he can easily judge their efficiency and correct them. If he does not watch them he may not realize where his casting is at fault.

A well-executed backcast will cause the fly to pass the angler below waist level. The line straightens at the end of the backcast as the rod is lifted.

In order to avoid the line's tangling with itself or with the fly or leader as it goes out and reverses itself during the casting, it should be made to go out on one path and come back on another, following the track of a very long and narrow oval. Unless such an oval course is planned, any slight variation in the course of fly, line, or leader, easily caused by a breath of wind, will cause contact between parts of the line travelling at different speeds or in opposite directions. The stronger the wind the wider the oval should be. In any case the oval should be wide enough to take care of occasional deviations in the casting.

PATH OF LINE SEEN FROM ABOVE

A full-arm stroke drives the line up and out for a long, smooth-looping forward cast.

In normal fly casting the line goes out in one direction under the pressure of the rod, then there is a period of waiting while the line makes its sweep until, at the precisely correct moment, an opposite pressure is exerted by the rod and the movement of the line is reversed. The changes of direction of the rod must be made with accuracy and precision. If the rod moves before the line has had a chance to straighten there will be insufficient weight of line in position for it to work with. If the rod movement is delayed too long the line will have straightened out and fallen out of good position.

Not only must the rhythm of this conventional fly casting be precisely timed but it changes with the length of line out. It takes longer for a long line to straighten out and be ready for a change of direction than it does for a short one. In order to teach beginners or to correct faults in others, I worked out what I call a "constant pressure system" which enables them to correct their own casting faults. To work with it the oval in which the line is cast must be widened abnormally. In order to insure a high back cast I did the unorthodox and rotated the plane in which the line travels by 90 degrees. Instead of working the line in a horizontal plane directly overhead it is worked in a more vertical plane beside the caster, low in front, high in back. While in conventional casting the fly follows a figure-of-eight pattern, in the "oval" it never crosses its own path.

The "constant pressure" pulls the line around behind the rod in the large oval, always with pressure on the line, instead of the forward-and-back motion with the difficult-to-determine waiting periods in between. There is no sudden snap of maximum force and then a complete relaxation of all pressure. The caster has something tangible to work with. He is dragging a weight of line around through the air. His rod movement and pressure must be just great enough to keep it moving around the circuit.

The tension on the line and the bending of the rod are never lost although they increase and diminish as the line makes its oval. If there's a loss of tension the caster feels it immediately and knows he's out of time. There's no worry about how long to wait because there's never any waiting.

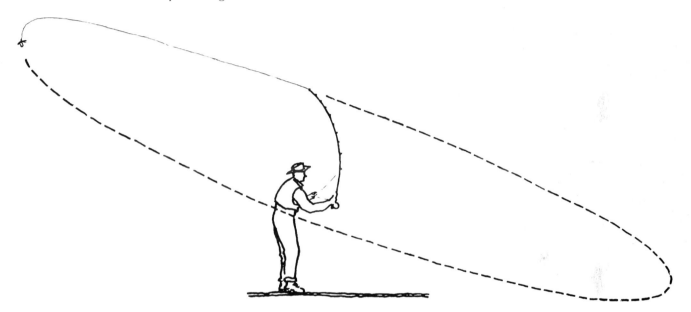

As line is let out through the guides, the oval automatically grows and takes longer to make. From the far point of the oval at the back cast the caster can drive it forward in a typical cast to the desired spot. Any caster whose timing is off will find the method of value. The combination of a constant pressure swing and a high back cast is a practically foolproof way to insure good casting. The caster can return to the conventional casting motions in an instant, if he wishes, by shortening the small axis of the oval and swinging the line's travel to an overhead plane.

Normal fly casting calls for a space for the back cast almost as great as the distance the fly is to be cast forward. By using the roll, or switch, cast the angler may make a forward cast of considerable distance without having any space available behind him. First step in the roll cast is to hold the rod vertical until the line hangs slackly from the tip. Move the rod tip slightly away from the body. Then the rod is switched forward and down using a good deal of arm motion. A big loop is formed which goes rolling down the line and which, upon coming to the end of it, picks up the tag end of the line and the leader and flips them forward, too. If a little slack is given just after the rolling motion is made each roll moving down the line will extend the cast a little farther until the limit of casting is reached, a distance from half to two-thirds of that which can be achieved by the overhead method.

In actual fishing roll casting is little used, being reserved for the difficult places where an angler cannot wade out far enough for a reasonable back cast and no boat is available. However the roll-cast principle is applied advantageously to another situation. When a line has sunk deeply in the water during the retrieve so that it will not lift readily for a back cast, the angler can save the trouble of stripping in line by sending a roll cast down his line which will bring it to the surface in perfect position for the lift-out. The forward roll and the back cast are then combined into one flowing motion. This technique is used by most capable fishermen whenever their retrieves come in low under the surface.

The roll cast can also be used as a short cut to learning to cast a long line or to cast at all. In desperation, I advised beginners at fly-fishing who might have only a day or two in camp, to use this stunt in order to cast the 50 feet or over that might be required to hook a salmon. There wasn't time to give them a more thorough grounding in fly casting.

Joan Wulff is shown here casting in the falls pool on the Godbout River.

They'd be placed in fishing position with plenty of space for a back cast and about 40 feet of line worked off the reel and out through the guides. The line would be allowed to drift down with the current or gather in the still water near them. Then they would be shown how to hold the rod upright until the line hung slack. (If the line isn't given time to slacken, the system—and the roll cast—will not work.) With slack line hanging from the tip, they were guided through a hard roll-cast motion.

Immediately upon its completion the rod would return to vertical for the time required for the line to slacken again. Another roll-cast motion would follow, and another. Eventually the line would straighten out on or above the surface, and at that precise moment they were taught to make a back cast and a forward cast with a line shoot at the end of it.

By using this method it becomes relatively simple to teach a well-coordinated but inexperienced caster within a matter of minutes how to cast far enough to catch a salmon. It doesn't look very graceful but it will get a wet fly out and take a novice over the first big hurdle. Having learned the roll cast and the essentials of the long cast he can polish up on his form *after* he's learned to catch fish rather than beforehand.

An important factor in fly casting is the ability to recognize the right length of line extending beyond the guides for best distance on the final back cast. When rod and line are balanced for the power of the caster, the full belly of a multiple taper line should be just beyond the guides. If too much line is out the weight will be too heavy for the power of rod or angler; if there is too little extended there will not be enough weight available to develop the maximum casting power of the rod.

The greatest casting distance is achieved by shooting line on the final forward cast. If the rod is working under just the right amount of line, maximum speed and power will be developed on the final back cast for the greatest total distance forward. It is possible to make a longer back cast but never a better one. A longer back cast will make too heavy a load for the forward drive which will then not pull out enough line on the shoot for a maximum cast. Anglers who are in good casting form readily recognize this point, but for those who may lose touch with their tackle periodically it is wise to mark the line (with a painted ring) for the back cast that will deliver the most power.

The difficulty of straightening out the leader at the end of the cast, often encountered with large, fluffy dry flies, results from insufficient power in the cast to straighten it out. When the angler realizes the line has slowed down too much to carry the cast through properly he can increase its forward drive if he pulls in a few feet of line or pulls the rod back away from the cast just before its completion.

The pulling in of the line will flip out and straighten a cast that would otherwise land with the leader doubled back. A slight roll, sent travelling down the line late in the final cast, will move it to the left or right as desired. A cast is not completed until the fly and line settle to the water. Until this happens slight corrections can be made by moving the rod forward or back, to left or right, or by sending a roll or twist along its length.

The hauling back of the line at the end of the cast which will increase speed will also increase the power of the forward and backward drives in the casting. If, as the rod is driven forward at full power by the right hand, line is also pulled in quickly through the guides by a jerk of the left arm, the forward line drive will be greater and the cast longer. The same is true of the back cast. The "double haul" is a method of adding impetus to both forward- and back-cast drives in order to get maximum distance. It complicates the casting and is only advisable when normal casting falls short of a particular goal.

There is one form of accident that happens more often to salmon fishermen than to any other type. Its result, when a salmon at last comes to the fly, is a momentary hooking of the fish but after anywhere from a second or two to a minute the fish gets off.

Sometimes an angler will miss or lose two or three fish in a row after working long and hard to achieve the rises, and only then will he be prompted to look at his fly to find the hook broken off just behind the barb.

Most salmon rivers swell with the spring floods and settle for their summer flows into channels winding their way through or around the great, gravelly beaches that make up the rivers' high-water beds. Salmon fishermen are called on for long casts, often in windy weather, and the combination all too frequently brings the fisherman's fly in abrupt contact with a stone. A back cast touching a leaf or a few blades of grass is not often damaging to the fly but the least tick of the flying point against a rock or pebble takes all the sting out of the angler's fishing offensive.

Anglers who, on less rocky waters, have fished with little thought to their hook points will suddenly realize the importance of checking them frequently when backed up by gravelly banks. There is no substitute for frequent inspections whenever there's even a bare possibility the fly may have touched a rock. Salmon rises are far too difficult to achieve to waste them on broken hooks. There is a gravelly bank on a Miramichi pool where a conservative estimate puts a 500-dollar value on the flies that were made useless because they touched it on a back cast last season.

The best time to check one's fly (and leader) is just *before* a salmon takes it. If you've just raised and missed a fish take a look at your terminal tackle before you try him again. Otherwise check your fly frequently for both broken hook points and cast-knots or weak points in the leader. If you do not check often enough, losing a salmon will surely remind you.

The occasional single overhand knot that an imperfect cast or a gust of wind can tie in a leader is not as great a cause of lost fish as is the broken hook, but it is still a large factor in losing salmon. The standard leader knot is designed to spread the strain of the union over a considerable surface area of the leader. That knot is but very slightly weaker than the rest of the leader. If the wind casts a figure-eight knot in your leader it will reduce the strength at that point by about 15 percent. If it ties a single overhand knot, which uses one turn to cut another, the strength will be cut almost in half at that point, and an angler using his tackle efficiently up to normal permissible tension is almost certain to lose his fish.

SINGLE OVERHAND

FIGURE EIGHT

While no great accuracy is required for simple water coverage, as soon as a fish has risen and it is often necessary, in order to interest that fish again, to repeat the identical cast the need for accuracy becomes apparent. Fly casting can be extremely accurate when the distance is moderate and there is no wind to deflect the line. The nearer an angler is to his casting limit in distance the smaller grow the chances of his being able to send his flies consistently to any given spot. Wind increases this difficulty.

Although the Portland Creek camps had a fine staff of guides, and it would be difficult to decide which of them was most capable, the records of fish taken pointed an unerring finger toward Ike Biggin. His charges caught more fish, season after season. Ike never propounded this theory to account for his success, but in watching all the guides and their methods I discovered what I believe was his secret.

Many of our fishermen at the camps were in the novice class; few were top-flight salmon anglers. The other guides would tell their anglers where to cast and often the wind or the length of line they had out would cause the fly to vary from a foot to several yards with each cast. Ike limited his fishermen to a very short line. He would not let an angler cast farther than his point of consistent accuracy, which might be no more than 30 feet.

Ike would work his charge into position by moving the boat until the fly would go to the exact spot most likely to interest a salmon at that lie. It would go there time after time after time. Consistent fishing is one of the fundamentals of catching salmon, and the uniformity of presentation he managed with all his sportsmen resulted in a very high ratio of rises. Other anglers whose flies were varying considerably from cast to cast may have enjoyed the pleasure of casting a longer line but they had fewer rises per hour of fishing. The angler who consistently casts beyond his point of accuracy is not fishing his best.

Controlling the fly at a distance through the exactness of the casting drive or length of line out are physical things, dependent to a great degree on muscular coordination. The control of a fly in the wind is mainly a matter of mind. It was a sort of shock to me as I learned each of two cardinal principles for accurate casting in winds, for I had been casting for many years before I learned them. As each one became apparent it was so simple I wondered how I could have overlooked it for so long.

The first principle lies in a recognition that wind is almost never constant. Only over the sea or completely level land can wind be steady. On a river it comes in gusts or other variations. The angler who casts uniformly, expecting a certain drive to carry his fly a given distance regardless of the exact moment the cast is finalized, is living in a dream world. He is casting but not thinking it through.

I think it was my experiences in flying seaplanes and bringing them in to the windy surfaces of lakes that showed the way. In landing a seaplane in heavy and gusty winds, a change of velocity of 5 miles an hour could mean the difference between smooth flying and a stall. An airplane, like a fluffy fly at the end of a leader, is a thing of the air, not of the earth.

In order to make perfect seaplane landings I'd come settling in slowly from a considerable height, watching where the wind squalls mottled patches of the water darkly. They usually had a pattern of sorts and there might be an area of a 100-yard diameter or more which would be under the influence of a hard and steady wind for a period of half a minute at a time. If I were just above the water as I came to the downwind edge of such a windy patch, and just above stalling point which would be reached within that patch of wind, when I settled to the water I knew the wind would soon decrease and that no gust would lift me above flying speed again before I slowed to taxiing speed. If I were to touch down at stalling speed in a quiet spot just before a gust hit I'd be flying again and have to make a second landing.

The answer to casting accuracy in the wind lies in the ability to judge the wind's strength at the moment of the cast. The wind's story is written on the water. The intense rippling of one patch indicates a higher wind velocity at that point than at another where the rippling is light or where there is none. You can see the wind gusts coming toward you across the water. Let the last of the gust help take your back cast out behind you and straighten it nicely. This allows you to snap it forward into a space of relative calm. It may be necessary to delay casting now and then until the gusts are right but good judgment in the wind will permit a high percentage of perfect casts, whereas systematic casting into a wind that varies in speed with each cast will result in impaired accuracy and fewer fish.

A wild fish is hooked in June on Harry's River.

In order to follow a fish, an angler must be at home in the river, almost part of it.

In time, the angler closes in.

Big fish hate the shallows and can be tailed much sooner in deep water than near the shore. BELOW: Victory, and the angler heads for shore.

The second important step in learning to control a fly in the wind came when it dawned on me that a false cast would take my fly right out where I wanted it but that when I followed habit and sent my fly out to a point above the surface to let it settle lightly, as it would under normal conditions, it was being blown away. On the false cast the fly is snapped forward and turned around in only the briefest second. If I could control my casting well enough to release the fly at the exact moment the false cast placed it perfectly, I would achieve my need.

It only takes a fraction of a second for a 30-mile-an-hour wind to whisk a small fly and light leader a dozen feet across the water. Only by forcing the fly right to the water and then forcing the line down into place can the perfect result be obtained. If the cast is stopped at a position A, as indicated in the illustration, the line, leader, and fly left floating in the air are subject to movement by the wind. When the fly is cast right to the water and the usual lifting of the rod that snaps the fly out at the false cast's conclusion is reversed to force the line down toward the water, too, the seemingly impossible has been achieved. It sounds more difficult than it is, and no matter how inefficiently an angler may be in completing such a cast, the result will be an improvement over his not having tried at all. Salmon rivers are often windy, and knowledge of how to cope with wind can be of great value.

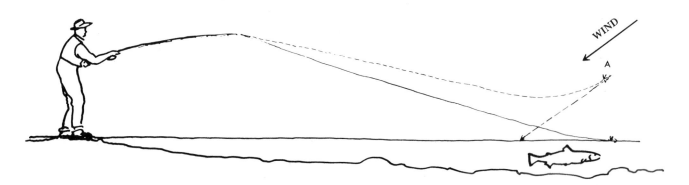

The direction of the wind has an effect on the destination of line, leader, and fly.

These two procedures for obtaining accuracy and distance in high and gusty winds came to me independently. The same thoughts may have come to others and they, too, may have worked along these lines. I do not believe they are yet common knowledge for it is a rare thing to find an angler who can put a fly where he wants to in a gale.

There is a third important factor in the ability to drive a fly into the wind which has to do with very small rods and the very fast cast they can give. It is tied up with the relationship between the fly's speed of travel in the cast and the speed of the air into which it must penetrate. This will be touched on later.

The angler should also remember that wind changes not only the casting, but also the fishing, picture. Salmon which would shy away from a heavy-splashing fly in a quiet pool will take it as a matter of course when it lands in the midst of wind-tormented waters. Then it would be more unnatural if it drifted gently down to the surface. And a salmon which would avoid even the finest leader on a still day will disregard a much heavier one when the whitecaps half obscure it. An angler will be much less conspicuous to a salmon above a rippled surface than over a smooth one and his casts need not be as long. Where a hundred careful casts on a beautiful day might leave a salmon unmoved, half a dozen may draw him to the barbed steel in a gale, for the waves often make a fish restless. When salmon are stirred to action by wind on the water a larger-than-usual fly and, in the opinion of many anglers, a silvery one, is most effective.

The foregoing has taken into account the times when the fly must be cast into or across the wind. Some lies may be fished easiest in a wind. Whenever possible the angler should make the wind work for him and, by putting it well behind him, let it help take the fly to the right spot.

It is best to have the wind come from the opposite side from which you cast. A right-handed angler finds casting easier if the wind blowing from his left tends to keep the fly line downwind of him as it makes its air travel on the forward and backward casts. A wind blowing in from the right tends to blow it against him or against his rod. If he must cast under these conditions he may find it preferable to cast over his left shoulder, keeping his body upwind of the line.

Wind from the right direction can be helpful in casting a loop which so bends the leader and line that the fly approaches the fish first. This is an aid in drawing rises. When the line or the leader comes to the fish first he is much more likely to notice it, seeing it well before the fly comes into his close vision. When the fly comes first and draws his attention, the leader following behind it may go unnoticed. By the time the heavy part of the tapered leader or the line has come close to him he has either risen or has already made a decision not to rise.

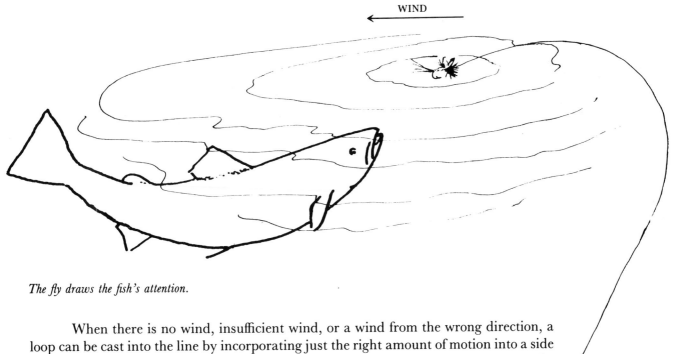

The fly draws the fish's attention.

When there is no wind, insufficient wind, or a wind from the wrong direction, a loop can be cast into the line by incorporating just the right amount of motion into a side cast. A right-handed caster can let his cast carry beyond a straight line in order to make a left-hand loop. He can let it touch the water just short of straightening out to make it loop to the right.

The slack-line cast is important for the dry-fly, or the patent, method. In this maneuver the line is cast out to its length at a high angle and snapped back partway by a backward pull of the rod. The line snaps back into a series of undulations or coils and gives a shorter cast in which the line is slack. All this slack may be used to let a fly drift freely with the current. It permits dry-fly fishing with long drifts over pocket water where no other casting method is so efficient.

A yank back at the end of the cast while it is still in the air will "snake" it out on the water with slack here and there along it. The slack that extends a fly's free drift *must* be *at* the fly. Slack anywhere else is useless once tension from a drifting line or leader reaches the fly. Therefore the best cast to give maximum slack is what I call the "plop" cast. It is a wide-looped cast which is not quite completed. Without quite enough power to straighten it out, the leader will fall in a pile with the fly. It will straighten out slowly as it drifts giving the fly a maximum free float.

The use of very light rods in fishing for salmon is a most intriguing thing. It calls for extra skill but it brings out a delicacy of action unattainable otherwise.

Fly fishermen have long believed that very light rods are not only hard to handle but won't make long casts. That used to be true, but modern techniques have made the featherweight fly rod much easier to use and have increased its range greatly. Important in these techniques is full use of the arm in casting.

Some forty years ago, in writing my *Handbook of Freshwater Fishing*, I described fly casting much as everyone else did, emphasizing movement of the wrist rather than of the arm, and warning against bringing the rod back much past the vertical on the backcast. At that time I had only limited experience with featherweight fly rods weighing between 1½ to 2½ ounces (scale weight of the complete rod). But since then consistent, season-long fishing with such rods has convinced me light rods are not only practical but that best results will be obtained with them when full use is made of the casting arm. Limiting the rod to the vertical point on the backcast hinders rather than helps the cast.

In 1962, as a result of disparaging remarks and writings from the long-rod exponents on the other side of the Atlantic, I challenged a long-rod exponent, Donald Rudd, who, writing under the pen name of "Jock Scott," was the premier writer on British salmon angling, to a fishing duel. He fished with his favorite Grant "vibration" 16½-foot greenheart rod, and I fished with a 6-foot, 1¾-ounce split-bamboo rod I'd worked out with Wes Jordan of the Orvis Company.

We fished for a week on the Aberdeenshire Dee in Scotland in stormy weather under poor conditions. There was some press coverage of the event, and when it was over, perhaps because football and baseball news was slow, there was a banner headline in the New York *Herald-Tribune* sports section saying "WULFF WINS SALMON DUEL 1–0."

A second satisfaction in the catching of that particular salmon was that Captain Tommy Edwards, British casting champion who, too, was scornful of my little rods, was standing on the bank. I was fishing with a #8 White Wulff, a dry fly, which British salmon were not supposed to take. When the fish rose Edwards said, "Hah! A sea trout." When it jumped and proved itself a salmon of 10 pounds he uttered a shocked, "Well, I'll be damned," shaking his head as if in lingering disbelief.

In an earlier chapter I described casting a fly line without any rod at all. A #8 fly line can be cast from 30 to 50 feet by hand. So let's start with the line and progress from there to its best use with a matching rod.

In casting by hand alone you must treat the line as if it were a rope. A rolling motion of the hand will send a loop rolling down its entire length. A sharp lift of the arm will pick up 20 to 30 feet and straighten it out behind you but a twist of the wrist, as used in normal fly casting, has practically no effect. Somewhere between the old style of casting and the casting of the line by hand alone lies the best casting motion for very light rods.

In the traditional method, length and stiffness of the rod provide the casting power. And since the combined weight of the longer rod and the line-filled reel is great enough to make full-arm movement fatiguing, casting is achieved by wrist motion. (All the early fly fisherman were told that the perfect caster can hold a book against his body with the elbow of his casting arm while he's in action.) But with short rods the limited power of the wrist simply isn't great enough to throw a light line.

The full-arm casting that would be hard work with a 9-foot, 6½-ounce rod is light work with a 6-foot, 2-ounce rod. And similar casting distance can be achieved with the latter by application of a new principle in fly casting.

I enjoy casting and always work my little rods relatively hard. And I cast them to the limit of my strength whenever there's a particularly distant spot I want to reach. In the past I could count on only about one month of life for a very light split-bamboo rod. Now, with impregnated bamboo, fiberglass, and graphite they stand up, season after season, with practically no breakage.

A third factor lengthening the casts of short fly rods is the forward-taper fly line. Its advantage over the old double-taper comes only when the line really begins to stretch out and 35 feet or more are off the reel. Then the lighter shooting line gets extra distance with the same amount of effort. Extra distance over a normal cast isn't so important with the usual 8½- or 9-foot rod but the long "shoot" permitted by the forward-taper line makes it possible to reach out to all normal fishing distances with a rod of 7 feet or less.

Obviously, the casting power of any fly rod is mainly limited by the weight of line it will handle in the air. And weight for weight you get more line length with the featherweight outfit. However, there is a weight limit for any outfit. But supposing it is reached at 55 feet, say, you can still add length to the casts, and yet not overstrain the rod, by using a long leader and learning how to snap it out.

Long leaders (mine range from 10 to 25 feet) will extend the line's maximum casting distance by about 80 percent of their length. Under the old elbow-at-side casting motion it was difficult to straighten out a leader, but with the full-arm motion—aided when necessary by a sharp pull back of rod arm, line, or both—a very long leader can be straightened out completely.

My casting motion resembles that of a pitcher throwing a ball. I start the backcast with my arm stretched forward, bring it back in a slightly underhand swing until the line is stretched out full length behind me, then catch the weight of the line, with my rod arm as far back and as high as I can get it, at precisely the proper instant to drive the line forward and down to the starting point. The light rod lifts it and directs it, but essentially it is the power and movement of my arm in its speedy drive that sends the line sailing forward.

The rotary effect of this line motion in a *vertical* plane has a number of advantages. First, the line tends to come in on a low level and go out on a higher one, lessening the chance of a tangle as part of the line drives forward while its end is still moving back. In standard casting tangling is normally averted by making the casting motion an elongated oval in the *horizontal* plane. With the short rod the oval lies in a vertical plane.

Often there is an obstruction on the bank which limits the backcast and thereby limits the forward cast as well. But by bringing the line in low and lifting it upward as it completes the backcast, you get good clearance above the ground or water at a point where you need it most. Thus you can get a full backcast at practically all times. When, under the same circumstances, the tail end of the backcast is lower—as it must be in the orthodox cast, when the line stays on a fairly level plane throughout—it seriously affects the length of the backcast and, consequently, the forward cast.

Still another advantage of the high backcast is that it helps make the forward cast low. A low forward cast leads to better fishing. It is more accurate, since the point of aim of the cast is closer to the water it is to land on.

To save effort, the pickup of the forward cast should be made with a typical roll-cast motion, pulling the fly to the surface, then picking it up immediately for the start of the backcast. This is a good labor-saving trick used by many fly casters. The angler with a featherweight rod will often have need of it.

Short rods will not pick up as much line as longer ones of the same proportionate power. This means more line must be retrieved before the successful pickup can be made. Overloading the rod on pickup usually spoils the chance of a good cast and, in the long run, is more work than the extra left-arm movement required to bring another yard or two of line inside the guides would have been.

The angler's grip on the rod is important. With the conventional wrist movement a grip in which the thumb rests on the top of the cork works very well. With small rods I lay my forefinger out full length on top of the rod for best results. This affords greater and more delicate control. It puts my hand at an angle where its overall grip on the rod is stronger and my wrist becomes a continuation of my arm rather than a loose joint.

Conventional casting calls for smooth, easy movement. Fly casters have long been judged by smoothness of line flow and easy grace of movement, even where changes of direction are involved. But all this goes by the board when you're using a featherweight rod. I drive out my casts with every ounce of power I can muster, seeking maximum speed. I depend upon timing to let me use full strength and speed for the necessary fraction of a second when the direction of line travel is changed. Here, as in the case of a baseball pitcher, one uses maximum strength and speed to move a light object.

Baseball pitchers have reached a throwing speed of over 90 miles an hour. That is the speed of their hand's movement, for the ball can move no faster than the thrower's hand. Hand speed is the key to distance with short, light rods. The need for snap and speed in getting the ultimate out of featherweight tackle cannot be overemphasized. Conventional casting with a light outfit will get moderate distance, but only coordinated speed and power will make it compete with standard outfits in covering the water.

Few anglers realize how fast a fly line can travel. Once I made stopwatch tests of the time required to straighten out backcasts and forward casts. I ran the tests first on my 6½-foot, 2-ounce rod and then on my 9-foot, 5-ounce rod. The amount of line off the reel in each case was the same, 55 feet, and each leader was 10 feet long. I made several runs of ten complete forward casts and backcasts during which the fly traveled 260 feet ten times, or a total of 2,600 feet of movement.

The average time for the featherweight outfit was a speedy 18.4 seconds, which was a rate of travel of 96 miles per hour. Peak speed is much higher, since the fly has to come to a stop and change direction at the end of each forecast and backcast. The average time for the 9-foot fly rod was 23.1 seconds, or a rate of travel of 76 miles per hour.

Kinetic energy, the energy of motion, is measured by weight and speed according to the formula $E = \frac{1}{2}MV^2$ where M is the mass and V the velocity. It follows, then, that if you double the speed you increase the energy by four times. The importance of line speed in casting with short, light rods cannot be overemphasized. Yet casting with them, because the time of power application is so short, is far less tiring than it is with longer rods.

Those of us who pilot airplanes know that if you increase the diameter of a propeller by even a small amount you cut down drastically the speed at which a given engine can make it turn. The resistance of the air slows it down, and for that reason, I couldn't make my 9-foot rod move through it as swiftly as I could the short, light one.

Most fly casters are convinced that it takes a heavy line to force their cast out into the wind. That's wrong. The solution is simple; send the line out with much more speed than the wind it faces. The featherweight rod with its higher speed will actually do a better job than a more powerful but slower outfit.

The featherweight rod should have a good stiffness right at the butt and be light in the tip. Here the so-called parabolic actions are not useful, since they have a pendulumlike swing. In the old casting method, this swing reduces the problem of timing, because the parabolic rod tends to settle into a rhythm easily felt by the angler and easily followed by him. However, such an action hasn't the backbone to deliver the drive necessary for a maximum cast with a light rod. Its virtues are smoothness and ease. I like a fly rod that takes the maximum amount of change of pace and delivers its full power in the shortest possible time.

Because the casting of the ultralight fly rods depends upon movement of arm rather than wrist, a number of variations are possible. When faced with a solid wall of foliage behind him an angler standing on a 6-foot beach or slab of rock can coil 40 feet of line and leader at his feet (working backward from the fly) and straighten it out in front of him with a quick snap of the roll-cast type.

The line can be cast in a big, vertical oval with its center well in front of the rod by varying the speed of the rolling arm motion. This keeps the line almost entirely in front of the caster, and as long as he has the feel of the weight of the line in the air he can pick the right time on any circuit to shoot the fly out 30 feet or more.

An angler's form in casting may be important to himself and to other anglers. To the fish, who will be the final judge of his prowess, form matters not at all. How the fly travels, what it looks like, how visible the leader is, how quietly it lands, how conspicuous the angler, . . . those are the only things with which a fish concerns himself.

Although all conventional fly casting takes the fly through a figure-of-eight path, my work with the short, featherweight rods led me to a new method. I'd had difficulty making very long, high backcasts by conventional casting, especially when wading deep. As I experimented I found I could get a better backcast by bringing my fly in so low that it passed me just above water level on the backcast. Then, by lifting my arm sharply, I could keep the fly and line well above the water and end up with my arm back and high in the position of a pitcher throwing a hard, fast ball. That is the best position to get maximum stroke distance and speed on the forward cast, and with it maximum distance.

In this cast my fly travels an *oval* course and never crosses its previous path. This also gives a wider loop in my casting and, therefore, a lesser tendency for the fly to touch the line and cause wind knots. More important, it was easy to develop a feeling of constant pressure of the line on the rod. This made timing a thing of feeling rather than one of guessing mentally exactly when to make the forward or backward stroke. With constant pressure the caster feels his line's drag continually as he moves line through the air; and he can sense through that pressure the loading of his rod for forward and backcasts. Although this oval pattern was developed in order to make longer casts with short, light rods this method will give smooth, trouble-free casts with longer rods as well.

Wading

Salmon fishing reaches its peak as a sport when the capture of the fish is achieved by a single individual rather than by a two-man team. Although an angler may handle his own boat or canoe in a pinch, it is difficult. In most cases the use of a boat or canoe implies a team of two men, both of whom will deserve a share of the credit for each fish landed, and either of whom may make a mistake that will lose a fish. To capture a salmon entirely on his own from start to finish, the angler should be able to wade.

Success in casting the fly, hooking the fish, and handling the tackle for salmon fishing are primarily matters of position. The angler who can position himself so as to reach a fish with a good fly presentation where other anglers cannot, has a distinct advantage. Where the catch may be only one fish a day or one a week, a single such opportunity may well double an angler's catch.

The fisherman who can manage, in playing a fish, to be at the right position for the critical moments can save him, while the angler whose mobility is limited may not. Almost always, the time it takes to land a salmon is seriously dependent upon the position the angler maintains relative to the fish. The ability to move with the necessary speed and direction is a primary requisite to good fishing practice. When an angler cannot move about well, and boats or canoes are not used, he is severely handicapped.

Wading, like present day basketball, favors a certain type of individual. It helps to be tall and long-legged. A short man will be up to his waist in water that will not rise much above a tall man's knees. A good wader should be heavy for, in a swift current, a short and heavy man can hold his footing where a taller but lighter man would be unable to hold his place. It is an advantage to be thin-legged and narrow-hipped but broad-shouldered and heavy above the waist. The submerged part of the angler has lost weight to the amount of the water he displaces and so is almost weightless. Only the weight above the waterline can help hold an angler in his position.

An angler who is willing to wade deep can use a short playing line, thereby maintaining the best control and exerting the most effective pressure on the fish.

Strength is another important factor in holding a position or wading against a strong current. Agility pays off in saving one's balance when a loose rock rolls underfoot. Good eyesight helps in discerning the depth and makeup of the bottom in order to place one's feet well. More than anything else, though, successful wading is a matter of judgment.

Obviously, the best physique for wading is that of the tall, broad-shouldered athlete. Failing to have been so blessed by nature that we can outwade all our brethren, we can at least wade to our own best advantage, and couple skill and judgment to give us good mobility within the limits of safety.

The man with hip boots is limited by their length to relatively shallow water where maximum strength of limb is not required. With the water at his hips, a man's entire trunk and at least two-thirds of his weight is above water. The angler whose waders come to waist or chest is more likely to get into difficult positions. When the waters lap up toward his armpits, not more than a third of his weight is left to press him down against the stream bed, and the water of the stream has a much greater area against which to press. One of my reasons for designing the original fully pocketed fishing vest was to have all the weight of my accessories above the waterline, as well as to have them readily available. Particularly when swift, deep water is to be encountered, the weight of spare reels and lines, raincoat, camera, and so forth make possible wading control in an extra inch or two of depth, which occasionally adds a salmon or two to the day's tally.

Following a salmon into fast water . . .

Will he fall?

A quick recovery.

Moving on toward the final moments of victory on the Serpentine River.

There is an old and persistent rumor that the wearing of waist waders is dangerous. Trapped air, it is said, will lift them quickly off the bottom in deep water and will hold a man's feet up, forcing his head under water until he drowns. From California to Quebec the story has been repeated with its local versions. I have heard of it happening in California's Kern River and in Newfoundland's LaPoile, and at various points in between. It must have been true that the men had waders on and did drown, but I am certain it was not because of anything inherently dangerous in wearing them.

One of the magazine editors of my acquaintance expressed uncertainty, and, in order to prove a point and give him an article, I donned my waders and dove from a bridge some 20 feet straight down into a deep, swift-flowing river. I entered the water head first, clad in beltless waders, with my fishing vest and all my normal clothing on. In that way I could be certain to trap the maximum possible amount of air in my waders and put myself in the worst possible situation, according to rumor. Had I waded in gently and in an erect position, which is the way most immersions occur, the water pressure would have forced all the air out of the waders by their pressure against the body and some critic would have claimed it wasn't a fair test. I had a photographer catch me in mid-dive, head down just above the water, to verify the situation.

I went deep, and, as I recall it, the water was cold, but there were no difficulties. There was air in the waders and it held my feet up beautifully, something ordinarily requiring a certain amount of kicking effort. There was no abnormal tendency for my head to go under. Swimming, though slowed down by the excess of apparel, was actually less effort than normal. It was easier to swim with the air in the waders than without it.

Then I waded into the pool from a sloping bank which took all the air out of my waders before immersion. They were still no serious problem. If air is trapped, it is an advantage. If not, waders or boots have almost no weight underwater since their specific gravity is not much different than that of water, and they can not seriously drag one down. They would be a nuisance for long-distance swimming, but the angler who falls in has but to paddle enough to keep himself afloat while he drifts to shallow water or swim to nearby shallows where he can stand up. A ducking is much more of a discomfort than a danger.

Many an angler must have inadvertently gone in over his depth or slipped and been washed by the current into a deep pool. Most of them must have been able to reach safe footing, for there are very few instances of mature, stream fly fishermen having fallen in and drowned. Where it has happened, it is most likely to have been caused by panic, inability to swim, a snootful of "Old Rotgut," or some other special circumstance not connected with the waders. A wading angler should be careful and keep dry, but should he slip, waders may not help him much, but they will not sink him, either.

Wading over sand and gravel is easy and the footing is good. As the gravel or rocks of the streambed become larger and less uniform, wading becomes more difficult. Solid rock streambeds or streambeds where the rocks are well established and will not roll are much easier and safer to walk on than those where rocks will roll easily under foot. Rough rocks, like sandstones and brecchias, furnish a better gripping surface for one's soles than the hard, smooth rocks of the granitic type. Smooth rocks coated with moss and slime are the slipperiest of all, and only chains or hobnails will grip on them.

Some wading shoes and boots and waders come equipped with hobnails, but most do not. Hobnails can be added to a smooth sole, but such a permanent addition may not be desired. Hobnail sandals or chain sandals which can be strapped on, are simpler. The latter type places three or four lengths of chain under the ball of the foot much as chains go on a tire. Felt soles are available on wading sandals, too, and any type of sandal can be strapped on or removed readily. Rubber soles, especially when worn smooth, are very slippery on many types of bottom, especially on hard rocks. Some sort of sandal is a good investment for use over smooth-worn rubber soles.

Although it is a nuisance to carry, a staff can be a help in wading. It gives an angler another point of contact with the bottom without getting wet. There can be no doubt of a staff's value in swift water or over slimy, slippery, large stones. If one is used, it should be tied to one end of about a yard of thong or parachute cord with the other end secured to the belt or jacket. The staff can float downstream from the angler in the current when not in use and will always be readily available when needed. If a wading staff is not secured to the fisherman in some manner, it is likely to be dropped and swept away at a most crucial time. There are now available sectional, folding wading staffs which, from a collapsed length of 9 or 10 inches, can be extended in a second or two to a sturdy 4- to 5-foot wading staff. They have strong central elastic cords so that when removed from the case or pocket, a simple shaking of the segments makes them line up rigidly. This is a godsend for the wading angler who seldom needs a wading staff but when he does, needs it badly.

Where an angler has a guide, the "buddy" system of wading is a sound one. In it, a fisherman and his guide lock arms while wading out across slippery bottom to the fishing position. Each one grips the other's biceps with one hand, leaving the other free. A wader usually falls because, when his balance is about to be lost, there is nothing to give him a slight support. Even a light pressure on something as stable as a man's arm will insure his staying upright.

It is possible to learn to read the depth of the water by the pattern of the eddies and currents on the surface, but only long experience can provide this ability. The average angler should wade very cautiously where he cannot see bottom, and he should always have an eye on where he'll go if he slips or falls.

It is easier to wade across a swift current by turning one's side toward the flow. Then the area presented to the current is only half as great as if the angler faced directly into it (one leg instead of two). By taking short steps, usually moving the upstream foot ahead first and following with the downstream foot, the area against which the force of the flow can work is held to a minimum.

Many excellent waders appear always to be on the point of falling in. They slip and slide and, somehow, at the last minute manage to recover. Recovering is an art in itself. If one swings his stern around into the current as he slips and pulls his feet up under him quickly in the same motion he may be able to put them down again solidly before the top of his waders has sunk below waterlevel. If one foot slips on a rock, a hop upon the other one may give time to find secure footing before falling becomes inevitable. These are tricks for the athlete and for the brave and the adventurous. For most wading anglers, there is no better advice than "be careful."

8

The Presentation

is choice may cover an entire wide-ranging fly assortment or just a single box of flies, all similar in size and shape but varying in color, but a competent salmon angler on a good river can safely say, "pick any fly and I will show you a salmon." It is no exaggeration that when the local-standby patterns are fished, presentation is three-fourths or more of the taking of a salmon. Specifically: the placing and movement of the fly are at least three times as important as the pattern.

It is this feature of angling for salmon that lets the individual, who understands the fish and the fishing, fish his season through with only half a dozen battered flies and yet take more salmon than any other angler on "his river." There are those who feel (and the writer is among them) that if they had possessed a wider range of flies and patterns and known when to use them they could have taken even more fish.

In any case there can be no question but that the presentation of the fly is the crux of this angling and that the moment of the taking rise heavily outweighs the moment when that fly was tied or purchased or was selected for that bit of fishing. Almost anyone can come by adequate tackle, can learn to cast, and, in time, to play a salmon well. To choose the right fly and fish it efficiently is a separate thing, a part of the difference between the ordinary angler and the expert. It is the difference between those who come closest to the mastery of the sport and those who are merely capable participants.

The supreme moment in fishing is the hooking of the salmon. If you can hook them readily, even if you are only moderately good in other phases of the game, you will have fine catches. However, if you can play them as well as anyone else in the world but cannot hook them, your talents will be wasted. Only to a gifted few is it given to really understand the art of both the choice and presentation of the fly and the moment of setting it, which makes up the true heart of salmon fishing.

The Wet Fly

The wet fly, fished according to custom, is cast across the current and downstream, usually at an angle of about 45 degrees. The current causes the line to tighten and swing an arc through the water, ending up by hanging directly downstream when the cast is fished to completion. Under the stimulus of the current the wet fly becomes a swimming thing, set apart by its motion and apparent life from all the many lifeless drifting things a river may carry. It is fished upon a tense and not a slack line. Therefore, for fishing the wet fly perfectly the cast should carry to a straight-line finish. Any curve or slack in the line subtracts from the distance the fly can swim.

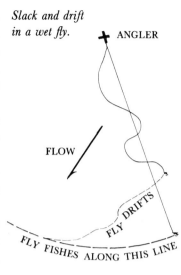

Slack and drift in a wet fly.

If the cast ends up in a straight line, the fly, under immediate tension from the flow, will begin its swimming as soon as it touches the water. If there is slack, the fisherman can take it up immediately either by stripping some line in through the guides or by lifting his rod. Otherwise he must wait for the current to carry the line downstream, which will cause it to tighten against the reel or hand and eventually cause the fly to swing.

One of the commonest wet-fly fishing faults is the failure to straighten out the cast, and then, having failed, to take no corrective action. Guides who can cast beautifully often must stand idly by and watch their charges cast out a loose line and then let it drift. This practice can result in the fly being fished about 20 percent of the cast's potential, and of not being fished through the water where the salmon lie. More often than not, the water at the far end of the cast is the best and, by losing it, an angler forfeits a large percentage of possible rises.

When a wet fly lands with a lot of slack and drifts freely, it is quite possible a salmon may rise and take it, but it is also true that only the most alert and able of fishermen will realize the fish has come to the fly and be able to set the hook before it is ejected. This drifting of a wet fly with the current has been developed into a special form of wet-fly fishing, to be discussed later. However, for the great bulk of the wet-fly anglers, a drifting fly means time and water wasted.

The wet fly has a distinct advantage over the dry, or drifting, fly in its water coverage. The wet fly automatically covers all the fishable water within an angler's reach as he wades down the pool. He simply makes cast after cast at a similar angle to the current as he progresses, and each cast automatically follows a course roughly paralleling the one which preceded it. The dry-fly fisherman must choose a particular line of drift to fish. The freely floating fly will cover only a small fraction of the water in the same amount of time.

The wet fly's complete and uniform coverage is the best one when all the water appears capable of holding salmon. Then the angler can make cast after cast with a step between casts until he has covered the pool. Preferred procedure would then call for a second passage over the same water with a different fly or the same pattern in a different size.

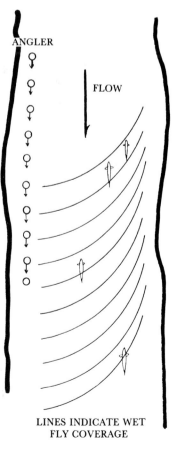

LINES INDICATE WET FLY COVERAGE

When there is no certain knowledge of how many fish are in the pool or where they lie, it is more logical to completely cover a stretch of water with one fly and go over it again with a second and perhaps a third, than to change flies at varying points on the passage through the pool. If a fly is given a chance at the whole pool, no matter how widely spaced the casts may be, and a second fly given a similar chance, the opportunity of taking fish with each fly is much the same. If, instead, one fly is fished for the upper half of the pool and another for the lower half only, one fly may take fish for the simple reason that no "taking" fish were lying in the unproductive half of the pool. It is also possible that if the patterns had been reversed in their order of fishing, the angler's catch might have been greater, for the fly which fished the barren water might well have been much the better fly of the two for that day and hour and place. It is reasonable and logical to try and give comparative tests to fly variations. If there is any point at all to changing flies, there is good reason to use one's fishing time trying to gather data about which patterns are most productive, in order that those most productive patterns come to be used most of the time.

When fishing large rivers where there is a seemingly uniform flow over a large area in which salmon may be lying at one point as well as another, it is customary to anchor the canoe or boat at the upstream end of the water to be covered. The first cast may be either to the right or to the left, and it is made with a short line. On each succeeding cast the line is lengthened a specific distance, usually from 6 inches to 1 foot, until the limit of the casting distance is reached. At that point the line is reeled in again, and a short cast to the opposite side is made. Again the line is lengthened, cast by cast, until a similar area on that side has been covered.

Then, if the water is to be fished more intensively, another fly may be used to make the same coverage. If the angler and guide feel it is wiser to cover more water lightly than go over the particular bit he has just fished more intensively, they will move on to the next anchor drop. In other words, the canoe will be so positioned that his first casts will begin where his previous casts ended. In that way, drop after drop, a stretch of water the width of the angler's casting will be covered as he moves downstream. The completeness of the water coverage depends on how close together the casts are spaced and how many times the water is covered before moving on.

We have considered the wet-fly cast from the point of view simply of covering the water in a uniform and thorough manner. In doing this, one should cast either as far as it is reasonable to cast and fish a fly well, or far enough to cover the likely water thoroughly, if that is a lesser distance. We have fished out the cast to a downstream position for two reasons, first, because it gives the most complete coverage and, secondly, because it is more efficient, all other things being equal, to make a long cast and fish it through. The fly cannot hook a salmon while it is in the air. It should be in the water and fishing the greatest possible percentage of time. The fewer casts and the longer water retrieves that can be managed without loss of control of the fly, the better.

Naturally, when a fish is raised but does not take the fly, the angler will concentrate some extra casts upon that area. Similarly, it is reasonable to concentrate the casting wherever one thinks there is the greatest likelihood of catching a salmon.

Fishing over barren water happens all too frequently, for it is rare in salmon fishing that an angler can be certain there are always fish under his line. Usually he must operate on the chance the fish are where he expects them to be. This is particularly true of the early fish which rarely leap or otherwise show themselves, and which are scattered throughout a far greater area than will be the case later in the season. In the early season a uniform coverage is most likely to produce well, and it is fortunate that the early fish are usually "good takers" and far more likely to take a fly on the first cast than on the second, third, twentieth, or two hundredth.

When an angler wishes to concentrate on certain areas or for any reason to fish less water than a full cast will cover, he loses fishing efficiency in the sense of area covered per hour; but if his judgment is good and he has given up barren or unlikely water in favor of a better chance at fish, he will be well ahead. The angler who is

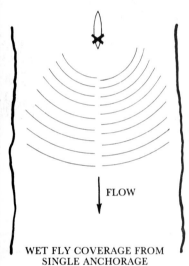

FLOW

WET FLY COVERAGE FROM
SINGLE ANCHORAGE

uncertain where the fish are lying should stick to a wide water coverage lest he concentrate on a poor spot instead of a good one. The angler whose judgment or whose guide's judgment is good can well afford to give up a little fly-in-the-water efficiency to keep that fly more constantly in front of some fish.

There are some fishermen, and among them some guides I remember on the Little Codroy and the Margaree, who liked to "spot fish." They achieved a considerable success raising salmon by dropping the wet fly just over the head of the fish and letting the current swing it away, instead of casting beyond the fish and letting the fly swing by in front of him. If they could either see a fish or knew, in relation to a rock or other identifiable part of the streambed, exactly where one should lie, they would concentrate on the fish with their casting, changing flies periodically, often resting him for long periods, but always keeping the same cast going out to him until, in many cases, he ended up by taking the fly.

Where there are few fish to work on there is soundness in this method. With a few fish in the streams, there can be only a few places worth fishing, namely, where the fish lie. The idea of putting the fly as close to the fish as possible on every cast, however, may not necessarily be the best course.

The first time I came upon such a spot fisherman, it was on the Little Codroy where, at that time, dry flies were rarely seen. My big, insecty, bucktail-winged floaters were new then, too. A local guide, unemployed at the moment, had been working over a salmon visible in shallow water over a gravel bar. He told me later he had cast a hundred casts right at the head of that salmon before I arrived. When my guide and I came to the pool he insisted I fish for that salmon. As he left the pool, I moved out with a dry fly and, on a practice cast while taking time to strip out enough line to reach the fish, I let the fly fall to the water a full 20 feet short of the salmon. The fish immediately left his position and swam straight to the fly, taking it down with a sucking noise. The other fisherman's mouth stood open as wide as the salmon's and I am sure from that moment onward he realized "spot fishing" is not always the best way to trick a salmon. Nevertheless, it is effective much of the time. It calls for accurate casting.

Somewhere between the spot cast on which the fly goes directly to the salmon and comes away for perhaps only 3 or 4 yards before being lifted again for the return voyage, and the fully fished-out cast, there is a wide casting range for the angler to use. The short-swim is the least efficient way to have a fly in the water, though it may be the best way to have a fly near a fish as often as possible. The medium-swim cast is the most common type. As the fly nears the end of its swing, it makes a quick turn into the current and then moves rather slowly in regard to the streambed, although its speed through the water continues to hold up. It is at this point that salmon have a strong tendency to take a fly. Many fishermen look for their strikes at this "bend" of the retrieve and try to bend them just upstream from the point where they expect salmon to be lying. It is safe to say that rises at the bend are more common than at any other time. Up to the bend, the salmon have some inclination to follow and, as the fly changes from a cross-stream to an upstream heading, they are impelled to take it. Rises after the bend has occurred are much less frequent than during the turn or before it occurs. Many anglers tend to pick up their fly shortly after it makes the bend on the theory that further fishing of the cast is unproductive effort which can be more properly applied to another cast. This is a fair assumption and the practice is common enough to show that many anglers agree with that thinking.

One definite exception to this rule is the late fish. When salmon have been long in the river, they have an increasing tendency to follow a fly, well back, and, if they rise at all, rise only as the fly is nearing shallow water or as it hangs in the current. Even for those who habitually pick up a fly after it has turned the corner, it would be wise to fish the casts right to the end when fishing late in the season.

Although a fly has ceased to move in relation to the streambed, it may be moving swiftly through the current. If it still has movement in relation to the flowing water, though it may look lifeless to an angler, it looks alive to the salmon (if he does not notice the leader). In his thinking, anything that can hold a position in a current or move through it without a visible connection to anything else is living and swimming.

Salmon will take a fly left hanging in the current. Such strikes have come after anglers have been standing talking for a matter of minutes with a line hanging downstream from an idle rod. They have come for fishermen who stopped to light a cigarette and let their lines trail. They have come for fishermen who purposely let a fly hang in good water or near a fish they could actually see. These rises to a hanging fly suggest that a fly should be fished until it hangs in the current, if it is going to hang within easy reach of salmon.

Up to this point we have been content to let the speed of the fly through the water be determined by the speed of the current. We have not taken in line to make it move more swiftly; we have not dropped the rod tip to slow it down. We have fished the simplest of all wet-fly casts, which sends the line out quartering downstream, picks it up when the current has carried it the maximum distance, and after a single back cast sends it out again at the same downstream angle. Where the current was swift the fly moved swiftly; where the current slowed, so did the fly. To let the speed of the fly become dependent upon the current is effective enough when the water is right for the fishing. Fortunately, most salmon like to lie in water having a generally suitable speed.

When salmon settle in quiet waters, either in lakes or pools that are very low, there is little or no current to move the angler's fly. Here we come to a condition which forces a departure from the normal. Under these circumstances (and under other more normal conditions as well), two groups of anglers are content to let their sinking flies drift with the light current either on a greased and floating line (greased-line method) or on a sinking line (Patent method). These variations, like the dry fly, cover less water than the normally fished wet fly does. The other alternative is to speed up the retrieve of the fly.

A lifting of the rod will speed up the fly; so will taking in of the line. An angler may well use a combination of the two. When the fly touches the water, if there is slack in the cast, he can lift his rod just far enough to put the fly under tension, and he can do it quickly. Lifting the rod will take up nearly a rod's length of line in a fraction of a second, much more than can be brought in by stripping line in through the guides during the same period. Once the tension reaches the fly he can adjust it to obtain the desired speed.

Although the rod takes up slack most quickly, it does not do it best. If the rod is raised to the ultimate limit in order to take up slack, it has passed the point of usefulness in applying pressure for the setting of the hook. Only a part of the potential rod lift

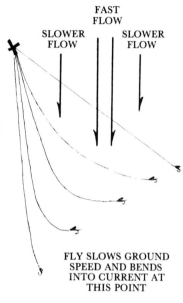

FAST
FLOW

SLOWER
FLOW

SLOWER
FLOW

FLY SLOWS GROUND
SPEED AND BENDS
INTO CURRENT AT
THIS POINT

should be used, always saving a little for setting the hook. The best procedure is to lift the rod only as much as one must, and, when there is still slack to be taken up or the speed of the fly must be increased, start taking in line immediately by hand. If the rod has to be raised at the start of the retrieve then the line should come in fast enough not only to bring the fly to the required speed but to allow for the lowering of the rod back to the normal extended position it held at the end of the cast. That is the position in which it has most power for the strike (or to take in slack if a salmon takes the fly, is hooked, and then comes toward the fisherman).

How fast should a salmon fly travel in still water? How high is up? It would be a fair guess that a fly should travel at about the speed it travels when fished on a perfect wet-fly cast over salmon lying in normal lies in normal water. Hardly an exact definition, but fitting in a sport in which few things need to be exact in the sense of predetermination. In essence, it suggests increasing the speed of the fly when the water runs slower than usual and decreasing it when the water speed is accelerated. A great many fishermen do just that and do it with considerable fishing success. There is a feeling among them that there is a "perfect" speed of a salmon fly through water, and they contrive to give their fly that speed as uniformly as possible.

By lifting the rod or swinging it upstream or downstream, by taking in the line, they increase speed. By lowering a rod or letting out line they decrease it. They may end a cast with the rod held high, then drop it down swiftly in order to slow the fly down. They may hold several coils of line in their left hand ready for a controlled release which will cut the fly's speed. They may use a combination of both line and rod to do the job, and they may speed up a fly at one stage and slow it down at another. A single cast over mixed water may call for several changes of pace with regard to the normal speed. Attaining a constant speed becomes a game within a game. Whether or not constant speed is worth the trouble is for each angler to decide. There is a strong indication that revising the speed of the wet fly toward the normal will pay off with more rises.

How deep should a wet fly travel? Another difficult question to answer. There have been days and places where competent anglers have, out of seeming necessity, fished a heavy fly slow and deep in order to take salmon while just above or below them another fisherman has taken fish with a fly which swam just under the top. Most of the fishermen who fish Newfoundland's Portland Creek with a wet fly use the "hitch" that originated there to keep their flies skimming on the surface, firmly convinced that if a salmon will rise at all he will come to the top. On their own waters they seem to be entirely correct. As a matter of principle, however, and taking all waters into consideration, it is also logical to believe salmon will rise 1 foot for a fly more readily than they will lift 2 feet or 3 or more from their positions near the bottom.

The most sensible advice would be to fish deep only when the fish are deep and listless. A deep cast is a slow cast. Fly and line do not sink readily. A fly that is heavy for its feathers, heavy enough to become, in a sense, a sinker, is a nuisance, or worse, to cast with, and it drags rather than swims through the water. A fly line, by its nature, will not sink readily. It needs a certain diameter to make handling easy, and if it were heavy enough to sink rapidly, it would be too heavy to cast very far. The larger flies on their heavier hooks do travel a little farther under the surface at normal speeds than do the smaller ones, but retrieving a fly deep usually calls for marked slowing down of its speed. When the fly moves only half as fast, the fisherman covers only half as much water. This slowing down is one of the penalties of fishing deep. A second is the awkwardness of casting heavier flies. To fish deep with a weighted fly is illegal. To take an unweighted fly down deep in swift water is impossible. Fishing deep is pretty well restricted to slow water.

When fishing dry the angler *must* watch his fly in order to be able to set the hook at the rise. Since he has to watch his fly anyway, watching the surrounding water for the telltale flash of silver, patch of color, or shadow that gives away a salmon's presence is fairly easy. The wet-fly fisherman, fishing in the conventional and usual fashion, can depend upon the pressure of the fish upon the hook to tell him when the fish has taken the fly and the battle is on. Between casts he often feels free to look around him while his fly takes care of itself.

I put marks on my line at the 30-foot, 40-foot, and 50-foot distances from the leader connection: a single, then two, and finally three rings painted black, respectively. When a salmon makes a false rise I look to locate one of the marks and establish it as being a certain distance from one of the guides or from the tip-top. By duplicating that mark's position and establishing the same direction by a shore marking I can duplicate the cast. Often, in a wide run of water, I have risen several fish and marked each one. Being able to rest the fish but come back to them with a cast identical to the one which intrigued them the first time, I feel these marking have had a great value in fish hooked.

Sometimes, when a reasonable rest brings no second response from a salmon that has made a rise to the fly, I check the stones on the streambed and line up directions to markings on the shore so that I can return to the exact spot and from there make a cast identical to the first one after I've fished somewhere else for a while. This, too, has helped me hook many salmon.

By measuring to the third spot from the reel, using my rod length as a measure, and adding the leader length I can, when the line and leader straighten out completely, know just how long the cast was. Some days casting seems easier than others. Often I check the marks to see if I'm casting the usual distance for a given effort. If my distance is short I check my power, stroke and timing and often find that my casting comes back to normal.

Whether an angler fishes wet or dry, the keenness with which he watches his fly and reads the water beneath it will have a serious effect upon his take of salmon. With inexpert fishermen, the guide must be depended upon to watch the fly constantly, whether it floats or sinks. Many salmon will make only a slight movement toward the fly the first or second time it comes over. If the angler is not aware that a fish has shown interest in his fly he will move along and leave behind him an excellent chance to hook a fish, perhaps the only chance of the day. It takes good eyesight and experience to recognize a salmon by the little signs that show he is there. An observant fisherman may well take three fish for every one taken by the salmon fisherman who only casually watches his fly.

When an angler sees a salmon rise to his fly there are certain things he should do. His first move should be to check the distance the fly is out. If he has some line coiled in his left hand he should reel up slack to the point at which the line was when the rise came. It is extremely important to have the exact distance. He should hold his position and check the direction of the cast while his memory is fresh. His best chance of getting that salmon to rise again is to duplicate the cast exactly. It may take a dozen casts or

A keen salmon fisherman keeps his eyes on the fly.

more for, on one, the direction may be wrong and, on another, the current, always changing a little in its flow, may not be the same. It is often some small vagary of the current where an eddy forms and dissolves again that gave the fly the particular motion which drew the rise. Just making casts in the general direction of the first one with a cast of different length will catch an eager salmon but not a truly fussy one.

One of the most common mistakes anglers make is to change the casting distance. In checking over the common faults of anglers with their guides, the habit of pulling off an extra foot or two of line as soon as a fish rose stands high on the list. For some reason when a salmon rises the instinctive reaction is to make a slightly longer cast than the one that had risen him as if, by doing so, it would put the fly closer to his lie. It is worth trying both longer and shorter casts but the length of line that drew the rise first can be depended on as most likely to draw him into a rise again. Best procedure is to hold the same position and guard the same distance.

A point of debate is the advisability of creating a motion of the fly over and above that of the current which makes it swing. Many good fishermen put a constant quiver in their rod while they fish their fly. This is a normal procedure with trout fishermen who are trying to make the fly seem more lifelike. It is normal with the bass fisherman who has a sustained wiggling action built into his plug or spoon. Still, almost all anglers who troll for mackerel, tuna, or any of the swift game fish of the sea with a "feather" or other artificial bait are content simply to let it swim a straight course through the water behind them.

As far as it is possible to decide such a thing, indications are that a good fly-twitching salmon fisherman catches no more than an equally good fisherman who lets his fly swing on a steady rod. From the point of temperament, a nervous angler might prefer to move his rod constantly while a more stolid individual would not. The choice, I believe, lies with the steady swing. A salmon rising to it has an easier target to catch than the fish rising to a less predictable, twitching fly and is less likely to miss on his rise.

When a trout fisherman is torn between one fly pattern and another, or cannot make up his mind which of three will catch a fish, he has a simple solution for the situation. He hangs a dropper or two off his leader. Then when they swing by him, the trout has a choice. One salmon angler of my acquaintance, who had risen a fish but could not hook him, decided to try two droppers for salmon. He had read La Branch's fine book on fishing the dry fly for trout. Taking a tip from this dry-fly pioneer and twisting it out of recognition, he said, "I'm going to create a wet-fly hatch. By the time the third one comes by, those salmon are going to think something unusual is going on and get excited."

Maybe it was the rest period while rigging up his line that increased the salmon's tension to the necessary point. I am sure it was not my friend's fly hookup, because the salmon never saw them all. He took the first fly to come to him on the first cast and was off in a smother of spray. The fish streaked for the tail of the long, quiet pool, and there complications began. A 5-pound sea-run trout grabbed the tail fly as the salmon towed it behind him with a most enticing movement. This so startled the salmon that he made a series of three great leaps, towing the trout along across the surface like a skipping blue marlin bait. It was something to watch while it lasted, but it could not last long. The salmon tore free, and my friend began reeling in the big trout.

If a trout will snap zealously at some light refreshment trailing behind a running salmon, another trout is likely to find a fly towed around by a trout even more irresistible. When the big trout was pulled back over the spot where he and some of his friends had been lying, another somewhat smaller trout took one of the droppers. For most of the way in, they nullified one another's efforts to go anywhere else, but at the last moment, the hook fell out of its well-worn hold in the first one's jaw. A dropper fly is a fine solution for an indecisive trout fisherman, but on a salmon river, it is best to keep spare flies in one's fly box. If a dropper fly is used it should be only to skim it along the surface as a more attractive lure. In this case the tail fly should be on a very fine leader which will break rapidly if taken by another fish or snagged.

The position of the wet fly as it comes to the salmon is worthy of consideration. Is a salmon more interested in a fly which is presented in a broadside position than one which is headed toward or away from him? Like most things about a salmon, that is practically impossible to determine. Salmon come from below to take flies hanging in

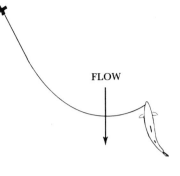

FLOW

the current, approaching them from the rear. Salmon take flies just as they land, sometimes so swiftly they must have started for the fly before it actually touched the water. Do salmon care whether a dry fly comes floating down head first, tail first, or sidewise? Few dry-fly fishermen could be positive. It is certain most salmon take wet flies which are broadside to them. And just as certain, most wet flies are broadside to them when they see them.

Couple a belief that a broadside view of the wet fly is most effective with the belief that salmon prefer a fly near the surface, and with a further belief that the fly should drift freely with the flow and you have Mr. A. H. E. Wood's greased-line fishing. This is a very effective method which Wood worked out in the British Isles, but which has a proven effectiveness on most waters, wherever tried.

The effect is to approximate the float of the dry fly with a wet fly. Approximate is the right word because the normal cast is across the stream and the fly, in its fishing, swings around to a position downstream of the angler identical with that which it would have reached had it been fished in the conventional wet-fly manner. The difference is that during the cast, where necessary, the line is "mended," that is, the belly is taken out of it. The fly travels, but it travels slowly and rather uniformly.

Wood greases the line for two reasons: to keep the fly near the surface and to make the line easy to pick up for the "mend." When a current or eddy puts a bow in the line it is lifted with a forward looping motion which is like a partial roll cast. This will pick up the line and correct or overcorrect the current-formed bend in the line.

The illustration shows how the line would be bent in normal fishing, and how the mend would revise the line's position. The mending of the line should be managed without disturbing the fly. It is a sort of side-roll cast which has force enough to lift most of the line out of the water but not so far as to seriously affect the leader and fly. The greased-line fisherman must keep a close watch on his line and correct the bending developments with the necessary mends. When there is no bowing of the line no mending is needed.

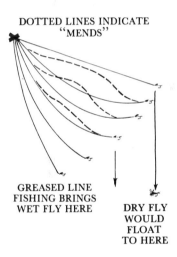

DOTTED LINES INDICATE "MENDS"

GREASED LINE FISHING BRINGS WET FLY HERE

DRY FLY WOULD FLOAT TO HERE

On some occasions, Wood suggested casting at an upstream angle which would, for a period, give a float identical with that of a dry fly. Indeed, sometimes his flies did float because of grease which worked onto them from the line and leader. He recommends a jerk of the rod to pull an inadvertently floating fly under for the normal fishing of the method.

His method is similar to fishing the dry fly in some respects, and he does not find slack near the fly a disadvantage. The fly is always very near the surface, and the alert angler sees the salmon as it comes up to take the fly. The rise is usually of the head and tail variety in which the fish comes from below, opening his mouth to take in the fly and continuing on in a roll which carries him half out of the water with dorsal fins showing high and his tail coming well out of the water as he starts downward again. The greased-line method does not call for a strike, but rather insists that the line be left slack, even that slack be given out if the line is in tension at the moment the fish takes. The hook is to be set not by the angler but by the pull of the line in the flow.

It works this way. The fly, leader, and line are all drifting downstream with the current. If the salmon takes the fly into his mouth and settles toward the bottom the fly's downstream motion is stopped. The line and leader continue to move downstream and soon bring a tension on the fly. The pull on the fly, instead of being directly toward the angler is at an angle well below him. Almost always when salmon are hooked by this line-drag, the hook will embed in the corner of the mouth, a good holding position, whereas hooks pulled directly toward the angler may hook anywhere in the mouth. The smaller hooks are more certain to embed under the pressure of the drifting line than large ones, because less force is required to set them and because the salmon is less likely to feel them and spit them out. Where large hooks are used the period of slack permitted after the fish is seen to take the fly must be a measured quantity.

One of the greatest difficulties in learning the system is controlling the natural instinct to strike when the salmon is seen to come for the fly. No strike must be made at that time and a definite period of slack is essential. One of the most difficult times to hook a salmon (according to Wood) is when a salmon comes to the fly that is almost directly below the fisherman and he is about to lift it from the water. The rod should be held high for the end of the retrieve, and if a fish is seen to come for the fly a few feet of slack are given by dropping the rod tip in his direction. This allows the fish to turn at an angle, and the line to pull the fly into the corner of his jaw.

When the fly is fished in relatively swift water with the greased-line method, and tension on the fly is likely to come too quickly, the angler is advised to carry a few feet of slack coiled in the left hand which can be released when the salmon takes the fly. This gives the line time to reach its downstream position before it pulls on the fly.

It is easier to mend the line when there is an upstream wind blowing. A long rod makes mending the line easier than a short one does. Wood's rods were twelve footers. The mending of a line calls for weight throughout its length, too. A very light shooting line extending beyond the guides would nullify the angler's efforts to mend. A double-tapered line would be preferable for this very specialized wet-fly fishing.

In considering the greased-line method it is important to remember that while it has been very successful, its main success has been in Europe where dry-fly fishing has not yet evolved. The dry fly not only reduces drag, but can completely eliminate it. A dry-fly float calls for the pickup of the fly at a point directly downstream from where it started or whenever drag occurs. The greased fly line, fished to a point directly below the angler, has to have considerable drag to get there. Some modern low-floating dry flies, not worked out or even used in this country or the British Isles when the greased-line method was developed, give the dry-fly angler an opportunity to meet the essentials of the greased-line method even more completely than Wood's tackle did.

Greased-line fishing can cover more water than the dry fly would because the term "drag" applied to dry fly means any movement of the fly over the surface, while with the greased-line fly, the slow swimming of the fly is permitted so long as the line does not belly. The "swing at the bend of the usual wet fly cast, preferred moment for most normal wet-fly strikes, is lost, but in its place, the greased-line fisherman has fewer misses and, under some circumstances, will take more fish."

A third established method of fishing the wet fly is the "Patent Method," developed by Col. Lewis S. Thompson in 1928 on the Restigouche. This method casts a wet fly out like a dry fly, but instead of floating freely on the surface it sinks and drifts with the current. Col. Thompson originated the method using large hair flies and, by thus drifting the fly, gained all the small activity of the hairs under the light pressures of the current.

The feathers or fibers of a wet fly normally fished and swimming through the water are forced back into a tight bundle by its pressure. The compressed fly has the apparent life that movement gives it, but it does not have any appearance of life within itself, no moving of legs or wings or feelers. The Patent method loses the appearance of life given by motion *through* the water but gains instead the appearance of life within the fly. This is also the essence of normal dry-fly fishing where motion is avoided except as delivered by the water's surface.

Hair flies ranging in size from #6 to as large as 3/0 to 5/0 are successfully used in this method. As with dry flies, quite large flies are effective, surprisingly large to anyone accustomed to fishing either of the wet-fly methods. Since the essential motion of the fly is within itself, it depends largely on the materials used. Hair seems to give the best results, but some other fibers "work" effectively. It is likely that any soft fibers of the right length and strength will create an attractive fly whether from animal, bird, or synthetic.

The fly is cast with a considerable amount of slack in the line. The slack can best be gained by stopping the rod before the cast is completed and ending the cast with the fly high above the water. The line, which was straight or nearly straight, will become wavy with slack. The cast may be made across the stream or at an upstream or downstream angle. The fly will drift properly as long as it drifts without drag. The word "drag" is used in the absolute sense, as with the dry fly, not as in greased-line fishing. At least, the method calls for complete slack. A personal opinion, based on a few experiments, is that salmon will take the fly in varying degrees between a pure drift and a normal wet-fly swing, with the no-drag condition the best. In any method of salmon fishing there is a certain amount of overlapping, and, although the originator or a confirmed disciple may successfully work a rigid system of fishing, there will be other anglers who will have success with variations which the strict interpretations do not permit.

When the hair-fly fished in the Patent method falls to the surface, it is at the will of the surrounding water. It sinks slowly and eventually sinks to the bottom unless drag, caused by the motion of the line in the current, takes over and starts it swimming toward the normal end-of-the-wet-fly-cast position. The system is one for tempting fish that have been located, such as fish that have risen but failed to touch the fly, rather than for covering much water.

Any salmon coming to the fly before it sinks deeply can be seen readily. After the fly has sunk very far, especially if the water is not absolutely clear, it will pass out of vision. Since the fly used is usually a large one, a salmon is likely to eject it quickly and the fisherman's strike must come right after the fish takes it, before he ejects it. Since the fly is always on a slack line when fished as the method prescribes, a strike is always necessary. The greatest danger of missing fish, however, is to strike too quickly, for in this method the fish will often be seen on the rise before they can get to the fly and close on it.

Arthur Perry, able guide and devoted fisherman, introduced me to his "riffling hitch" when I first fished Portland Creek. It originated there, and having been taken into the repertoire of anglers who have fished there as the Portland Creek hitch, it is spreading slowly to all salmon waters. It is a method of looping or "hitching" the leader around the head of the wet fly and pulling it, skidded, across the surface instead of letting it sink under.

Early anglers visiting Portland Creek in almost every instance had to resort to this hitch to take salmon. The Portland Creek guides were almost unanimous in believing a salmon could be taken in no other way. Such a rigid interpretation of the whims of a rising salmon was difficult for me to accept, and I continued fishing my wet flies in the conventional manner. I did catch an occasional salmon but not as many as the anglers who were in other respects no more capable fishermen. I had felt the Portland Creek anglers had never given the conventionally fished wet fly a fair trial.

On subsequent trips I fished with both the normally tied-on and the hitched flies and caught salmon on both. The hitched fly, although fished less frequently, took more fish, and I had to admit it added an exciting moment when a big salmon poked his nose out of the water in a burst of speed to catch it.

When I decided to establish the fishing camps there I was still undecided as to the comparative efficiency of the two methods. The turning point came on an afternoon when the cool wind was blowing up from the sea. I had fished the stretch above the Low Rock and reached a lie where another groups of rocks curved upstream in a U-shape. In Portland Creek the salmon make a habit of lying ahead of, instead of just behind, the rocks. I can think of no reason for this except that when the ice jams up against the larger rocks the churning current, working underneath it, digs out a deep hole on the upstream side. Much of the river is shallow and without pools, with the depressions in front of the larger rocks holding most of the fish.

Fishing had been slow and I had covered several good lies without a rise. I was ready then to stick at this one good spot and succeed or fail there in the half hour remaining. I fished the wet fly, attached normally, under the surface in the accustomed manner. I tried #4s, then 6s and finally 8s. I watched closely, for if I should miss the almost insignificant gleam of silver as a restless salmon moved slightly under the passing fly I would fail to make the necessary dozen or more identical casts that would bring him to the hook. I was alert to what happened, although it was unexpected.

As the #8 Jock Scott swung its arc—with the fly just beneath the surface where the salmon usually like a wet—it happened that a leader knot several feet ahead of the fly was just creasing the smooth surface and sending out a small V of wake as it did so. A salmon drove up from the depths and struck the knot, insignificant as it was in contrast with the fly. If the riffled knot would draw a rise from the fish, I decided, so would the riffled fly. My fingers threw the hitch on the Jock Scott, and on the second cast a salmon hit it hard. Ever since that moment I have fished the hitched wet fly more than the conventionally sunken one on Portland Creek.

No one now at Portland Creek claims to have been the originator of the riffling fly, but here is the accepted story. Long ago, warships of the British navy anchored off the stream, and officers came ashore to fish. They left a few old-style salmon flies, which had a loop of twisted gut wrapped to the straight-shanked hook to make the eye.

Soft and pliable when in use, the loop enabled the fly to ride more smoothly on its course and avoided the stiffness and canting which accompanied any solid attachment of the stout leader to the eyed fly. But the gut loops grew weak with age, and many a good salmon, when hooked on an old and cherished fly, broke away with the steel and feathers. To play safe, anglers often gave away old flies. To most recipients they were Trojan horses. Only to the Portland Creekers were they a boon.

Quickly realizing that a salmon hooked on a gut-looped fly was likely to break free, they made sure the fly would stay on by throwing those "hitches" around the shank behind the wrapping. The fact that the fly skimmed instead of sinking bothered them not in the least, for they were practical fishers of the sea. They fished the flies on spruce poles with makeshift reels or none at all. They cast them out and drew them back. And because they had no proper flies with which to fish they developed a new technique.

The making of the hitch is important. Arthur Perry, in common with most Portland Creek guides, makes his so the monofilament pulls away from under the turned-up eye at the throat. This will make both the single- and double-hooked flies ride correctly (hook down) on the retrieve. Such a hitch is effective on standard salmon-fly hooks with turned-up eyes but awkward if the eyes are turned down.

I use the same throat hitch for double-hooked flies, but with my favorite—the single-barbed iron—regardless of whether the eye turns up or down, I shift the hitch 45 degrees to one side or the other, depending upon which side of the current I cast from, so that on a crosscurrent retrieve the fly will always ride with the point on the downstream side. This position seems to give it much better hooking and riding qualities.

Using this method, it is easy to learn how to fish *any* wet fly correctly, whereas it usually takes years before you can watch the water under which the sunken fly is travelling and guess correctly just where it is and at what speed it is moving. Too much speed or too little will not draw a salmon's interest. The most perfect speed is that at which a hitched fly riffles best.

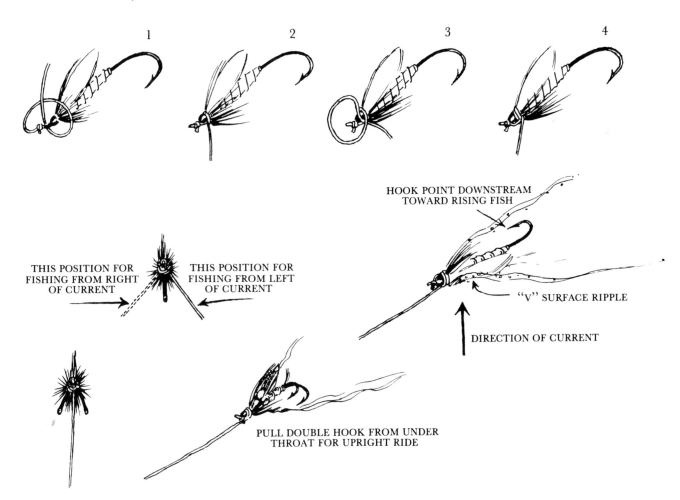

1 2 3 4

THIS POSITION FOR
FISHING FROM RIGHT
OF CURRENT

THIS POSITION FOR
FISHING FROM LEFT
OF CURRENT

HOOK POINT DOWNSTREAM
TOWARD RISING FISH

"V" SURFACE RIPPLE

DIRECTION OF CURRENT

PULL DOUBLE HOOK FROM UNDER
THROAT FOR UPRIGHT RIDE

If the speed of the retrieve is wrong, the hitched fly will either throw spray or sink below the surface. If one of these things happens, a strike is most unlikely. Since the fly is visible at all times, the angler can slow down if he sees the fly making spray, speed up if it starts to sink. Almost without conscious effort, he learns to maintain his fly at the right speed through fast water and slow, matching the speed of the retrieve to the water the fly is in. Through crosscurrents and eddies, on glassy glides, the lifting or lowering of the rod to speed up or slow down the retrieve soon becomes automatic.

Thereafter, it is not difficult to match these tactics to a sunken fly which, though still invisible, can now be readily visualized as it travels through the water. I think it is largely because of this that the guides at Portland Creek have been able to teach novices to catch salmon almost as well as old-timers.

With the riffling hitch, fish are hooked about as readily and held just as securely as when the fly is tied on in the conventional manner. They are so sold on it at Portland Creek that 95 percent of all wet-fly fishing done there is with a hitched fly.

It has worked out well on many other salmon rivers, too, like the Humber, the River of Ponds, the Miramichi, the Eagle, the Adlatok, and on rivers in Scotland and Iceland. I find myself using the hitch more and more instead of normal wet-fly fishing simply because it thrills me to see a fish break the surface in his strike. As compared with the dry fly, the riffled fly moves faster, since it moves across the flow as well as with it. A trout or a salmon can wait until the dry fly comes to him, then quietly rise up and suck it in. With the riffling fly, the fish must not only rise to but *catch* the fly; and a big salmon, in doing so, rolls up ahead of him a wave of water one never forgets.

Are skittered dry flies as good as the hitched wet fly? Experience at Portland Creek denies it. Granted, the hitched fly stays up only because of its motion, the fluffy dry fly rides at a different angle and height, and develops little wake.

Like any relatively new method, riffling the wet fly will be especially effective where the fish have seen a lot of flies presented in the old way. That is why the original dry flies, which were essentially only greased and floating wet flies, brought such remarkable results when first used over trout and salmon, and why long, thin floating bass bugs, shaped almost like streamer flies, made such wonderful catches.

Various sorts of insects skim across the water instead of flying over it or swimming through it. Water spiders, bugs, and striders or skaters, as well as stalled-out land bugs, slide their way over the ripples and eddies. Many an injured minnow flutters his way across the pool, nose breaking into the air and tail lagging downward, until a game fish takes him down. Hence, to imitate such action with a riffled fly is both natural and effective.

There is a generally held opinion that a wet fly is more effective when reduced in speed for slow water, especially when it is low and clear under midsummer conditions. Wood's greased-line method evolved from the normal difficulties of taking fish in the slower, warmer waters of the late season. So did dry-fly fishing, for anglers were loathe to experiment when a normally fished wet fly was working effectively. Most anglers work a very slow or drifting fly under all low-water conditions.

It is surprising, then, to realize that under these same circumstances, other anglers have been able to entice salmon to a fly which is moved with inordinate speed. It was once my privilege to see a demonstration of the speed with which a salmon fly can be fished and yet be effective. The pool was small, lying between steep sloping banks at the foot of a falls. Salmon, waiting in the depths for a sufficient flow of water to climb the falls, were listless, and now they rested in the midafternoon sun. Two of us had fished it periodically for a number of hours, casting for short periods, resting it for long ones, taking but one fish near the start.

A local fisherman, crudely equipped, came down and, at our insistence, tried the pool. He fished it carefully with the normal wet-fly fisherman's technique. After a thorough coverage of the water he suddenly changed his tactics. He ripped a cast back through the water so swiftly that it made a whistling sound. I look at him, amazed. He made a second similar cast and hooked a fish. I was prepared to find the fish foul-hooked, but when he beached it the hook was fairly in the fish's mouth.

He went back to fishing again. I came to stand beside him and found it difficult to follow his fly in the water because it moved so swiftly. It would land, and he would give it every bit of speed he could produce. Three or four more casts and another fish rose and took the fly. A real fast retrieve, he allowed, was worth a try when the fishing was dull. I have tried it and made it work, although I do not like to fish that way. Knowing it will work keeps one from being smug about the slow retrieves, if nothing else.

Neither this book nor any written word can describe exactly how a salmon fly should look nor how it should move to lure a salmon. To do so is no more possible than to describe adequately the taste of a particular apple or the shape of a cloud. Words will not do it but experience will so condition a fisherman that he can look at a fly as it is fished, either his own or that of another angler, and know that it is "right" for the fish. Lacking experience in judging the speed or drift of the wet fly, an angler would do worse than to study closely the fly of a competent angler and imitate him a well as possible, until he has some real experience of his own to go by.

These, then, are the accepted methods of fishing the wet fly. They overlap to a degree. The plain truth is that no matter how a wet fly is thrown into the water and retrieved, if it is continued long enough under fair fishing conditions, a salmon will take it. Some salmon will seemingly take any fly presented to them, others resist all offerings. Between these two extremes are the great bulk of salmon making up the sport, and there is a remarkable consistency in their tastes. A well-developed method which works is far to be preferred to a constant changing of methods without plan or pattern. It is best to stick to one method until it is mastered before trying another. Success with one method is easier to achieve than with many. The skill and judgment required to use, in their most effective manner, all the methods of fishing the wet fly is something reserved for no more than a few salmon fishermen, but the eventual ability to use several methods effectively adds interest to the sport.

The Dry Fly

The simple matter of drawing a fish up from the depths to the top for any surface fly is more of a thrill than having the same fish take the fly well under and getting first indication of his presence by a pull on the tackle rather than by sight. In the words of Jack Young, guide of the Serpentine River, "I don't believe there's a more beautiful thing in the world than to see a salmon rise to a dry fly."

Another thrill is the taking of a good sized salmon on a very small fly. Nowhere in all angling is there a situation which places a greater demand upon tackle skill. One of

my most rewarding moments was the taking of a 27-pound fish on a #16 dry fly, a floating wisp of a feather, and a hook so tiny most trout fishermen think it too small for trout of ordinary size. To intrigue a great fish with so slight a bit of material is a satisfying pleasure. When the angler casts such a fly on an appropriate leader (4-pound test or under) over a salmon, he is striving for a pinnacle of the sport.

I was one of a small group, fishing at a camp on the Moisie in 1964, that formed the "Sixteen-Twenty" Club, a charmed circle of anglers. We formed it before any one of us or anyone we knew had caught a salmon of 20 pounds or over on a single hooked #16 fly. I'd taken a fifteen-pounder on a #16 and relating the experience had led, first to a discussion of how big a salmon could be taken on so small a fly and then to the idea of the club.

We tested the #16 hooks we had in our fly-tying kits, ranging from prewar Alcocks to modern Mustads. Uniformly they either broke or bent out at a pull of 4 pounds on our scales. We knew we had a challenge ahead not only because of the breaking and bending but because of the tendency of the fine wire to cut through its grip on a salmon's flesh, as well. We all set out to qualify as members of the club by catching twenty-pounders on sixteens.

While waiting for supper I tied several flies of a new pattern, a skater with a snoot of bucktail which I felt would give the maximum bulk that could be crammed onto so small a hook. It might, I hoped, have a flip-flopping action when jerked across the surface which would be more attractive than the usual in-line pulls. When cast out that evening the fly did tumble a bit on the water, and it was effective.

The sun was low when we started fishing but before it had set, Alain Prefontaine, our host, hooked a good fish. It was solidly dark before I tailed that salmon a quarter of a mile downstream. The scales in the flashlight's glow read 20½ pounds, and the Sixteen-Twenty Club had its first member and president. He caught the fish on the new fly I'd tied so we named it the Prefontaine. I lost a good fish on a #16 the following day, and two days later I landed two twenty-four-pounders, both on size 16s, to become the second member.

I'd been landing my salmon that trip at about half a minute to the pound on my light, split-cane rod and 8-pound test leaders. These fish on #16s took me 32 and 38 minutes, respectively. Playing them was a very sensitive thing. So delicate was the controlled tension that I seemed almost to sense their heartbeats.

When they were fresh and wild I played them gently, lest the hook start to cut through the flesh of its hold and enlarge it so that later, when slow but solid pressure must be applied to enable me to hand tail them, it might fall out or tear free.

Lucien Rolland, another of the group, caught a 19½-pounder that almost gave him membership. It was not until two years later that he caught the 21-pounder that brought him into the club.

Somehow the others never quite managed to bring in a twenty-pounder on the dimunitive fly. Many qualifying fish were lost in the last moments before the net. My feeling is that, as in flying where a mistake that can kill you is usually made long before the crisis arrives, the extra pressure that loosens the hook's hold is made early in the fight but has its weakening effect in the final moments of play.

Over the years I have taken thirteen salmon of over 20 pounds on #16 flies, each an exciting adventure in the playing of a great fish. The largest, a twenty-seven-pounder, took the fly on a sunny morning and only fifty minutes had passed before I was able to take his tail in my hand. I relive the final moments of that struggle where I had him in close, time after time, knowing that the guide behind me on shore with the net could have had him safely in the net while I was still waiting for the hand-tailing grip, but I was stubbornly determined that if I couldn't take him, alone, with my bare hand he could go free.

Lucien has taken three now. I watched him take the third, a twenty-three-pound fish in the Parsons Pool of the Grand Cascapedia. I still fish with #16 flies most of the time when I think I'm in the presence of big salmon. I keep hoping that somehow I'll hook and land a thirty-pounder on a #16. As far as I know we three are the only ones to have met the club's standard, and the little, gold lapel medallion I wear at times has a deep meaning, a feeling of treasure.

Once, a few years back, I rose a fine salmon to a #16 fly but after that he steadfastly refused to come to look at any of my #16s. Lunchtime passed, and finally, I felt I must give up and leave the pool. Before leaving I decided on a final cast or two with a #6 fly to see if it would make a difference. It did. The fish rose and was hooked. When I brought him to the scales he drew them down to a full 31 pounds. Next time I'll stick with the #16s when a fish I rise is big and conditions are fair for ultralight fishing.

When the water is rough and high and the fish are deep, a good presentation cannot be made with the dry fly. These are the conditions normally prevailing at the start of the season. Despite this general rule and the reasons for it, fresh-run fish can be taken on the floating fly. I have taken them at the very beginning of the run in Newfoundland, Nova Scotia and Quebec with sea-lice still clinging to their sides.

Here is a simple rule about when to start dry-fly fishing. Fish wet in the early season until you see a fish "porpoise," or make a surface roll, bringing the upper half of his body out into the air. This gives away his exact location in the pool and tells you he is surface-minded. A porpoising fish in the early days of the salmon run is an easy mark for a properly presented dry fly. Later on, when the salmon porpoise much more freely, these surface rolls will not have the same significance. Also, in the early season, if you can determine the exact position of a fish as indicated by a jump or a swirl at your fly, present a dry fly to him when the wet one fails. The biggest handicap to dry-fly fishing in the early high water is the difficulty of presenting the fly to enough fish.

What flies to use and how to fish them? These are matters of angler's choice. Perhaps the simplest way to show the trend of my dry-fly thinking would be to let you stand beside me, in imagination, as I start to fish Lent's Run in Portland Creek. We stand near the center of the river, shallow water behind us and a deep and moderately swift, steady flow passing between us and the evergreen-clad bank a hundred feet away. Broken cumulus clouds, pushed by a southwest breeze, alternately screen the sunlight and let it through. It is late July; the main runs of fish are in the river, and the water is at normal summer level. My watch says six-thirty, with three and a half hours of daylight remaining. Conditions should be good to take a salmon, but the water has been fished all morning from seven-thirty till one P.M. by an angler who reported one good salmon rise to a dry fly, another reported rise, perhaps the same salmon, came to a wet fly. During the time one grilse was captured on a White Wulff number eight.

My feeling is that if a fish rises now he will not take the first time he shows himself but will make a false rise. If, however, I can locate a fish, I will have a pleasant evening working over him and have at least a fifty per cent chance of bringing him to my hand. My first fly will be one to draw him out and make him show himself. A number eight Grey Wulff is my offering. With it I work the fifty yards of stream on which I plan to concentrate, covering the water swiftly on my first passage through, with but a few repetitive casts at places where I know salmon are prone to lie. Otherwise I make a general coverage of the water and take a step or two between casts. The first time through I see no movement of a salmon in the faintly brownish waters over which the fly has floated.

Are they sleepy? I will wake them up. To the end of the leader goes a big White Wulff on a number one hook, larger than any available in the stores. My guides have nicknamed it the "seagull." It is as big as a humming bird and as hard to cast. It goes out over the same water in the same kind of coverage. The sun is getting lower, but it will be more than an hour before it sets, and the big fly is startlingly conspicuous in its slanting rays. This time I think I see a flash of silver under the fly as it floats down. Half a dozen casts to the same spot are made without result.

Now the fly is changed for the Surface Stone Fly on a number four long shanked hook, yellow body, black tipped brown fibers at the front with a long single wing of dark brown bucktail for it to float upon. The fly goes out low to the water and skips to rest. On the first cast, a salmon comes up in an active rise but, although from my position he seems to have taken the fly, he is not hooked when I give a short quick strike. The next two casts are directed to another spot, then the fly goes back over the risen fish. The fish shows briefly under the fly and turns away, making no move to take it. Now I have a salmon located. He's watching the surface, and any fly I put over him will interest him to some degree. But he is wary and will probably take considerable coaxing.

Although I think a number 16 spider the best bet, I'd like to have him on a little larger hook. I use a fat-bodied all black fly with a small amount of hackle and tail. It's a lumpy, buggy looking affair of no particular shape nicknamed Midnight. With the interest he's shown, I know now he'll see a gnat if it goes over. I can hardly see the little spot of black in the rippling waves as he comes up to it the first time over. This rise is not as vicious as the first one, and I could see the small fly still floating after his head had broken the surface and gone down again. I let the fly float on.

The next few casts go to another spot and draw nothing. Then the fly goes back over the fish. No movement shows him, and the next dozen casts directed to the same place bring no action. It's time to change again.

This time I put on the fly I probably should have used before, a brown number sixteen spider. The fourth cast brings him up and, because I cannot see whether or not he actually has taken the fly into his mouth, I strike lightly but find he has not taken it. More casts go out over him with the spider. Ten casts later he comes up again and turns down again without quite breaking the surface. He had a good look at the fly, and the water rippled over him but did not break. I'd rather have him on a larger hook if I can manage it and, as he appears to be a very good fish and one likely to go downstream through rough waters before he can be landed, I decide to go back to a larger fly.

A number ten White Wulff goes out next for more than twenty trips before the salmon comes up under it, deep, to flash his side of silver. Twenty more casts show no sign of movement.

Because the hardest rise has been to the Surface Stone Fly, I send it out again and, at the third cast, the fish noses up under it but fails to break the surface and take it. The low-floating fly bounces up and down on the rippled water caused by the fish's close approach and drowns, but I do not strike and let it drift well below him before making the pick up.

The little black number twelve goes on to the end of seventeen feet of leader, and on its third drift the salmon rises and is hooked. I think he might have come a little sooner to the smaller spider or to a skater which would have both shocked and intrigued him much as the Surface Stone Fly did, but I wanted him on something larger than a sixteen hook. As I play him and worry about the big sunken boulders in the flow, I am glad he is fast to nothing smaller than a number twelve. He goes out of the pool at the end but comes in shortly to shallow water where I can tail him and take him ashore.

Most of the daylight is gone and, for the rest of the evening, there is no other rise. Had I not shocked the fish with the very large and unusual flies, he might never have shown himself. The big fly started his train of interest. The unusually long, large, almost submerged shape crystallized his desire to rise, though inaccurately. A tiny spider, one hundredth as big as the Surface Stone Fly, held his interest and finally, the non-descript black fly which had interested him only slightly at first was his undoing. If that fly or other small flies only had been fished, it is doubtful if that salmon could have been taken, judging by my previous experiences.

Reel maker
Stan Bogdan
casts on the Godbout.

The surest way to success with dry-fly patterns is to have a variety in size and shape. The primary need is in the range in which experience has proven most successful for the waters you intend to fish. Then, by having flies both larger and smaller, both high floating and low floating, you have a good range with which to work. Where wet flies, in order to take salmon, must be held to a relatively narrow size limitation, dry flies need not. A confirmed and successful wet-fly fisherman whose experience has taught him that only flies between size 8 and size 4 will give results under certain conditions, would hardly expect a salmon to rise to a great fly as big as a small mouse. If left to his own devices without some special urging, he isn't likely to try it. If you fish with widely varying sizes of dry flies, you may be ridiculed in some quarters, but you will be more attuned to the living, vital stage of salmon fishing and to the future, than to the past.

There are many rules or principles by which good anglers choose their flies. Some will insist upon a light fly for dark days and a dark one for brightest light. This practice will have some adherents who will believe a light fly is more visible to the fish on a dark day and a dark one more visible in sunlight. This is hardly true. The sky is always lighter than anything else, and the fish practically always sees the dry fly against the sky from his position below it. A light fly is less conspicuous against a light background than a dark one. If the light is poor, it would seem best, from the salmon's point of view, to try to attract him with a dark fly. When the sun is out on a bright day, all flies will be more conspicuous and it will be easier to see a light fly against a light background then, than when the skies are dull and all visibility is limited. Thus, from the fish's point of view, dark day—dark fly, bright day—light fly. The real reason for using a light fly on a dark day and dark fly on a bright day is that it is easier for the *angler* to see the flies in question. There is a great tendency to take one's own thinking or reaction and assume the fish's will be the same.

Salmon will take a half-sunk dry fly in a heavy rain. They will take an all-black dry fly at night when the light is too dim to see anything more than the barest outline of the trees lining the shore. These things I know, and from them it follows that though the dark dry fly may be better in good light, it will work in any light, even no light at all.

It is good to fish a light fly when it is so near dark, for any other fly will be too difficult to watch. Similarly a dark fly is good when the day is dull and the water silvery. At these times a white or light fly will blend in with the silvery sheet the surface presents, while a dark one will stand out sharply in an expanse of silver reflections.

One should fish a dry fly too small or too dark in color to see only when such a fly will take fish and other, more visible flies, will not. These are decisions each angler must make for himself. Let him, if he is to be truly successful in his choices, always make them first from the viewpoint of the interest of the fish, afterward for his own convenience or efficiency.

One of the commonest mistakes of dry-fly fishermen is to fish with too short a float. Unless working one particular salmon, short floats are inefficient because of the small proportion of time the fly is within reach of unseen fish. Floats should be as long as possible, consistent with having them continually over good water.

I like to work over fish briefly at first, limiting myself to a few casts after a rise, then concentrate on them perhaps ten minutes after a ten minute rest. After that period if they have not been pricked, rest them again for a longer period and then fish them steadily for a 20-minute period. The rest periods, of course, are used to work on other fish or search the water for new ones. If a fish is hooked and played, by taking note of one's fishing position as established by the crossing of lines from four points on the surrounding shores before leaving it, I can go back to the same spot from which I was casting and, by using the same direction and distance as before, continue to fish for the other salmon that had been located from that spot earlier.

A very good trick for identifying lines, first thought of by my wife Joan, is to put dots of paint on the lines near the point where the front taper reaches the belly of the line. Six dots for a #6 line, seven dots for a #7, and so on. Then if you have two or three lines of the same color but differing weights it is easy to tell which is which.

The accepted rules for choice of flies will guide the beginner into a generally good pattern of fishing. They can never lead him to the heights. To reach these he must develop within himself a feeling or judgment as to which flies will work, in which combination and under what casting or fishing variations. It is one thing to go out and simply cover good water with the dry fly and quite another to present the fly to an individual fish. How many times should it be cast directly to his head before casting it upstream for a long, tantalizing float down to his lie? How far over his back should it float before you give up hope that he will suddenly turn downstream and take it? One has a vision of a fish lying in his parlor, while the fly comes down, fifty times right over his head and then, tantalizingly slow in its approach, approaches from far upstream to make him rise.

It is my belief a certain pattern of fishing will be more effective than another, that it is not just a matter of dividing up the fishing time among so many different dry flies but upon how the casts with each particular pattern are spaced. Just as a melody may be made up of a certain group of notes which, if played in different order, would be discordant, each angler must make his own fishing pattern which can be varied from fish to fish to suit conditions or the fish's progressive reactions. To follow the musical concept, those who turn out the most attractive "melodies" will have the most rises.

It may seem that this is going beyond reason in fishing procedure, but how else can one explain two anglers, both fishing over salmon, using the same flies in approximately the same intensity of fishing, having widely different catches; that one angler will consistently outfish the other, and that their presentations of each fly will appear equally capable?

When should one change from wet fly to dry fly and vice versa? It is wise, I believe, to change whenever it is necessary to retrace one's fishing steps for any distance. In other words, when an angler has worked his way up through a stretch of good water with the dry fly and wishes to work over it again on the surface, he will gain by fishing a wet fly down through the water as he returns to his starting point. Or, if he has been fishing wet and wants to repeat the same coverage, he should fish a dry fly up to his starting point. This way he makes good use of his travelling time. He may move as swiftly as he wishes or as slowly, making many casts close together or a few widely spaced.

Fish showing interest but refusing to take wet flies may succumb to the dry fly or vice versa. While walking back over a stretch fished thoroughly with a wet fly but casting a dry fly out casually as I travelled, many a salmon, which had not shown

himself before, has suddenly come up to take the floater. Before giving up on a fish that has risen to either wet or dry, it is good policy to try the other type, as well as to vary the basic casts and approaches.

With rare exception, most dry-fly anglers are sure a dragging fly will put down a salmon. The usual fishing method which works most effectively is to let the fly float with the current's flow entirely without any pull from the line. I think it is the course of wisdom to avoid drag completely except in very unusual circumstances, as with a skater.

I never think of any discussion of drag without remembering a scene on Nova Scotia's Luscomb River back in the early thirties when dry flies were rare on salmon rivers. There, at a deep, wide pool below the falls, I found a local angler fishing with a large, brown bivisible. He was casting it out from a position on a rocky ledge above the water halfway down one side of the falls. His casts were the same as they would have been with a wet fly. They went out onto the current, and he dragged the fly around into the slower water and finally picked it up again to duplicate the cast.

I saw a salmon take his fly, and later, as we stood over the fish, he told me the fly had been a gift, the only one he had ever seen. Knowing no other way, he had fished it as he did his familiar wet flies. He had taken nine salmon on it up to that point and was careful to use it only on a heavy leader (which floated just as did his line) so that he would not lose it now that he knew how good it was at taking fish. The whole performance was shocking to a dedicated dry-fly man, but it proved again that almost anything will work with salmon, if you try it hard enough and long enough and believe in it yourself. Inasmuch as he was catching more salmon than anyone else at the time, I failed to see any necessity for enlightening him about the accepted dry-fly technique.

The skating or skipping of a fly is unorthodox in fishing the dry fly. It violates the cardinal principle of most dry-fly fishing. The skater, very fluffy and light, is cast out and retrieved across the surface in a series of jerks. It is a tantalizing thing, originally calculated to draw up a big brown trout when conventionally fished dry flies would not, a feat it can often accomplish for salmon. This skipping of these fluffy flies across the surface often will pull a salmon to the steel. It will draw them to a strike reasonably well but has a greater value, I think, in softening them up for some other fly later on. It makes them conscious of surface action and of fly movement. The mere fact that a skater or spider has been skipped across in front of a salmon a few times can make him take the dry fly he has been indifferent to for the preceding twenty minutes.

A fly called Whiskers, developed by Lou Butterfield and Charlie Wade on the Miramichi, is one designed for skimming across the surface. It, too, is a tantalizer but it has the advantage of being tied on a larger hook. It is heavier than a skater, lies lower to the water, and slides, rather than glides, across the surface as the skater does. Both flies have a place in the well-equipped dry-fly fisherman's vest.

A common fault of dry-fly anglers is their failure to get the last full measure of their float. The fly, sailing gayly down over good salmon water will be dragged under before it need be because the fisherman is holding his rod at an angle upstream (or downstream) from the direction in which the line is going away from him toward the fish . . . . or because it is being pointed at an angle up into the air.

To give the greatest length of line for a float, the angler, at the end of each cast, should have his rod at an angle very low to the water and pointed in the direction the line is leaving it. An inch or two of extra floating will often bring a salmon to the fly. It is foolish to waste it.

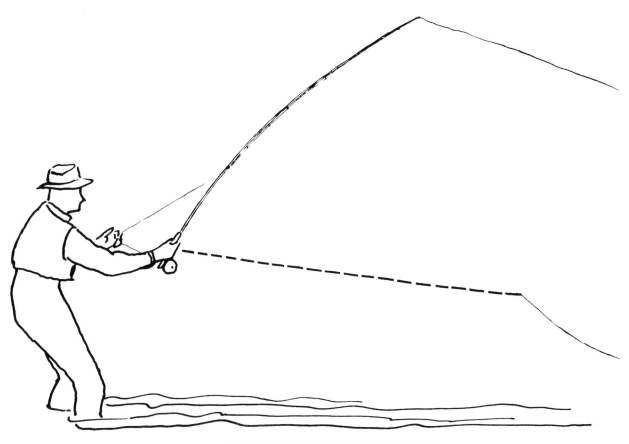

DOTTED LINE INDICATES ROD POSITION FOR MAXIMUM FLOAT

Line can also be pulled off the reel and slipped out through the guides to extend a downstream float. In that way a fly may be fished to a salmon beyond the reach of an angler's cast whenever he can get above the fish and the water is suitable for a long downstream float. This method of getting lines out to a fish is also suitable for extending the wet-fly cast.

The wet-fly fisherman works downstream as he fishes in order to reach new fish, leaving behind the water that has seen his finished casts and the picking up of his line. As each cast falls farther downstream, it comes closer and closer to a fish lying ahead of him until, finally, it comes right ahead of his nose. If he were to work upstream as he cast, the fly would come over the salmon's tail before it passed in front of him, a less satisfactory approach. The angle of the wet-fly fisherman's cast is determined by the direction of the flow and, unless the fly is to float absolutely free of line tension, the cast must be made across or down the stream. However, since the dry fly is designed to float at the will of the current and is fished on a slack line, it is possible to make the cast at any angle across the current. The usual tendency is to work upstream. Consider the following points.

If the angler stands abreast of his fish, he may not have to strip in any line between casts, in any case, stripping will be reduced to a minimum. This position makes for the easiest casting and puts the average point of the fly in the float farther away from the caster than at any other angle with the flow. The angler is well in the fish's vision, perhaps at the more conspicuous point. This, however, may be far less important than that the fish is more visible to the angler for the cross-stream flow position. The importance of seeing a fish move under the fly or to see him clearly as he takes it cannot be denied.

The quartering downstream wet-fly cast angle is not good for dry flies as the fisherman moves into the fish's vision behind the fly at an angle that makes him fairly conspicuous, but if he uses a long line this will not be of too great consequence. When the angler fishes a wet fly he is always at full cast distance from his fly. The dry-fly fisherman can cast his dry fly out to the full length of the cast and then have it drift back toward him over fish that are lying half a cast's length away or less. In other words, the dry fly fishermen is usually *closer* to his fish and therefore it is better for him to be behind the fish and out of his field of vision than in front of the fish where he can be readily seen.

The directly downstream angle has some of the same difficulties applicable to the directly upstream cast, except in one important way. The first cast over a fish can always be a perfect one, because on such a cast dry fly, leader, and line all land above the fish and approach him fly first. If he takes the fly it is fine; if not, then the fly, leader and line must come back right over his head to make the second cast, and the entire length of the fly's float must be stripped in before a similar cast can be made.

It is one of the virtues of dry-fly fishing that the angler may stand in a broad stretch of river and fish effectively in any direction. He may work on a dozen different fish at a dozen different directions without moving out of his tracks.

The wet-fly fisherman, having raised a fish and wishing to "rest" him, is limited in the areas to which he can cast while he waits out his resting period, unless he moves from his position. He needs the current to swing his fly and is more or less limited to downstream casting.

A leader is less conspicuous under the surface than above it, but sinking it is often quite a problem. With any grease or water repellent upon its surface a leader will float, and it is difficult to keep grease from getting to the leader when the fly is oiled or the line is greased. Grease from the hands, picked up from line and fly, is deposited on the leader where it spreads along the surface.

Leaders float more readily in warm weather and on smooth water. It is particularly difficult to sink a fine leader on a warm, windless day. The speed of the leader's travel through the air at the end of a long line during the cast tends to whip it dry, and, even without the aid of grease or oil, it is likely to float. Fine monofilament does not have enough weight to break through the water's surface tension. Only when the leader is coated with a substance which will eliminate this surface tension will a leader sink readily.

Rubbing a leader with strong soap of the laundry type will clean off grease and help break the surface. Lacking soap or any of the prepared substances, rubbing the leader with crushed alder leaves will be fairly effective. Soaking monofilament or any other leader having some absorbency will cause it to sink, and if it is not cast with such snap or speed as to dry it out, it will sink readily.

A short yanking of the line across the surface will often pull the leader under if the water is choppy or the line itself has sunk. When it is necessary to sink a leader by this method, it should be cast well above the spot to be fished and then the quick yank on the line may be accomplished at a sufficient distance from the fish so as not to alarm him. The fly only should be floating as it comes to a finicky fish.

It is customary to use a floating line when fishing a dry fly. There are certain obvious advantages. It is easy to pick up and makes casting simpler than a sinking line does. The floating line does not tend to pull the fly under. It is possible on a long float for the sunken line to pull under both the leader and fly. With the entire length of the line floating the angler has no worry from this source.

It is easier to pick up a floating line than a sunken one. There is less drag getting it into the air, and a caster can pick up a longer length of floating line than of sunken line. When a sunken line is used, the angler must often take in two or three extra coils of line with the left hand for the pickup, which would not have been necessary with the floating line.

Grease on the line makes it slide through the guides a little easier. It cuts down friction between line and guides thus saving wear on the line. This friction is especially important when a final "shoot" is used to extend the cast.

My own floating lines almost always sink a little, because I grease them only for skaters. I am willing to sacrifice a little on the ease of pickup, a little on the life of the line, and a little of the distance on the shoot to achieve the following compensations:

A barely sunken line can be used to pull a leader under and, with skillful handling, will sink the leader without sinking the fly. Although a greased line will shoot a little farther, this advantage of the greased line is partly offset by the extra distance gained by higher specific gravity. The essential difference so far is that the sunken line takes a little more casting work to cover the same water. It demands more line handling to shorten pickups for the backcast, but the angler gains the ability to sink his leader, a problem almost impossible to overcome with a fine leader on which grease has gathered from the line or guides. A sunken leader will capture a fish which a floating leader will scare.

Admitting to somewhere near equal benefits on this point brings us to the real difference. Suppose there are salmon lying in a pool as illustrated below. When the angler fishes for the far fish, his line must cross over the backs of the near ones. No one doubts that a floating leader is far more visible than one that sinks. The same obviously holds true of the line, but probably in a vastly increased proportion due to the line's greater size. Dragging the line across the surface over the heads of the salmon is sure to have a damaging effect, for a dragged floating line makes a serious scar on the surface. The fly, dragging along behind the line, has little, if any, attraction for the fish, and few fish are ever caught on a dry fly at such a time. In effect, the angler's retrieve of the floating line over some of the fish in the pool damages his fishing prospects.

Contrast the sinking line that comes back under water. It makes no ripples or scarring of the surface. It brings behind it a sunken leader and a dry fly, sunken, which

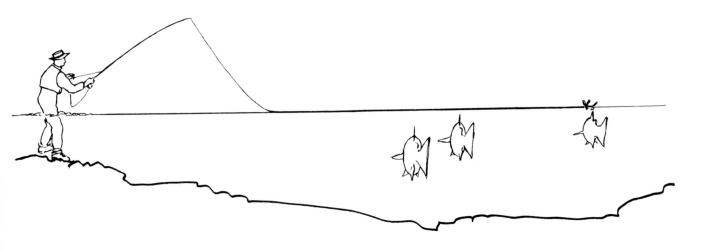

will often draw a rise from one of the fish a floating line might scare. A hair dry fly or any dry fly suitable for fishing the "Patent" method, when submerged, can be pulled under purposely and left to float leisurely down over a listless fish. Such a fly as a Surface Stone fly or a big Gray Wulff will work effectively under the "Patent" method, and will sink much more slowly, giving a longer period before it goes down out of view and must be retrieved. The use of the slowly sinking line calls for more work on the part of the angler, but I believe it will bring him more fish. I prefer to use an ungreased floating line, which will sink very slowly, but will give easy pick-ups and pleasant casting.

In the broad view, fishing the dry fly is harder than fishing the wet fly. The loose line caused by the float of the fly must be stripped in, and there are false casts to be made when the fly is half-soaked and must be dried out. The angler *must* watch his fly if he wants to hook a fish, whereas the wet-fly fisherman may rest his eyes upon the scenery after his cast is made and use them again only when he feels a fish or must make a new cast. But, with the dry fly, he can see where his fly is and what it is doing at any given moment. If he fishes at all he finds himself fishing with all his faculties concentrated upon the fly. But then, he should, by rights, fish the wet fly with the same intensity. The method, after all, should be decided from the prevailing conditions. The angler should fish the methods he thinks best suited to the day and hour in the proportion he thinks they will afford the best possible catch.

When to Use Dry—When to Use Wet

There is a general impression that dry-fly fishing is effective only in the late summer under warm, low-water conditions, and that wet flies are best when the rivers are high and cold. There is a certain truthful generality to that premise, but it is not precisely bounded. It is logical to believe that if a salmon can be drawn to within a few inches of the surface to take a wet fly, he can also be drawn to the top for a floating fly. Experience supports this, so let us consider the use of the dry fly and the wet fly as being roughly similar in their power to pull rises when both are fished in the conventional manner on or near the surface.

The real reason why the wet fly is more effective than the dry fly in high waters is that the dry fly covers but a small stretch of water on a single cast, while a wet fly covers a good deal. When the rivers are high, there is a much greater spreading out of the fish in the river. Then it is difficult to cast a dry fly and know it is drifting over or near a fish. However, when the rivers are low and the salmon have become grouped together in tight knots in the pools, it is relatively simple to put a dry fly within their reach. If a wet-fly fisherman casts completely across the good water of a pool, then, by making each succeeding cast 2 feet below the previous one as he moves down through the pool, he can be certain he has brought his fly within a foot of a point directly over every salmon there. It would take a dry-fly fisherman, with his much slower-moving fly, much longer to make the same coverage.

When the rivers are roaring in the spring, it is difficult to know exactly where salmon will be lying. Let a salmon porpoise, showing his back in an easy surface roll, and he gives his position away. A dry-fly cast to that fish is as likely to be effective as a wet fly, if both are equally suitable. Because of the wet fly's greater coverage, it is the most logical type to use in early or high-water fishing. However, when a salmon rises and misses the wet fly and refuses to rise again, it is also logical to make then an equally serious presentation of dry flies to the same fish before giving him up. Although dry flies are normally fished across the stream or at an upstream angle, it is possible to cast them at the normal wet-fly angle for a short float over a well-located fish without changing position.

The speed of the dry fly varies with the speed of the flow which, in high waters, is at its peak. Thus, in the early season, a dry fly sweeps by a fish without giving him as much chance as it will later. A wet fly's movement through the water in relation to the streambed can be controlled by the angler. He can give slack line, lower his rod, or fish at a steep angle downstream to slow down his fly. The dry-fly angler must take the current as he finds it and entrust his fly to its flow.

Because the wet fly depends upon its motion through the water for its appearance of life, slow water detracts from this factor or else makes the angler work harder in stripping line to maintain speed. The dry fly, which depends upon a "look" of life and no actual motion of the fly relative to the flow, has no such problem. All these factors favor its effectiveness in the low waters rather than in floods. They may be minor points, but every thorough salmon fisherman will want to consider all such details in planning his strategy for taking salmon.

The well-equipped salmon angler should have both wet and dry flies available at all times. In the high, cold-water times, he may well carry a preponderance of sinking flies. When the rivers are low and clear, his preponderance may be dry, but except on unusual waters, there is no time when having both types on hand may not result in taking a fish that would otherwise not have come to a fly.

It is reasonable to assume that when conditions are normal, with floating and sunken fly about equally effective, it would be most productive to use wet and dry flies more or less equally on a time basis, and that an angler's stock of dry flies and wet flies should be nearly equal in variety and numbers. This is seldom the actual case. Wet flies predominate, principally because there are more tried and true wet-fly patterns available. Still, the logic of the situation unalterably calls for an equal emphasis on both types, provided the angler is able to fish both with equal skill and enjoyment.

I know many anglers who prefer dry-fly fishing to such a degree that once conditions are suitable for floating flies, they refuse to use anything else. There are others who insist a wet fly is all that is necessary to take fish and find greater enjoyment in subsurface fishing. It is reasonable and right to fish as one chooses since the enjoyment of the actual fishing may be the sport's greatest reward, but to insist on fishing only in one way, either way, is to create for oneself a definite handicap. Exceptional skill may result in fine catches by one method only, but the same skill applied judiciously with both methods could produce even better catches.

A letter from the late T. B. Fraser in speaking of the Grand Romaine and Coacoacho Rivers on the North Shore of the Gulf of St. Lawrence says, "We are getting more and more fish on the dry fly. Both places have developed into excellent dry-fly waters, or let's say the fishermen have graduated from wet fly to dry-fly fishing. We do not get spectacular catches, one to one and a half fish per rod per day through the season, but our gang have a lot of fun. Your Wulff patterns, Cosseboom dry, and Rat Faced McDougall are the favorites on our waters." It may take quite a bit of time and patience to catch salmon by the accepted methods, and when the dry-fly method is new, it may take considerably more time and experimenting to find the patterns and sizes and methods most suitable to any river. Until the ice is broken, as this comment suggests, there may be prevailing opinion that dry flies will not work.

There are few rules about salmon fishing that hold with any real degree of consistency. One of the few is: "When the air is colder than the water, fish won't come well to a fly and rarely to the surface." It is often more positively stated. Like all such rules about salmon fishing, it is not completely true, but it is worthy of being remembered.

Such conditions may occur when a sudden cold front pushes through in normally warm weather. It may happen at low water or high. At such times, a wet fly fished slowly and deeper than usual is most effective. This, like any other such statement, is open to question. It is backed by some personal experiment and considerable checking in the field with other anglers. The only logic to support it is that when fish are listless, a fly brought close to them will draw rises where a fly farther removed will not. "Air colder than water" is a good excuse for going beneath the surface. A heavy hook sinks farther than a light one at the same speed of retrieve. The slower the retrieve, the deeper the fly sinks, also. A heavier than usual fly with a slower than usual retrieve is recommended for this condition.

Bright weather is generally thought to be better for dry flies than are overcast or drizzly days. The thought behind this is that the sun's brilliance makes the dry fly, whose motion over the water is slower than that of the wet fly when normally fished, more easily seen by the salmon. Light is a prime factor in visibility. Motion also draws the eye. Since the dry fly has less motion, most anglers feel it needs more light.

The Patent method of fishing, which casts a sinking fly upstream in such a way that it comes down to a salmon at his own level in the stream and quite close to him, is another technique used sometimes for listless salmon. It can be used effectively only when the lies of the salmon are definitely known. Where salmon can be seen and cast to, it is quite effective. Where they cannot, but the water is low enough to concentrate them in a few pools, it is reasonably good, also. When the water is high, or the bottom rocky and filled with eddies, the Patent method has little value . . . and may cost its user some of his flies when they snag on the bottom. He may also commit the most unpardonable of salmon-fishing sins: he may foul-hook an unsuspecting fish.

The conclusions to be drawn here are that the wet fly will cover more water and can be brought closer to the fish. The dry fly, perhaps more tantalizing in its effect upon the salmon, covers less water but is effective to some degree under practically all fishing conditions.

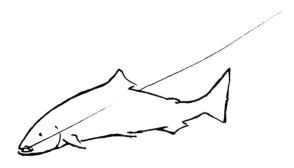

9

The Rise

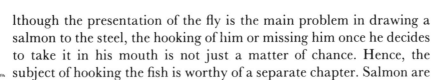lthough the presentation of the fly is the main problem in drawing a salmon to the steel, the hooking of him or missing him once he decides to take it in his mouth is not just a matter of chance. Hence, the subject of hooking the fish is worthy of a separate chapter. Salmon are extremely temperamental in their decisions to rise, and taking advantage of this is an important facet of the sport.

The fleeting instant at which a salmon takes a fly into his mouth may be the most important one in his capture. The moment requires maximum judgment and control by the angler. An angler who has spent an entire vacation fishing under relatively poor conditions and has had a few rises from salmon, all of which were missed, needs no convincing on this point. Such an experience may leave him baffled. However, it is not an unlikely circumstance especially when the fish may have already spent their early exuberance and have been and perhaps been pricked or hooked by the flies of other anglers.

The Wet-Fly Rise

How important the hooking of a fish may be was well illustrated by an event at the Portland Creek camps. When I started them, the river was rarely fished. The proportion of fish hooked was about half of the rises, a very good average. As the fishing became more intensive, the proportion grew lower. During the second year of operation, we hit an August slump, when, for a two-week period during which we had rains and high water, only a few fish came into camp. In talking things over with the guides in search of a solution, their consensus was that the fish were rising but the fishermen were not striking them properly. The guides, all able anglers, were certain that if they themselves had been handling the rods the catch would be nearly normal.

As it happened all the anglers in camp ended their trips on a Saturday, and new anglers were not to arrive until Monday. It gave me a chance to let the guides have a day off. Since all the guides liked to fish and were often uncertain as to whether to have a job and not be able to fish for salmon, or fish for them and not have a job, I saw a chance

to help along their education (and mine). In announcing the day off, I also suggested they fish the river for the day, and I put up a bottle of rum as a prize for the guide who would bring in the biggest salmon.

Six of the guides went fishing . . . and the bottle of rum went to the guide who caught a six-pounder, the only fish taken by the entire crew. It was the first time some of the guides had ever fished under conditions where salmon make false rises or come short, a situation that usually develops where fishing is intensive and when the fish have been long in the stream. It gave the guides a new appreciation of the problem their sportsmen faced.

Those guides were unanimous about one thing. They believed a fisherman should strike when the fish takes his fly. This strong feeling may have been born of their earlier fishing, much of it done with a spruce pole cut in the woods, a line of sorts, guides of telephone wire, and a questionable reel lashed to the heavy end of the spruce. For the most part, they fished short lines with such tackle, using short leaders. The salmon, being close in, were perhaps frightened as they spied the angler during their rise, ejecting the fly quickly and making a strike advisable.

They were certain a salmon would spit out a fly instantly, rejecting the contention that if a salmon really closed his mouth on a fly moving through the water at approximately 2 miles per hour he would have to be mighty fast to spit it out before even a very slight drag would sink the hook point into the flesh. Just the barest touch is necessary with a sharp fly point to have it penetrate. Once the point has penetrated even to the slightest degree, any further pressure only makes more certain the setting of the hook past the barb.

If a salmon takes a fast-moving wet fly into his mouth, he is practically certain to be hooked or at least pricked by the point or points of the fly. Striking prematurely is likely to take the fly away before the salmon can get it, or at least before he can close his jaws on it. The premature strike is a common fault, especially with anglers accustomed to catching any but the larger trout. (With small trout a quick strike is really necessary if one is to hook his fish.) If a choice must be made between an early strike or a late one, where the conventionally fished wet fly is concerned, the late strike should be the choice.

Where the hook is small and sharp, requiring very little pressure to set it, no strike at all is needed. As the hook size increases, so should the pressure when the fish takes the fly. In any case, on the normal retrieve, there is no need to make any change whatever in the retrieve until the actual touch of the fly to the fish is felt. Then the tension should be increased to the necessary degree.

Many anglers feel the need to strike no matter what the fly or the method. Others are confident the salmon will hook himself on a wet fly. Must one strike with a wet fly? The answer is yes, and no. Yes, when the wet fly is moving slowly or is on a large, dull or double-pronged hook. No, when the fly is moving swiftly or the hook is small or sharp and requires little pull to penetrate beyond the barb.

How do you program yourself to strike when necessary and to strike with suitable vigor or restraint as the occasion demands? The need is to set the hook beyond the barb so it cannot draw back. The main variable is the size of the hook, the key to the power required to *set* each particular fly. A second factor is the strength of the leader which enters into the picture only when it is relatively light. Obviously the strike required to set a small hook like a #12 is a gentle one; the strike needed for a 3/0 double hook must be fierce.

The strike may well be quite hard without danger once the point has touched the fish. A hard strike is perfectly satisfactory if it comes at a time when the fish has the fly in his closed mouth. It is all right, regardless of circumstances, if it hooks him. It is all wrong when it pulls the fly out of his mouth or, for any other reason fails to hook him.

The spread of power variation depends upon the spread of the hook sizes and rods the angler uses. If he always fishes with strong leaders, all his strikes may well be as strong as his tackle will stand. If he ranges down under 10 pounds for leaders and into the small-fly range he'll have to vary his strikes accordingly.

If the fish is docile, strikes on the hard side won't cause too many problems, but if the fish's reaction is as swift as the strike, and just as hard, even the strongest leaders will break and hooks will tear right through a grip that would hold under ordinary circumstances.

The foregoing does not take into account the uncertainties every angler faces. There will be times when the hook point strikes bone and will not penetrate, when a turn of the fish or a vagary of the current causes the point to scrape the flesh rather than embed itself. Not all solid rises result in hooked fish. The percentage of strikes missed, where the salmon actually takes the conventionally fished wet fly, should be low, not more than one in seven or eight.

There was a great salmon in a Serpentine River pool late one season. I fished for him every morning for close to a week. Almost every time I fished I was able to bring him up for a look at the fly. Although I tried all my tricks, he always rose to a hitched wet fly. He would come from downstream, rolling a great wave of water ahead of him. Finally, on the sixth day when he surged to the fly, I felt his pressure upon the line. I lifted the rod in a quick, hard motion to set the hook, then dropped it to relax the tension while I took time to reel in the loose coils of line from my left hand. When the line ran directly from reel to first guide, I lifted the rod again in anticipation of the solid pressure and strong movement that would surely follow.

Some spectacular leaps!

There was nothing but slack. The hook was free. I have long pondered the situation and only one explanation makes sense. The fish, I believe, missed the fly, but it touched him on the outside of nose or jaw or gill cover where there was gristle or bone. The fly could not penetrate. Although normally hard, my strike had lacked power to sink the hook beyond the barb and when the fish received slack, it simply fell off. If true, I would have lost him in any case. The next day a rise of water caused the fish to change position. We never located him again. If he did not really get the fly into his mouth, I do not begrudge his escape, but if, in setting the hook, I failed to give the proper pressure, I feel a lasting regret for that particular inadequacy.

Fishing a fly by the greased-line method should result in an even better average of hookings. Assuming it is their intent to take it, fewer fish will miss the slower paced, single-hook fly when they rise.

In fishing the Portland Creek hitch, there is supposedly a greater likelihood of missing a fish. If a hook, designed to be the perfect device for securing a fish, has gone through hundreds of years to a peak development, it may be illogical to believe a radical change in the point of connection of the leader and the angle at which it is connected could do anything but impair its efficiency somewhat. Yet the percentage of fish hooked is apparently as good in this method as in the two preceding ones.

When a fly is moving under tension from the line, it is hard for the fish to eject it without being hooked. It is when the fly is drifting slack and when there is little movement of the water that the danger of having fish actually take a fly into their mouths yet not be hooked is greater. The Patent method poses the greatest difficulty for the angler in the hooking of actual rises.

When the rises are false, either through misjudgment on the part of the fish, or a last minute decision on his part not to take the fly, the angler cannot hope to hook the fish except accidentally and, most probably, foul. An occasional fish will be clean hooked under such circumstances. These might have escaped a nonstriking angler, but these occasions are too infrequent to suggest a strike where the fly is not taken.

False rises are a problem. Under some circumstances, they are easily recognized. At other times, it is impossible to detect whether the fish actually tried to take the fly or turned away short. Most salmon rises occur at quite a distance from the angler, nearly the length of a cast away. At a distance of even 25 feet, the actions of a fly and a fish under water are difficult to discern. At 10 or 15 feet, however, when the water is smooth, it is easy enough to see what is actually happening.

For a period of several years, I practiced the stalking of salmon before attempting to fish for them. A squirrel will watch a hunter sit down and, after not too long a time, if he remains motionless, the squirrel will decide there is no danger and start to stir. A deer has a longer memory and a greater caution. Watching a hunter sit down, he will stand sometimes for hours in immobility and then, instead of sneaking away, may relax and feed. I decided that salmon, like game animals, would relax their vigilance after something which had moved into their vision stayed there in relative immobility for a reasonable period of time. It was possible to accomplish this relaxation of the fish in open water but much easier where there was a rock or other obstruction already in the stream which would hide my legs and part of my body. The time required was proportionate to the visibility at first approach.

Salmon, like most wild things, will not live in a constant state of fear. If they are frightened, they leave the area or, as a last resort, may hide. They may hold in a position they consider safe, in water of satisfactory depth, with deeper water or open space adjacent, even though aware of possible danger. However, their memories are short. Salmon relax after a period ranging from twenty minutes to more than an hour, during which I would sometimes stand motionless, sometimes fish. My rod was very light and small, it cast almost no shadow and my movements would be slow, deliberate and held to a minimum.

By waiting beside a rock which rested in about 4 feet of water and protruded for a foot or more above the surface, until the salmon on the far side of it were relaxed, I have had them rise to the wet fly with nothing but 6 or 7 feet of leader extending beyond the small rod. I have seen them come from their resting spot on the bottom to within a few feet of my head as they made their rises. They have risen up to the fly and taken it cleanly; they have also risen up to the fly and simply turned away at the last moment. In some cases, a miss was made with the mouth opening as it to take the fly. Some put their nose within an inch of the fly without touching it.

From such a close stand, it was possible to see a fly disappear into the salmon's mouth. A few times, when a strike was made as soon as the fly went out of sight, the fish was pricked but not hooked. In no case, when the fish was allowed to set the hook himself, was a rise missed. Since the water was in summer flow rather than at spring height, my flies were small and easy to set. It is possible that with double hooks or large singles a strike would have been of some advantage in avoiding a spit-out.

One of the puzzling things about a salmon's rise to the fly is the speed with which he can make it. In seeing a salmon's rise only at the surface, they seem lazy and deliberate at the moment of taking the fly, but often their movements between the time they leave their resting place near the bottom until they are in position, openmouthed, on the surface, are so swift the eyes cannot follow them. Like a tennis player who speeds across court to the right position and then leisurely returns a shot, the ease with which the fly is taken belies the speed required to get there to take it. When watching a salmon in his lie while my fly swam over to him, the fish would be plainly visible in a few feet of water under a bright sun. Suddenly I would see the fish on the surface taking the fly before I knew he'd left the bottom, even though I had been expecting the rise and had been watching for any sign of movement.

This unbelievable speed of movement, which most anglers never see, may explain the salmon's ability to take a speeding fly. Only those who have watched salmon make this sudden lift from the bottom, or who can vividly imagine the speed they develop in only a few feet of water to carry on into a vertical leap of a dozen feet, can credit a salmon with his true ability in this regard.

The dry-fly presentation is almost always with a completely free drift. But, even though it may seem to flash by the salmon lying in or under a swift run at too great a speed for them to catch it, that's rarely the case. I'm reminded of a pool on the Adlatok where the water raced over a lip at the tail and carried on down through fast broken water too rough to follow a salmon through. Ted Rogowski was flicking out a dry fly preparatory to casting up into the pool. His fly dropped to the swift tail-race run and was whipped out of sight in a fraction of a second. But, in that brief instant, I thought I

saw a flash of silver deep down under the water's race. At my suggestion, Ted dropped his fly in the race again, and again I saw a movement beneath it. The third cast brought a spray-throwing rise. The fish was hooked but it was an exercise in futility. He turned down into the rocky chute and left a broken leader behind him. It was also a lesson in how swiftly a salmon can move. Many times, since then, I've fished dry flies in unbelievably fast water and hooked some salmon where they could be landed in spite of the fast water conditions at the point of the rise.

In considering whether or not to strike, it is worthwhile taking into account the possibility of a second rise on the same cast. I remember a long, deep pool on the Restigouche River where a 20-pound fish missed the fly shortly after it touched the water, missed again as I continued a normal retrieve and was hooked on the third attempt to take it in the single, normally fished-out cast. If the fly had been snatched away from the fish on his first miss, there might never have been a second try either on that cast or on following casts.

During my stalking of fish in order to fish to them from short distances. I had many follow the fly only to turn away again. A fish may follow from a distance and never really approach the fly. On the Coxipi River in Quebec I had one fish follow the fly twelve times, each time coming a little closer. On about the seventh closely followed retrieve, I stopped the retrieve and his momentum carried him beyond the fly. He did not take it. The next follow was farther behind. By the twelfth, he was coming in as close as before. Again I stopped the fly and again he overran it but did not take it. Then he refused to follow it or any fly I changed to. Normally, when a fish showed interest in a fly, I was able to coax him into taking it. This fish was the exception.

When waters are low and the fish well accustomed to their rivers, it is wise to stay well back from the shoals and bars upon which the salmon may rest, and sometimes to fish a fly right to the river's edge.

I have a vivid memory of a pool on the upper Margaree, where I stood well back from the pool to cast and retrieve. My fly had almost reached the dry, gravelly bar at the shore when a tremendous swirl and a flash of silver disrupted the pool behind the fly and splashed the water up on the dry rocks. The salmon fell short in his last-minute drive to reach the fly. His back fin came out of water and his belly fins were rubbing on the rocks as he turned away. Two casts later, that 23-pound fish rushed into shallow water just as the fly appeared to be escaping, and this time was hooked . . . and landed. This occurred only a short time after another fisherman had fished the pool unsuccessfully, from a position in full view of the fish.

I believe that any salmon which shows interest in a fly can be taken, and if it is not, that the failure lies as much or more in the angler's choice of flies and presentation than in any change of mood in the fish.

This is not an absolute rule. I should say it holds when other fish are being taken and conditions are generally normal. There are times, usually before a rain, when salmon may make a pass at a fly, often a savage one, but from then on show no interest whatever. If this happens with one fish, it is likely to happen with several. This is an expression of the moodiness so much a part of salmon and so important to understand when fishing for them.

Salmon seem moodiest just before a rain. While working on a documentary film for a paper mill at Corner Brook, I fished the Lower Humber River in the evenings when the sunlight began to fade. By the reactions of the salmon, I was able to forecast the weather for the following day's photography with more certainty than the available weather reports, which often failed to take local variations into account.

It is the opinion of many that leaping salmon will not rise readily to the angler's fly. It is easy to locate a fish that leaps periodically, and yet, although they are the fish that are cast to most often, it is more likely to be a fish lying quietly at another spot in the pool that finally gives the angler his rise. If leaping fish are not good prospects, the rolling, or porpoising, salmon certainly are. When a salmon rises up to the surface showing his back fin and sometimes appearing to take something from the surface before he goes down, prepare for action.

The porpoising fish is a restless fish and is very likely to rise to the angler's fly if it and its action please him. The sight of such a fish has furnished many a break in otherwise monotonous days and given fresh hope to jaded anglers. These surfacings of the salmon may be almost as regular as clockwork. When timed, they have proven extremely accurate for several periods in sequence. I have hooked many by casting to them just at the time they were due to rise again. Too often the angler makes his casts to them just after they have risen, grows weary before they show themselves again, and moves on only to come back and fish again after the salmon breaks the surface the next time. These anglers have fished at the time when the salmon would not rise and have missed the time of greatest opportunity when he was due to come to the surface again.

Rather than take for granted the reports of others on salmon behavior under actual fishing conditions, I have attempted to watch them for myself. I can recommend this business of becoming a part of the background and waiting until they are relaxed before trying the effect of certain flies or leaders or methods. Sitting with binoculars on a high bank or a bridge can take the place of positioning close to the fish and is much easier, though there is always the distortion because of the magnification which may make distance between salmon and fly appear different than it really is.

The Dry-Fly Rise

My studies of salmon taking the fly started with wet flies but reached its peak in observing floating flies. One morning on the upper River of Ponds at a pool where the river flowed over some sandy shoals into a lake, Bob Reedy and I climbed onto a rock centrally located in the pool. The river had been relatively unfished up to that point in the season. Water was normal for early summer, a good flow that promised good fishing. The day was bright and sunny. Bob had a movie camera and I had my tackle.

A salmon and a grilse lay almost beneath us beside the rock we stood on. They had flared away as we climbed the rock from the shallow side but drifted back into position again within a few minutes. In order to set up a pattern of slight motion so they would not only be used to us but used to the fishing motion as well, I started casting a 50-foot line to another part of the pool. Our object was to get moving-picture sequences of salmon rising to the fly.

After a half hour of casting to the far fish and raising a few, but letting them work free on the barbless dry fly, during which time Bob was taking jumps with a telephoto

lens, we decided to try the fish at hand. Bob switched to the 1-inch, or normal, lens, and I shortened line until only the rod's length of leader extended beyond the tip guide. I let the white fly drop to the water just above the two fish and drift over them. On the first cast the salmon lifted a little from the bottom.

On the second cast, he came to the surface, poking his nose slightly above it but with his mouth closed. The fly bounced in the ripple he made, almost touching his nose, then went floating on. On the third cast he broke the surface once more, touching the fly but turning downward again without taking it. The camera was grinding during both false rises, giving me a further chance to study them when the films were shown. On the next cast he probably would have taken the fly, but I slipped a little and leaned against Bob. Then, to save pushing him into the water with the camera, I slid in myself. It is not at all strange that those two fish did not return to the rock that afternoon, nor were they there the next morning.

The patience it takes to bring a salmon to a close-in dry fly is well rewarded. If watching a salmon come to a wet fly is enlightening, then seeing his actions with a dry fly is little short of amazing. The question of when and how to strike with a dry fly had been under considerable discussion during the years previous to my decision to try stalking. Salmon anglers had been more or less agreed, then, that the best way to handle the salmon rise was to treat him as if he were a big brown trout, for the big brownies tend to rise with a deliberation paralleling that of the salmon. It is a good rule and can be improved upon only by a most careful watching of the fly, and a realization of when the salmon is fooling and when he is not.

Salmon ranging from 5 to 20 pounds have come up and pushed their heads out of water to bring their underjaws down upon floating flies and sink them. These fish never made any attempt to open their mouths. As with a leaping fish, the watcher often seems to see and hold the action in his mind longer than it takes to happen. So I remember, graphically, watching a twenty-pounder's nose poke up and lift my #10 dry fly, balanced upon its wet and rounded surface. He carried it up until his whole head was out of water before his momentum slowed and he settled to the water again. After coming up under the fly a number of times, once drowning it with this tail and making a turn as he went down as if to look and see how well he had managed to sink it, the fish finally took and was landed.

This habit of salmon, which is readily recognized and easily studied in some waters, casts a question to those who insist salmon rise to a fly for food, for the taste of its juices, or for the feel of its carcass in their mouths. As the season settles to late July, and the fish settle into pools for a moderate residence, this characteristic becomes very pronounced. It will usually take at least three rises without result for every one that brings a fly in contact with a fish. Sometimes an angler may have twenty rises from a single fish yet never touch him.

In the early season, the dry-fly fisherman may treat his dry-fly rises with all seriousness, worrying about the timing of his strike rather than whether or not the fish managed to get the fly into his mouth. When the water is swirling through the pools, high and deep, it is almost a foregone conclusion the salmon is trying to get the fly. He may miss it, but he is not likely to miss it out of playfulness or whimsy as he will later on.

The false rises made by salmon have thrown a good many inexperienced dry-fly anglers off the track. Salmon rises are rare, and on many rivers, two or three a day is considered good. Consider the novice angler's situation. He has heard conflicting reports on the timing of his strike. One acquaintance has told him he must strike quickly, as soon as he sees the rise. Another has insisted a strike is not necessary and the fish will take the fly down with him and hook himself. Still another insists a salmon's rise is like that of an old brown trout, and the strike should come as soon as the fish has the fly in his mouth and starts downward.

When the novice gets his first rise, he strikes quickly . . . and misses. Next time he tries striking a little later . . . and still he misses. Finally, he lets the salmon take his fly down with him and feels a gentle tug but fails to hook the fish. In each case he has done the wrong thing and is still no closer to the solution of when to strike. His first two rises were false, and he should not have struck at all. However, in the excitement from seeing so large a fish boil up under his fly, he was unprepared to make a thorough check on the small matter of making sure the fish actually took the fly. His third rise was a real one, and because he failed to strike, he also failed to set the hook.

To set the hook with a dry fly, which floats on a slack line, a strike is necessary. In testing out the idea of giving slack to set the hook, as is done with the greased-line fishing of the wet fly, my experience is that the fish did not hook themselves frequently on the dry fly and were missed much too often. There is too long a time between the salmon's rise and the time a dry fly, cast with an upstream loop, gets any tension from a current-pulled line. The line, upstream of the fish and drifting toward it, creates slack instead of building up tension. So one must strike. The question is how?

The spring of the rod is the cushion on which an angler depends for the taking up of shocks. The hard thrust of the salmon is absorbed by its bending. If there were no rod, and the pull came directly to the reel, the spool's inertia would offer enough resistance to snap the leader or tear out the fly. The same cushioning effect so useful against the fly's swift movements is just as deadening when the angler makes his strike. The line tightens up slowly.

The usual wet-fly strike is to lift the rod and thus increase the pressure enough to set the hook into the fish's jaw. In it, an already slight pressure is simply increased with a rapid buildup of pressure. This is the time-honored strike, the most often used for all fishing. The conditions under which the dry fly is fished are not identical with those of the wet fly, and there is reason to believe the simple wet-fly strike is not adequate, and that its inadequacy may be blamed for a good many missed fish.

There is a basic difference in the two sets of conditions. The wet fly is under slight tension. The dry fly is floating free. If it only takes a very light movement of the rod to put the fly in tension, the two conditions may be considered similar. However, if there is, for instance, 15 feet of slack, even a hard movement of the rod will not suffice.

A conventional mind may complain the comparison is not fair, that no one should fish with that much slack. Let me counter with the fact that salmon *can* be hooked on that much slack and more, and that if one were to limit himself in the amount of slack used when fishing dry flies to a few feet, he would catch far fewer fish. Let us look at it from the other view. Slack is necessary in dry-fly fishing. How can one set the hook at the strike no matter how much slack the line has in it? There is a way.

Consider a clothesline lying on the floor in a loose and sprawling pattern. If one end is lifted up slowly, the far end, still under slack, will not be moved. However, if one end is given a quick, sharp yank the entire line will move a little all along its length. It need not be straightened out completely in order to impart a slight movement to the far end. Even the slightest of movements, an inch or two at most, is enough to sink the point of a small sharp hook into a salmon's flesh beyond the barb. After that, if there is slack for a while, it does not matter. Slack will not cause the fly to fall out. Freshly set, its grip is good, and any movement of the fish tends to trail a little of the leader and line behind him and the water resistance on them will maintain a slight pressure. Slack may be a factor in losing fish when they are hooked on a large and heavy fly or lure, or after they have been played long enough for a hook to cut a hole in the flesh. It is not a problem with a freshly hooked fish on a well-embedded fly.

To give the line a movement designed to carry on through its length to the fly when there is considerable slack, the hand gripping the rod can be snapped back, away from the fish to arm's length.

A better way is to lift the rod in a conventional strike and, at the same time, make a hard down-and-back pull with the left, or line, hand as a caster does in a double haul. This swift movement of the line will usually travel its entire length and help a great deal in moving the fly just the fraction of an inch needed to sink a hook beyond the barb. A rod is a delicate instrument, designed to cushion shocks not to give them. The line has little strength, or give, and a motion initiated at one end travels its length faster and has a greater shocking power than the lift of a delicate fly rod. Mastery of this strike opens the way for an angler to fish long floats of the dry fly on a cast where 60 feet of line has been stopped in mid-air and condensed to 30, and he still is able to hook a salmon that comes up and takes the fly the moment it hits the water.

Both types of strikes have value. The lifting of the rod is the simplest, and the one to be used when there is little slack in the line to be taken up. When there is more slack than the lifting of the rod can take out, then the backward yank of the line or rod butt is the only one to use.

Memories of my first dry-fly salmon are still vivid. He rose almost vertically in the clear waters of the Hut Pool on the Margaree. His jaws just came to the surface, opened, and closed on the fly. I could see the flash of his gill cover, and thought I saw the few black spots that lay upon it. Then he sank back, tail first, into the depths again as my rod came up and the reel began its song. Another time, that same season, while fishing from a high bank, I watched a salmon swim 20 feet to suck down a dry fly with a noise like that of a 5-pound bass taking a bass bug. Salmon have been hooked in the side after a fly had been ejected with the rush of water through the gills. Salmon will often take a dry fly in the beautiful head-and-tail rise with which they frequently take a wet. They will sometimes come well out of water. I recall a great male salmon that rose to a floating fly in the Humber during a thunderstorm, poking straight up beyond his forward fins as he took the fly. I remember, too, that I missed him and never rose him again. I have motion pictures of a salmon making a clean leap and taking the fly in his mouth as he came up out of the water. It is hard to conceive a method of taking a fly a salmon may not attempt.

An Atlantic salmon's acrobatics.

A fine fall salmon from the Miramichi.

There is, of course, only one right time to strike for the dry-fly rise. It is after the fish has taken the fly into his mouth and before he spits it out. There is no way to be sure of this other than watching at close range. When one cannot see what has actually happened, one should strike if it appears the fly has been taken down.

A thirty-pounder on the Serpentine came to a big white dry fly with great deliberation. His back showed out of water. His great jaws opened. Fortunately, with a fly so large, it was easy to see that when he closed them again the fly was still outside, floating along by the silver of his side. There is nothing in all salmon fishing requiring greater control and restraint than watching a salmon roll up to a dry fly and wait, with striking arm cocked, to see if he will take it or let it pass by. My tense arm was controlled that time. The fly went on, and the salmon sank from sight. He came again, similarly, without taking the fly, an hour and a half later. It was nearly as long again before he rose once more, in the same lazy fashion, and pushed his open mouth forward to engulf the fly. An insulting yanking of the fly away at either of his two false rises probably would have precluded the third.

There was an old male fish in the Miramichi that made a rise I will long remember. I was close to him and I could see him come up. His jaws seemed slightly apart, but his mouth was closed at the nose where his hook bill overlapped. His nose came just short of the surface and his back lifted the water in a little roll but did not break it. Turning downward on his side, he sank and, in sinking, waved his tail until its upper tip broke the surface where the fly was riding and sank it. Three times he made the same kind of rise, twice more drowning the fly and nearly doing so the third time. Then he would come no more. He was playing with me; not I with him.

There is one dry-fly rise perhaps more difficult than any other, and it is a fairly common one. It usually occurs when a fish lies in shallow water, and often, the angler knows the fish is there and has been watching him closely for any reaction to his flies. It occurs most often when after a series of casts the fly landing just in front of the fish has floated over him and has been picked up just behind his tail . . . short, quick casts, designed to make him nervous. Then, a long cast puts the fly 20 feet or more above the fish and it comes floating down to him. It is a big fly, and he can see it well a long way off in the clear and shallow water. He can see the angler, too, as well or better than the angler can see him. The fly draws near with tantalizing slowness, but he waits and shows no sign. Finally, after a normal rise is impossible, he is suddenly irritated beyond measure. He swings around—the turn is always away from the angler—and comes at the fly from beyond it toward the fisherman, with his movements churning the water harshly. His mouth is open and he takes the fly. More often than not, the angler will lift the fly right back out of his open mouth before he can close it! Had the fish been facing in any other direction but right at the fisherman and had there been less confusion than there always is, the problem would not be as great. This seems to be an instance where, if the angler had left the line slack instead of striking, the fish would probably have hooked himself, in the manner of greased-line fishing. In this case as he takes the fly the fish is completing a circle to head back into the current.

On one dull and misty evening below Stag Island on the Lower Humber the great river spread wide as it flowed by the canoe. I was fishing a large dry fly and covering the nearby water in a general way, for it was all some 6 or 7 feet deep with a dark bottom below its own dark, peaty color. Dusk was coming on, and there had been no rise nor any sign of salmon. I was covering the water downstream from the boat, dropping the fly almost abreast of us and letting it float away, stripping line out through the guides to give it slackness as it went.

In the eerie light, I saw a sort of pearly glow which rose and grew beneath the fly. Then, unexpectedly, a salmon's head showed and the water broke as he head-and-tailed to take the fly. It was the luster of his under jaw that had shown so brilliantly in the dark water and had seemed to be a thing apart. Nothing else about the fish had been at all visible until he came to air. I missed the rise and failed to get the fish, but I have never forgotten the little spot of light that shows on a salmon when he is tilted up, head toward you. I have seen it since on fish that did not otherwise show themselves to me and, knowing it for what it was, have stayed on to cast that spot, and eventually to hook a salmon.

10

The Action

Many an angler has come in from the river with a story of a monster salmon he could not hold. His tackle is broken and the inference is that he was fast to an extraordinary fish, and that no ordinary angler could have saved him. The statement indicates a complete lack of understanding of the technique of playing a fish. The tackle includes a reel which is there to hold the line and to let a fish run. A fish of 5 pounds can break a leader just as quickly as a fifty-pounder. Anyone who tries to stop a fresh salmon of *any* size from running will break his tackle. He has failed in the whole idea of playing a fish, which is to give line whenever the pressure calls for it and *before the tackle breaks*. He is blaming the fish for his own shortcomings and advertising his own ignorance.

In order to have a consistent pattern for playing a fish, an angler can reasonably assume his fish is well hooked. If he does not, he may lose more fish through babying them than he will save. Only when an angler can see the hook has a poor hold, or when a salmon has been played for a very long time on a very small hook, should he worry about the hook coming out. Otherwise, he is borrowing trouble.

If he breaks a leader, he must assume it was his fault, for had he been using perfect judgment, he would have released the tension and avoided the loss of the fish. Admittedly, with ultrafine leaders and flies, there are circumstances where tackle breakage is to be expected, but it is a sign the fish or fishing conditions, or the ability to handle the tackle at the moment, were beyond the capabilities of the angler. This holds true for any breakage of tackle except for defective units.

If a leader was weak, it should have been discovered by previous testing. If a poor cast in the wind tied a knot in it, the angler should have checked it and retired or replaced it. If the reel overruns and jams, the angler had not set it at the right tension or had failed to brake the reel hard enough to match the pressure. If the tackle is not right or is not handled effectively enough, it is the angler's responsibility. By trying to blame the fish for his own shortcomings, the angler only closes the door on his own improvement.

The angler can bend his rod to maximum pressure when the fish is tired and holding steady. Photo by Joan Wulff

This large salmon from the St. Jean River has been played to the point that the angler has only to grasp and twist the hook to release it.

No amount of reading, listening, or talking will teach an angler what sort of a pull his tackle will stand. If he tries to find out by fishing, he will either lose a good many fish or fail to put his tackle near the limit of its power and, consequently, fish poorly. It is easy enough to test the breaking strength of a leader in the hands, but having determined it, it is very difficult to translate that pull into the pull to be exerted at the rod butt to equal it. There is a most sensible way to learn about the tackle's holding power. That is to hook a fly on a bush or root or fencepost and, with 20-odd feet of line out, pull upward with a bent rod until the leader breaks.

Almost every angler who tries it for the first time is amazed at the strength he must exert. Some anglers find themselves unable to break the leader or straighten out the hook without using both arms or shortening the line in order to pull directly with only a slight bend in the rod.

That heavy pressure, almost to the breaking point of the tippet, is safe to use only when conditions are *static*, when neither the fish nor the angler are moving, or when both are moving in the same direction and at the same speed.

Other anglers often disbelieved me when I said that if I am free to move to the right positions my salmon never sulk, in spite of my very light tackle. To hold his positions when I am downcurrent from him putting on a maximum pressure, the salmon must, essentially, swim in place. He must work to hold his position under the strongest pressure my tackle can give, and that is more difficult for him than running against a light drag. No fish will put up with that kind of pressure very long. Naturally, if an angler uses the same light pressure on a sulking fish that he does on one that is moving, he may spend hours playing a fish that could have been brought in in minutes.

A few years back a new pool, the Brush Pile, was formed on the Grand Cascapedia. A swift run over a ledge created a deep, dark hole where, we were told, a salmon hooked in the run would go and sulk. It had taken hours, we were informed, to work a fish out of that sulking position a few days earlier.

I was anxious to see the place, and when I hooked a good fish in the run, sure enough, he raced down over the drop-off into the deep hole and took up a steady lie. I moved downstream and put on the maximum safe pressure I could have put on if my 8-pound-test leader had been tied to the wall behind my house. It was devastating. In less than two minutes the fish broke into runs and leaps, and from that point, acted like an active salmon in a normal pool. He came to hand in twenty-one minutes—a twenty-five-pounder.

Too few people know how much strain is safe to use when a fish sulks and you're below him. Many dare not use it for fear they will hold it too long when the fish makes a sudden break. The angler's rod is his cushion. It's slightest bend warns of a fish's sudden movement, a movement that must be sensed instantly so that the reel may be freed to give out line. It is worth mentioning here that I use only a strong enough click to keep my reel from overrunning and put pressure on with my fingers. It was for this reason that I designed the "Lee Wulff Ultimate" reel (manufactured for a time by Farlow), a design which has since been incorporated in the Orvis CFO and reels of other manufacturers. The mechanical advantage of braking on the reel rim instead of the shaft is a great one, and when finger pressure is released the reel reverts to its very light click setting to prevent overrun. Those who cannot sense the sudden movement of a fish as soon as it begins will never be able to use maximum pressure or coerce sulking fish . . . they will never become top artists in the playing of salmon. It is rarely the steady pull that breaks tackle, but rather the sudden jerk. The rod is designed to cushion that shock but, for the angler with slow reflexes, it may not. Such an angler dare not approach the tackle's safe strain until he can speed up his reactions. When an angler does learn to release pressure quickly, he can work his fish harder, subdue them more quickly. It is wise for a novice to take an hour or more to play out a salmon if, by exerting more pressure, he fears he will lose his fish. But when he really learns what his tackle will take and learns to pass that pull on down to the fish, he will find himself in the middle of the "minute to the pound" fishermen. There he will be surprised how little his playing time varies from fish to fish.

One of the weapons the angler has in his struggles with the salmon is to create in the fish's mind the fear that an inescapable force has attached itself to him, a force he can neither escape nor understand. The fly becomes a nagging thing, driving him from one acrobatic feat to another until the full reservoir of his immediate strength is expended.

The wise angler can make his salmon run a fast, grueling race, with never a moment of rest, instead of just letting the fish work where and when he will, simply resisting him.

When a salmon leaps, he should be given slack so that he does not have an opportunity to get in a solid yank at the tackle. Usually, the dropping of the rod as the fish comes out of the water is sufficient to take care of this danger. A light drag should be used until late in the struggle, when the salmon's runs and even his leaps will be slowed down. Slack rarely results in the loss of a fish. It is much safer to run the risk of slack than of an extra heavy pull.

Salmon must face the current or swim faster than the water around them in order to keep the flow of water coming through their gills. The greater their exertions, the faster their gills must work, and the greater the quantity of water they need for breathing. Thus, when they turn to go downstream with the current, they must swim considerably faster than the current or they will suffocate. For this reason, they cannot run downstream for any great distance, against the tackle's drag, without a tremendous drain on their strength. Lack of breath always forces them to turn periodically and face the flow again.

An angler can make a salmon work harder on a short line. A long line in the water tends to cushion both the pulls of the angler and those of the salmon. In the early part of the fight, a certain amount of line should be out for best playing conditions, for, at that time, the speed of the fish's runs and changes of direction are most likely to take an angler off guard. After he has tired and begins to start off on his runs more slowly, the shorter the line, the better. The angler can put the greatest pressure on the fish with a short line, and he can hold it high enough to keep it free of rocks rising up from the streambed.

A long time ago, a friend and I, driving back to our cottage for lunch, crossed a bridge on the upper section of the northwest Margaree River in Nova Scotia. We saw a fisherman standing on a sandbar with his long rod bent and a grim expression on his face. Behind him, on the pebbly beach, sat a woman, watching. We stopped the car and walked down to stand beside her. "How long has he had the fish on?" we asked.

BELOW: *Beaching a salmon requires patience and skill—and a truly tired fish.*

With an 9-foot rod, the angler needs a long reach to apply the thumb-and-forefinger grip behind the forward fins of a tired grilse such as this one.

With the air of one who does not understand the seriousness with which the male of the species may take his fishing, she replied, "He's been standing just like that since ten-thirty this morning." As if to punctuate the remark, a fine, bright salmon left the water in a flashing leap, and the reel sang a short song. "It's the first salmon he's ever hooked," she added.

From the fisherman himself, we learned he had the fish on a double-hooked #4 Silver Grey, and that his leader was brand-new and fairly heavy. In our rich wisdom of a few seasons of salmon fishing, we told him of the standard technique to start a fish moving again when he stalled, as practiced by the local guides. This was to throw stones whenever he sulked. Then, with his permission, we threw out some stones behind the fish to stir him to action, which would soon drain his strength. The stones rocketed out to the placid waters of the pool and sent up high splashes which settled into ever-widening rings. The salmon was so impressed it streaked upstream as only a fresh-run salmon can, leaped ponderously, and fell free! The fisherman reeled in his Silver Grey, and, with the feeling that our popularity in those quarters was definitely on the decline, we departed without another word.

In all likelihood, that salmon would have escaped anyway, but from that moment on I have had a strong reluctance to do anything to stir a salmon to activity not originating with the angler. Stones thrown near a salmon will scare him and often make him run, but it instills him with a wild panic, not a depressing fear, and he moves suddenly. Instead of starting slowly, he breaks away at top speed, making a much more difficult tackle problem for the angler to manage. A poorly aimed stone may even strike the line or leader and yank the hook free. There is a better way to make a sulking fish move.

One of the great fears of the salmon angler is often that his fish will sulk. For this reason, many have used far heavier tackle than necessary in the belief that sheer power is necessary to move a fish, and that a sulking fish can continue the practice indefinitely. Usually, when he has to work against the tackle to hold his position over and above the effort of bucking the flow, he will not try, for too long, to stay in one spot. If, on the other hand, the fish is given the privilege of bracing his body across the current at an angle below the angler, the current will push water through his gills, and he need spend very little energy. From this position, a salmon can tax an angler's tackle for a long, long time.

If the hand grip is not secure a salmon will try to dart away for another run, creating a wild splash like this one. Photo by Joan Wulff

In holding a salmon in a pool where one is unable to follow him downstream or get below him, the angler must sacrifice some time in playing him out. It is not possible to make a fish work as hard from upstream as it is from a downstream angle, yet in many cases it is essential that a fish be held in a pool. When a salmon goes to the brink of the overflow and is held there, the angler is faced with the problem of working him back to the deep water. It is a strange thing, but a steady pull will bring him back while an unsteady one will not. When the angler tries to reel him up against the stream, he is very likely to turn with the flow and go down. But the same angler, holding his rod and line steady, can walk upstream along the bank, and the fish will follow docilely.

The vibration of the rod under the influence of the turning reel seems to frighten a fish, but the steady pull of equal intensity rarely alarms him. In making a test to see how far a fish could be brought, I used to hook fish a quarter of a mile below the camps, and when they tired, lead them upstream under a steady pull, like a dog on a leash, to end up alive in our little pool. Getting them through the rapid runs was not half as much a problem as getting them to come up over the shallow bars.

A high position is a good position for playing a fish in a deep pool, as Joan Wulff demonstrates in this photo taken at Pool # 5 of the Lierasveit River in Iceland.

With a fish in deep and steady water, or in water that is deepening as one goes upstream, there is usually little difficulty in "wading" a fish upstream. It is even possible, by using the same steady pull, with some fish, to bring them upstream right after they are hooked, to a guide who waits in a boat or on a rock or steep bank beside the deep water and have him gaff or tail them in a matter of seconds rather than minutes. This whole thing is pure trickery, from the salmon's point of view, and depends upon a steady pull, deep water, and a sure and steady-moving guide. The fact that it can be done occasionally indicates the control possible over a fish under certain conditions.

Most salmon fishermen, in playing a fish, use their rods as a lever to lift with. They think of a rod as up or down, and in the angle of the rod, they read the pressure it exerts upon the fish. To turn the rod, they turn with it. This is right as far as it goes, but it does not go far enough for perfection. A simple lifting pressure is all right as far as pressure control goes, but fails to give maximum turning ability to change a fish's direction.

The simplest way to test the efficiency of lateral rod action is to use it when a salmon is tired and is swimming slowly at a slight upstream angle in a position about 45 degrees downstream across the flow from the fisherman. It is taking all his strength to hold his position and create drag for the tackle. He is not taking line. A sort of stalemate momentarily exists. His strength and the push of the current against his body creates a strain that is as much as the angler dares place upon the tackle.

This deadlock may be broken by lateral movement of the rod, either upstream or downstream, as the angler wishes. If the rod is swung downstream, the fish must change his direction to turn farther into the current, like a sailboat holding the wind. As the rod's pressure continues to move downstream, he is forced to head farther and farther into the current, until his strength will not support the increased swimming effort—and the same tackle pull will draw him toward the fisherman.

If the rod is pulled laterally at an upstream angle, the fish must head farther and farther away from the direction of the flow and will be unable to maintain his pressure against the tackle. He will eventually either head into the flow or turn downstream and usually continue right around in a circle toward the shore again. In this maneuver the angler gains line and has the fish under complete control.

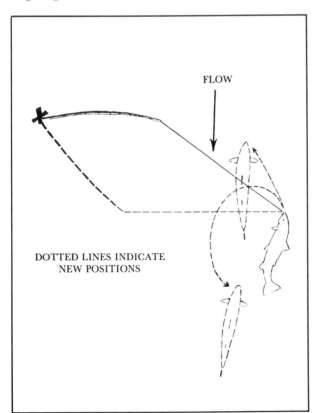

FLOW

DOTTED LINES INDICATE
NEW POSITIONS

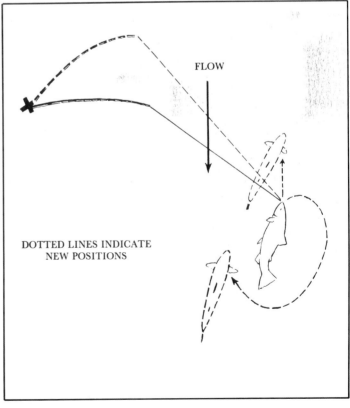

FLOW

DOTTED LINES INDICATE
NEW POSITIONS

Until an angler has experimented with the possibilities of turning and directing fish, even though the pressure be only momentarily applied, he will find it hard to realize how great a control can be exerted upon a strong fish by a relatively light pull. On any reasonable tackle, the salmon has strength enough to go where he wants for the better part of his fight for freedom, but if he can be coerced into going where the angler wants him to, his capture can be simplified. Some fish are stubborn beyond such directional proddings, usually the type that head downstream for the sea at any stalemate. With most all others, directional pressure is effective.

The hook's hold in a salmon's jaw may be either a solid or a very light one, a point which the angler cannot determine until the fish is finally captured. While playing it, under the assumption it has a good grip, he should still do everything possible to favor its hold. One important point is to remember from which side a salmon is hooked and play him accordingly. The fish is normally hooked on the side toward the angler with the fish headed upstream. The hardest pressure should be put on the fish from the direction in which the hook was set. Pressure from the other side, as the illustration shows, is much more likely to unseat it. It behooves the fisherman to be careful when either he or the fish changes to the opposite sides of the current. This may happen while following a fish downstream or playing him from a canoe. The longer the fish is played, the more likely the hook is to loosen its grip. Guard against a tired fish close in. It is very likely to circle the angler and cause a change in direction of the pull on the hook, which may pull it out.

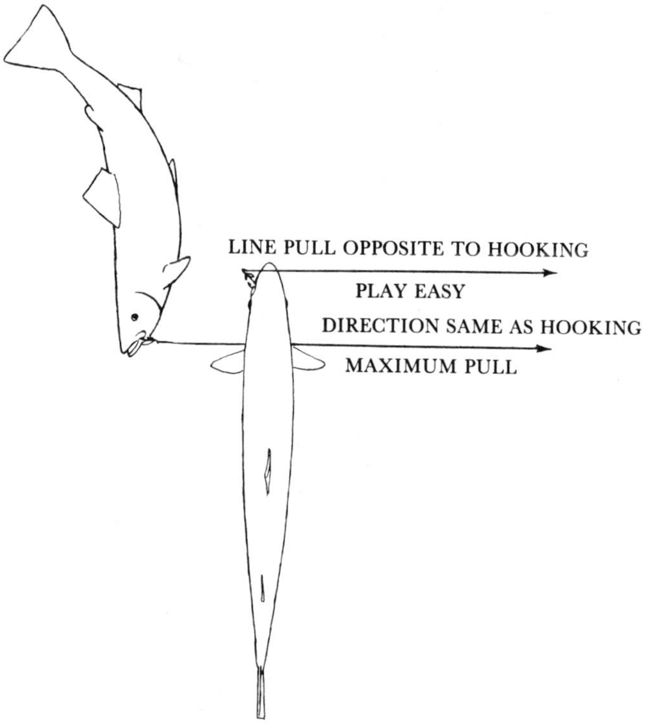

LINE PULL OPPOSITE TO HOOKING

PLAY EASY

DIRECTION SAME AS HOOKING

MAXIMUM PULL

When a fish is inadvertently foul-hooked, he becomes more difficult to play. There is an unusual fighting action to a foul-hooked fish which is usually easily recognized. (If he is hooked near the tail, the vibration of his swimming can be felt.) He will usually run farther than a fair-hooked fish, and his first run is likely to be a very long one. He will try to shake off the hook with speed rather than leaps, as a rule. He will usually head downstream and, since the angler's pull must haul him back sideways or tail first, rather than lead him head first, he cannot be brought up against the current.

As far as playing out goes, the time required for a foul-hooked fish as against a fair one should not vary much if the tackle is strong. The main difficulty in handling the foul-hooked fish is the inability to bring him in close enough at the end of the struggle. When the tackle is fine, an angler may have to do considerable maneuvering to make the capture.

However, when a foul-hooked fish is played in still water, there should be no difficulty landing him. Other than the length of his runs, he should offer no particular problem. In still water, holding the fish steady or bringing him backward suffocates him quickly.

There are times when a leader must be knotted to a line, and that knot will pass into the guides when the fish is nearly subdued. Even the smallest knot can catch upon a guide. There is a slight chance of the line catching at each metal loop and a strong pressure against it if it does. When the salmon surges away, perhaps with the last bit of his strength, and a leader knot or the knot of line to leader catches in a guide, there are several things the angler can do. He can push the whole rod toward the fish, trying to slacken off tension enough to shake the knot free from the edge of the guide. He can do nothing and pray the leader will hold . . . or he can simply turn the rod over so that the guides are pointed upward and the line is pressed against the rod along the top of the bend for its entire length. To do it, one must be fast, quick enough to free the knot before the fish can free himself, but it will almost always work. Many a salmon has been lost at the last minute, when victory for the angler was all but complete, just because an insignificant knot or even a connection as smooth as locked loops of line and leader, caught for that brief instant it takes for a near fish to tighten a leader and snap it.

The easiest place to control salmon for tailing, gaffing, or netting, is in water that is slow and as deep as the net, gaff, or tailer will allow. Still water makes the salmon use strength for every inch he moves in any direction, but a steady flow helps him to drift away with it. The deeper the water, the more secure the salmon will feel, and the less fright will cause him to move away from the angler or guide. A tailer or net works well in deep water. The gaff, requiring greater precision in aiming its stroke, works better in shallower depths. One of the secrets of bringing in a fish swiftly, when the angler plans to do the job himself, is to get out into water of a depth between his knees and hips. A salmon can be brought right alongside at this depth minutes before he can be drawn into the shallows.

When a guide is going to land the fish, there is always the possibility of his getting in the way of the line, stretching at its oblique angle from rod tip to water. Deeper water will let the guide stay closer to the angler, making it easier to pass the line over his head in case the fish makes a sudden sweep and the guide is in the way of the line. Where the angler is far back from the fish, and the guide must either duck under or step over the line when a fish moves, the problem is much more difficult.

A guide's tenseness as he leans down low to the water in an attempt to sneak up to the struggling fish unobserved, often gives him a sinister look. It is as if he were stalking with the knowledge that if the fish observed his approach it would flush like a bird and be gone for good.

*The paralyzing hand grip
on the tail makes it easy
to carry a salmon
from the water to the shore.
Photo by Joan Wulff*

True, it is very often possible to sneak up to a fish, especially one that is preoccupied with the pressure of an angler's fly and tackle, and gaff him with a quick stroke. However, in the best procedure, the fish should be brought to the guide. There should be no need for him to stalk the fish.

The guide, when he has taken position, should remain immobile but in readiness until the angler brings the salmon into position. There should be no uncertainty, no false moves. If the fish does not come well at first, the attempt to land or gaff him should be delayed until he does. Normally, passing up an uncertain chance to secure a fish is the best course. If the guide remains like a statue, and the salmon passes reasonably close once or twice without harm, he is less likely to shy away on successive attempts to draw him in. If, however, the guide makes a gaff stroke and touches the fish without securing him, it will be very difficult to bring him back. It pays to take a steady stance and wait.

Furtive movements only serve to alarm the fish. When best performed, the tailing, netting, or gaffing job is not one of stealth, but one of quiet and deliberate action.

Beaching a salmon is a sound way to get a fish to shore when a suitable beach is available. It should slope gradually at the water's edge. When the fish is tired enough, he can be headed into the beach and slid out onto it. It sounds simpler than it sometimes is. The fish will react violently to the shallowing water and try to turn away on either side. If he does manage to turn, he cannot be pulled up on the beach without "horsing" him, which is likely to break the tackle. When he succeeds in turning in water deep enough to get swimming power, the angler will have to let him go until he can be headed to the beach again for another try. The fish, in the successful beaching, is headed to the shore and held in that direction until he slides out on the dry beach. With a heavy fish and a fairly light leader, the task must be done with delicacy. By holding a steady pull at the leader's safe strain, the fish's own flopping will help work him up to a safe position. Then the angler can secure him with a grip on gill cover or tail.

A salmon's tail is much like a human's wrist in structure. A man's hand can hold it in a secure grip once the fingers close tightly about the narrow point, just as the tailer's noose will grip it. A salmon, gripped securely around the tail, usually becomes rigid as if from paralysis, making it very easy to lift or drag him to the shore. Once the grip is released, or if he escapes from it, he usually becomes active once again. There is a fine satisfaction in being able to reach down and grasp a salmon's tail, when you have tired him enough, and take him to the shore. It can be a fitting conclusion to one of the most difficult and delicate fish-playing feats in all of angling.

Many years ago on the Ecum Secum River, a lanky, raw-boned guide, named Dan MacIntosh, reached over and picked a tired grilse from the water with his big hand. At the time, I was accustomed to using a net or tailer to land a fish, and was surprised that a man's hand could grip and hold so strong and slippery a fish as a 5-pound salmon. I tried it, and, from that moment forward, rarely used a net for big trout or grilse, which are difficult to noose in a tailer because their tails are not as stiff and well developed as are the salmon's. I wrote about it and showed the technique in films which led many others to follow and eschew nets and gaffs. The grip comes down over the fish's back, just behind the head. The forefinger and thumb press into the slight indentations behind the pectoral fins. The grip should be a steady one, with all the fingers pressed tightly against the fish and toward the thumb's opposing pressure. This does not in any way injure a grilse and is a satisfactory way of either lifting them to the safety of a canoe or to the shore or to hold them briefly while a hook is removed.

There is much discussion of the hurt done to the fish while they are being released. The surest way to release a salmon is to cut the leader and lose the fly. The hook will not hurt him seriously, and he will work it free in time. Salmon flies, especially those proven successful with salmon, are often too precious to lose, however.

The best way to release a fish, I believe, is accomplished without taking him from the water and, often, without actually touching him. If the fly can be reached readily, and the angler can get a firm grip on it, either with the fingers or with a pair of pliers, the hook can be pulled out with a quick yank. With a good finger grip on the shank of the hook, in the case of a grilse, the lifting of the hook, point down, bend up, may even lift the fish clear of the water. A shake of the hand or a shake by the fish usually separates the two quickly.

When the fish is tired, the tailer may be carefully moved into position . . .

. . . then pulled almost as if it were a rope noose or lasso . . .

. . . until it tightens perfectly at the base of the tail, temporarily paralyzing the fish.

Barbless hooks with a bend instead of a barb make releasing a fish a simple matter, too simple sometimes. They are used by some anglers but require special ordering of the flies, as the flies on such barbless hooks are not otherwise available. A barbless hook will not allow the angler to give his fish slack to the same extent he can with the barbed variety, but there is no great problem to playing and landing salmon with them. Most anglers will, on occasion, want the best holding power possible in the fragment of steel they have set into a salmon's jaw. The grip of the conventional hook will not damage a salmon's jaw appreciably more than a barbless one. It is not too difficult to remove, especially with the aid of pliers. Even among salmon fishermen who release almost all their fish, there is general agreement that barbless hooks are not worth the trouble it takes to get them. They can be made, of course, by flattening the barb on an ordinary hook with a pair of pliers, but such hooks are very difficult to land a fish with.

There is a practically foolproof system for playing a fish. It is for the novice, and it looks a little ridiculous, but, if anyone is willing to admit he does not know how to play a salmon and wants to land one, it will work. One of my camp guests asked me if I thought his nine-year-old girl could catch a salmon. I said I thought she could, and she did.

I put her in a boat and soon had her working a short line in a fairly consistent cast. By changing the position of the boat until her fly was touching down at the right spot, she hooked a salmon. I had cautioned her to keep her rod vertical, or as near to it as she could, and as soon as the salmon pulled her rod down into an arc, she had promised to take her hand off the reel handle and not put it back again until she could hold the butt of the rod vertically. She had strength enough to hold the rod vertically against a light pressure, but as soon as the pressure grew heavy, she would have to let it go down and would immediately take her hand off the reel to let the fish run.

The salmon leaped and ran all over the pool, but he stayed in it. More than half the time her rod would be pointing straight up into the sky with slack line hanging from it while she reeled frantically. The fish could never get enough pull against her tackle to break it, and young angler caused him to run and jump and work against gradually increasing periods of light pressure. It took a long time, but the fish did tire, and eventually, she brought it within reach of my tailer. If a salmon cannot get a solid pull at the tackle and thereby break it, if he is well hooked and does not foul the line, and if the fish will stay in the pool, then, with a little coaching, anyone should be able to land him.

Slack bothers salmon so little that I have often worked a good gag on fishermen at the big, spread-out pool in front of the Portland Creek camp. Sometimes, in the evenings, when they had organized a "pool" about catching the first fish, with none yet caught and little time left before dark, I would find a place to slip in among several fishermen and cast a fly. The best time on that particular pool, which was fished far more heavily than any other on the river, was just at dusk. If fish were going to be caught there, it would usually be then. If I was lucky and hooked a fish, I would give him slack immediately. He would settle to the bottom in the slow flow, sometimes shake his head a little, but do nothing else. I would stand with my line trailing off downstream, just as if the thought had only then occurred to me, and say, "How about letting me get into your pool?"

Usually the reply would be, "You'll have to pay double. It will cost you two bucks." And they would all stop to look.

As soon as the words were said, I would say, "O.K.," give my rod a twitch, and the salmon would go skyrocketing up into the air. My reel would sing an accompaniment to, "Hey, that's not fair," or, "It doesn't count!" and I would play the fish on down toward the dammed-up pool in the tributary brook.

The most difficult salmon to play is one that simply holds his place in the current and shakes his head. Most salmon relying on that tactic escape. If they do not run, they waste little strength. The yank, yank, yank, of the fish against the hook will eventually work it free or weaken the leader to a point where it will break. If the angler gives slack, the fish simply rests, and when he tightens, he simply gives the fish more time to weaken the hook's hold or the leader's strength by his yanking. The only tactic I know to capture a fish dedicated to this head-shaking fight, is to slack off and get directly downstream each time it is tried. A salmon must be sideways from the angler to head-shake effectively. When the angler is below him, the head stays the same distance away right through the shake, and the pressure on the tackle stays fairly steady.

To release this 30-pounder back into the St. Jean River, the author grips only the hook and does not touch the fish.

Perhaps it is a psychological reaction that causes a fish to slow down when pressure is suddenly released. Giving slack when a fish rounds a snag and tightens the line against it will often cause him to pause, and if he feels free, he may retrace his course and swim back into the open water again. At other times, a fish feeling the slack will immediately stop to rest and, in that way, give the angler a chance to change his position and perhaps overcome the difficulty of a snagged line by maintaining complete slack until he is ready to start the struggle again. A fish that has passed through a narrow passage through which he does not return of his own accord, can sometimes be coaxed back through it by a nagging series of light twitches, convincing him he has a better chance to avoid them in the open water.

It was Ed Hewitt, a master of tackle tactics, who first wrote down the system of giving slack line to a fish racing downstream in order to turn him back. If a fish feels a sudden slack, his first instinct is to stop and head into the current. If even a short section of the line can be carried by the current to a point downstream of a fish, it will pull at him from below and almost invariably head him upstream. There is as much psychology in a tackle maneuver like that as there is in a quarterback sneak.

Salmon can be led into a landing position before they have spent their full strength. With appropriate handling, they find themselves weary and discouraged sooner than usual. The shorter the struggle, the more humane it is. If a fish is to be released, he will have a better chance of survival if he has been played out quickly. Playing a fish should be a game of fine skill, not one of torture. To play with a fish as a cat plays with a mouse is to prolong its agony. The more swiftly a man can bring in a fish on specific tackle, the greater his tackle skill. To the fastest driver in the road race, to the skier fastest through the slalom sticks, goes the trophy. Playing a fish is like a contest of action rather than a game of momentary precision like golf or rifle shooting. Skill will save time and cut the chances of losing your fish.

Most salmon do not like to leave a pool, especially in the smaller rivers where the runs between pools are narrow or shallow, but one can never be sure of this. How swiftly and how fast a salmon may run downstream toward the sea was graphically illustrated to Reg Sinclair. He had gone out with his guide to fish at the Benches, an excellent pool on the Portland Creek feeder where water poured over a falls into a long deep pool. Entirely independently, another angler and guide had headed up the same tributary for the afternoon's fishing, thinking the first pair would be fishing the upper pools by that time.

Reg Sinclair hooked a salmon of about 10 pounds, which, after a brief flurry on the surface and a few leaps, streaked for the tail of the pool. The guide shouted for him to follow the fish, but Sinclair was slow to start in the belief the fish would stay in the pool. The salmon kept right on going. Fortunately, there was plenty of backing line on Sinclair's reel, and he belatedly started to follow. The other angler, fishing the head of Jack Williams's pool two hundred yards below and around a sharp bend, was startled by the sight of a salmon swimming by him at a distance of only 10 feet. He turned to his guide to remark about it. It was almost a minute before Sinclair and his guide came into view following their fish, which had passed right on by the second angler and through Jack Williams's pool into the pockets of rough water below, where, eventually, he was landed.

*Playing this salmon
on the River of Ponds
with the 3-foot tip of
a 9-foot cane rod . . .*

. . . gets the angler close enough . . .

. . . to hand-tail easily.

. . . a bright 17-pounder.
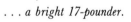

Salmon will often relax and hold under a steady pressure. Jim Reid, of Corner Brook, was fishing the Shellbird Island pool of the Lower Humber one summer evening. The river stretched out before him well over a hundred yards wide, a smooth ribbon of water channelled deep enough on the far shore for a seagoing tug to steam upstream, and ranging from 3 to 5 feet in depth for the 200 feet nearest him. The tide was nearing flood, and its effect was to raise the waterlevel where he stood. It was nearly dark, and the few other anglers who had been there earlier had left. Jim hooked a fish.

Within fifteen minutes it was dark, which made the playing job more difficult. His backing line had been showing for a full five minutes. Then, just when he thought he might work the fish in close enough to see his casting line again, his reel jammed. The fish hung in the current while he tried to loosen it. Five minutes went by, then ten. Jim finally gave up hope of fixing the reel, and with sudden inspiration, cut the line at the reel and tied it to a birch limb hanging out over the water.

We hurried to his car and drove rapidly to Corner Brook, 6 miles away to find his friend, Ted Bugden, and borrow another reel. Bugden was not at home but was finally located and, three-quarters of an hour later, we returned to the bending birch limb, put Ted's reel on Jim's rod and passing the line out through the guides, tied it to Jim's. Jim tightened up, expecting to find the line snagged and empty, but when he built up pressure enough, he felt the fish move out in the darkness and heard him leap. Fifteen minutes later, Ted gaffed a twenty-five-pounder for him.

Now, suppose you put yourself in my waders at the moment a big fish is hooked. The fly is a floater on a #10 hook, and the 14-foot leader tapers down to 4-pound test at the tippet. The rod is an ounce-and-three-quarters, one-piece, six-footer of Bakelite-impregnated split bamboo. The fish, a 27-pound Atlantic salmon, has taken the fly at the head of the Eastern Run on Portland Creek half a mile above salt water.

The river is at summer level, shallow enough to let you wade well out from the bar dividing the river's flow. You can cast almost all the way to the eastern bank. As you set the hook, your 50-foot line marker is at the first guide, and 20 feet of line hangs in loose coils from your left hand. The fish has risen in a downstream turn, sending a heavy wave creasing across the rippled flow. At the bite of the steel, he dives downward in a quick roll that puts his head upstream again. At this point you give him complete slack.

The #10 hook will stick to his jaw without any line tension, and it is your hope the fish will not take any real alarm from its bite in the brief moment you set it. You need a few seconds to get those loops out of your left hand and onto the reel. Loops have an unfortunate habit of tangling and jamming at the first guide, or of catching around one's fingers or the reel, if the fish makes a sudden swift rush as soon as he is hooked. You want him to realize his danger slowly and only after he has spent some of his strength. Many a salmon is lost in the first wild flurry of action that follows when he not only feels the hook but is subjected to heavy pressure, and perhaps catches sight of the angler as well. Panicky, then, and possessed of amazing energy, the fish whips out line so fast, the slightest error in tension will let him break free.

This fish of yours, however, is not yet frightened. He has felt only a slight pressure, perhaps the equivalent of one-half a pound of pull, for a fraction of a second— just enough to set the hook beyond the barb. He settles back in his regular resting place to figure things out. You have given him full slack, yet there is still some pressure from the force of the water against the line. It now begins to tighten.

Slack in the line is held between the fingers to maintain the tension until the strike; then . . .

. . . the line is allowed to slide through the fingers while reeling in until it is taut and then the fish can be played directly from the reel.

Your rod is always in your right hand, whether you are casting or playing a fish. Logically, you use the best hand for the most difficult job. Reeling requires far less strength and coordination than holding the rod, so you do it with your left hand. The more capable fingers of your right hand, thoroughly trained by their normal use in precise work, are the ones through which the line passes and by which the pressure is controlled. The right arm, much stronger than your left, holds the rod and varies its position as necessary. You reel rapidly, taking your eyes away from the still-spreading waves of the salmon's rise, to make sure there will be no tangle as you gather in line. A light pressure between the first two fingers holds it gently where it comes from the first guide; that way, the fish can at any moment draw out line by a slight pull. (The illustration on p. 183 shows how the two last fingers of your right hand put a tension on the line as it goes into the reel.) The coils of line from the left hand have been dropped to the water to straighten out in the current. When the line comes tight, either through reeling or a run of the fish, there should be no tangle, no loop of line around any finger.

You are alert. If the wind should whip the slack line into a tangle, there would be nothing to do but pray and work fast. A few quick steps toward the fish might gain enough extra time to untangle even a serious looking knot. But no knot forms and the line tightens. It now goes directly from reel to fish, so you relax.

The quick look you had at the fish as he took the fly, plus the heavy wave his body created on the surface, make your heartbeats speed up a bit. He is a big fish, all right, and you are determined to make no errors in playing him. Very gently, you increase the pressure until the rod is in a moderate bend. For thirty seconds the fish holds his position, then moves slowly away through the deep water toward the bank.

This first slow swim takes him 30 feet before he pauses. Next, he goes into some violent underwater twisting which he climaxes with a half leap. After the flurry, he settles toward the bottom and slowly eases his way back to his original lie.

Your finger and thumb still put a very light tension on the line. Behind that pressure, the reel is set at its lightest tension. The bend of the rod is easy, and the pull of the fly on the salmon's jaw is less than half a pound. Ten seconds go by before the fish shakes his head and moves away a few feet to hold again like a rock. Twenty seconds, thirty . . . then he moves upstream and away from you to the far bank, swings downstream until your backing begins to show. Now he heads upstream again and passes under the belly of the line in returning to his old resting place. You tighten up and hold steady. Three minutes have gone by.

Up to this point, everything has been going your way. You have managed to keep the salmon from taking flight, yet his exertions have used up some of his energy. You know the sudden speed the Atlantic can deliver when he is completely fresh, and you know most salmon are lost in the first few minutes, because the angler applies too much pressure, or because the tackle simply is not good enough to take it and the reel overruns.

Because the fly-casting line matching your 8-ounce rod is very small in diameter, it offers very little drag to the fish when he pulls it through the water. And when he stops, you can hold it in a shallow arc across the current's flow. The light rod is less tiring, both in casting and in holding, while you are playing the fish. Its depth of spring, the range between no pressure and the point where it breaks, is not great, but quick reactions and practice let you cushion the shocks completely.

Canoes and early-morning mist on the famous Moise.

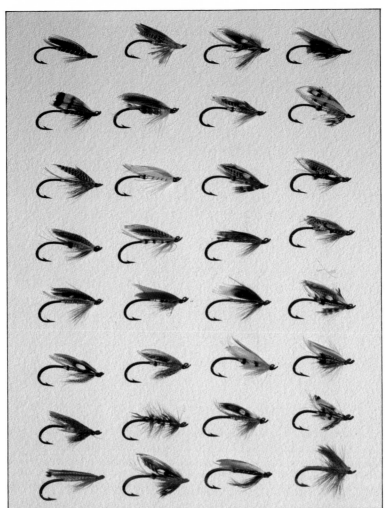

Blue Charm	Blue Doctor	Black and Gold	Black Prince
Black Ranger	Snow Fly	Blue Highlander	Moray Downe
Silver Blue and Jay	Yellow Babnet	Bull Dog	Black Dog
Lemon Grey	Beacons Field	Nicholson	Blue Jock Scott
Spring Blue	Jock o Dee	White Tip	Greenwell
Fotler	Childers	Canary	Limerick
March Brown	Jungle Hornet	Wilkinson	Black Dog
Sherbrooke	Jock Ferguson	Duchess	Lady Caroline

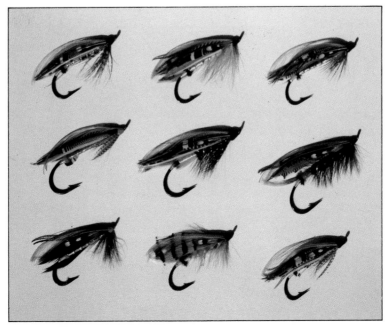

Mar Lodge	Green Highlander	Dusty Miller
Silver Doctor	Jock Scott	Black Dose
Night Hawk	Durham Ranger	Silver Grey

Traditional Atlantic salmon flies *(left)* and hair-wing versions *(right)*.
Top to bottom: Green Highlander, Dusty Miller, Black Dose, and Jock Scott.
All flies tied by Ed Van Put.

DEFEO SALMON NYMPHS

Scott   Silver
Brown   Grey

Four of the author's favorite wet flies. From upper left to lower right: Haggis, Cullman's Choice, Lady Joan, and Black Bottom.

Streamer-type wet flies with forward fin action: Muddler Minnow and Surface Stone Fly.

Some nymph-like flies used by the author.

Wretched Mess	**Teal**
Stone Fly	**Shrimp**
Grizzle	**Nymph Spot**

The original Wulff flies, tied and originated by the author.

White Wulff   Royal Wulff   Gray Wulff

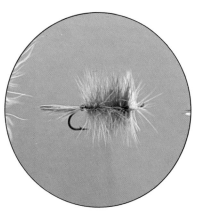

Brown Bi-Visible

Special flies for surface drift or action:

Prefontaine   Wulff Skater

Surface-film floating flies

Harry Darbee's Rat-faced McDougall   Surface Stone Fly
Looped-hackle Moth   Bomber

The most dramatic moment of all . . . the rise of an Atlantic salmon to a dry fly.

Big fish should always be played directly from the reel. Loose loops of line are booby traps, and any temporary advantage in stripping in line is more than offset by the danger of having it tangle. No rod, however long and springy, can hold a salmon when he wants to run. Now our salmon leaps twice, and, each time, you lower the rod and thrust it at arm's length toward him, to provide as much slack as possible. When he follows the leaps with a short run, you point the rod directly at him to minimize the drag. Just plain swimming will tire him, and the lack of tackle drag gives him less chance to loosen the hook. As soon as he stops, the rod, of course, comes up into a normal playing bend. The fish's early easy exertions have taken the edge off his wildness. He is already a bit used to the pressure of the fly, so when you twitch the rod lightly in a sharp pressure, he does not become frantic but tries a high, clean leap, dropping back to the water on his side after one complete end-over-end turn.

For 70 yards upstream, the water is deep, but beyond that big boulders break the flow. Downstream there is deep water, over 100 feet wide, for 200 yards. A few big rocks are scattered through the pool, but none breaks the surface, nor will any catch the line unless the fish dives close to the bottom just beyond one. The flow is steady and moderately fast. Below the deep water, there are only rapids and treacherous going. There is no deep eddy, no quiet water anywhere between this pool and the head of the tide.

The leap has shaken up the salmon, and his failure to achieve freedom sends him into a state of real alarm. He goes in for some violent head-shaking, which, to your mind, is the salmon's most effective maneuver. Now, if you hold the pressure steadily, no matter how lightly, you will gradually wear a hole where the bend of the hook works against the fish's flesh. To increase pressure, in the hope of making him change his tactics, is merely to increase the risk of enlarging the hole enough to let the hook fall free, or such pressure may break the leader with a sudden pull. So you drop the rod and give him slack. The current, carrying the line downstream, tightens it again in a deeper arc between rod and fish. As the tension builds back to normal, you feel his head start shaking again.

That is your signal to move downstream swiftly. If the big fish simply holds his spot while you stay abreast of him, and keeps on shaking his head against even moderate pressure, he will either break free or work the hook so loose it will drop out before he can be landed. The only solution, you have found, is to get almost directly below him, so that the movements of his head do not change its distance from the rod, and therefore do not dangerously change the pressure.

As long as there has been no serious working of the fly in his jaw, you do not hesitate to give him complete slack while you wade downstream to the new position. Fifty feet below him you tighten up. At this renewal of the tension from another angle, the fish heads upstream in a swift run to the big rocks at the head of the pool, where he holds steady while you follow. The upstream run, wherein the fish bucks the current as well as the tackle, is one that takes the most zip out of him in the shortest order, and you have held just a touch of drag against his run.

Before you can get to the preferred position, with a short line at a downstream angle from the fish, the salmon bolts downstream and passes you to the accompaniment of your screaming reel. You head shoreward from the water that is halfway between your knees and your hips, and hit gravelly beach on a dead run in order to follow faster.

Left-hand reeling proves its worth again during the salmon's long downstream run. With the rod in your right hand, you can move freely over the slippery rocks while still applying delicately controlled pressure. That would have been difficult with your relatively clumsy left hand.

The salmon stops at the tail of the pool where the shoal white water starts. Big fish prefer to stay in the deep pools, but you have a hunch that yours came close to going right on down out of the pool. Had he made a wild run like that when first hooked and fresh, chances are you would have lost him.

More than 100 yards of backing went out in that run, and you are relieved when your end of the fly line lifts out of the water again to hang 15 feet off your rod tip as the fish steadies. That places the salmon over against the far bank where a few dead tree trunks jut into the pool. Salmon are fish of the open water, however, and rarely foul a line deliberately by swimming into a snaggy spot, so the trunks are no cause for worry.

The fish now works upstream in a series of short runs. Each time he pauses, you pull him back and work him closer to your side of the flow. His runs are tiring him, and so are his efforts to hold his position while you pull him downstream after each burst against the current. *He cannot sulk,* for the mere holding of his position against the tackle's strain from below is as tiring as making a run. It will whip him just as quickly. If you were to follow him upstream on these runs and try to hold him from a point abreast of him, much of the tackle's pull would be absorbed by the current. The fish could, without additional effort, set his body at an angle with the current to increase the load on the tackle.

Keeping him down toward the lower edge of the pool is risky. Holding him near its middle would give you a greater chance of keeping him in the steady water when he gets an urge to go back to sea. However, you know you can tire him most quickly by working him hard from below, and you count on his hesitating at the tail of the pool before going over.

Trying to reel a fish back against the flow while standing above him would not work, because the rod vibration caused by your reeling would excite him, and he would start to run. But ninety-nine out of a hundred salmon will follow your *steady pressure* and can be led upstream by a wading angler. The last big fish you took from this run, a twenty-five-pounder, turned at the lip after three downstream runs, and, each time, you waded him back, eventually landing him in the middle of the pool.

This time, you have guessed wrong. The big, tiring salmon, sandwiches two leaps into the middle of a lateral run across the stream to the far bank, and then drives downstream into the fast water, putting you in the worst possible position, with half your backing already gone and the fish in rough water below you.

Hurrying downstream over the gravel, you get to a point on the bar slightly below the fish, plunge into the stream and wade out to within 40 feet of him. You are wringing wet, more from exertion than from splashing water.

Only skillful handling and a short line can keep the fish on in this water, and you know it. A long line would surely be carried down around the rocks of the stream bed and fouled up. Your cue is to wade back and forth across that rough flow, always below the fish, always pulling him downstream. He is tired now, and you can put a 2- to 3-

Gene Hill fishes a pool on the Delay where he can't let a fish run downstream.

pound pressure on him consistently. You are sure he does not have the snap left to make one of those fantastically fast starts that can break your leader almost before you realize he is on his way.

He grows so tired that whenever you pull his head into a downstream turn, he quickly faces into the current again and tries to hold his position. From here on the playing follows a pattern. You keep the fish in close, sometimes bringing the leader (locking loops connect it to the line) into the guides and letting it slide out again when necessary.

Although he has not yet turned on his side, he is tired, and you reach back with your left hand to unsnap the tailer from its place at the back of your neck. Holding the rod, line, and tailer in one hand, you set the spring with the other. Then, tailer in left hand, and rod in right, you close in. Line goes out against the tension still being applied by the thumb and forefinger of the right hand. You reel line back in with the finger and thumb of your left hand, which also holds the tailer.

When the salmon is in close, all of the angler's movements should be slow, deliberate, and sure. Photo by Joan Wulff

It is most important now to have your rod at the correct angle in relation to the fish. If he is going away slowly across the current, you know that moving the rod downstream with arm outstretched will turn him back into the current, nine times out of ten. The tenth time, you can take a few steps downstream toward him and, by bringing his nose around in a half circle, turn him back into the current again.

You have learned to keep your feet together those last few moments when a fish is close in. A short rod lets you work him in very close for landing. Just how close, you learned fifteen years ago, when a salmon darted right between your legs. Instinctive action saved both rod and fish. As you felt the little rod bend dangerously, and saw its tip start between your knees in the wake of the fish, you automatically stretched your arm forward to ease the bend of the rod and let it follow the fish between your legs. Your left hand came around and grasped the rod grip behind you just as your right hand freed it. An about-face and a change of hands on the rod put you back into position to finish off that fish, but you don't want to try it here in fast water.

You wait now until the salmon holds steady in a good spot, then you slip the tailer up to his adipose fin and tighten the noose around his tail. The contest has taken twenty-three minutes.

A tired fish may be only a half a minute from surrender, yet he can be lost by a pull of the hook in the wrong direction, or his own sudden surge of speed in the right direction.

11

Guides

good guide is an essential for all but the wisest fishermen in order to locate the salmon in a river. Even for the most expert salmon angler on a strange river a good guide is a wise investment. The great worth of a salmon guide lies in his knowledge of the positions salmon take up. He must know them thoroughly, not just under one set of conditions but under all of them. By knowing his riverbed at the time of dry spells when low water shows the locations of the rocks and ledges that form the best resting spots but only make a slight ripple in the surface when the high waters that bring in the salmon are coursing down the streambed, the angler can be told just where to drop his fly with a certainty that it will pass over one or more salmon. Stones of peculiar color on the stream bottom and various landmarks on the banks become his markers, and the words, "Now if you'll drop your fly about 10 feet downstream and a little to the right of those two white rocks and let it swing . . ." have a familiar ring.

Your good guide will know all the vantage spots from which he can view the pool and spot the fish that lie in it without disturbing them. He will know just where, under the dark depths the eye cannot penetrate, the salmon should lie and how their favored spots in the pool will vary with the rise and fall of the river's volume. He will watch your fly as closely as you do yourself, and when a salmon shifts his position as the fly passes over him, he'll tell you to be ready for a rise on the next cast. Such a man is skilled at making out the gray-blue shadows that are so easily lost in the background of rock and sand below them. And knowing where to look for fish, he will spot a salmon that a man of equal experience and ability, but lacking a thorough knowledge of that particular river, would overlook. Be sure, also, before hiring a guide, that he knows the river you plan to fish, for a guide who doesn't is little or no help to any experienced angler and not much more to the novice. The worth of local knowledge and experience can be well understood when I recall that I have found anglers fishing industriously on pools whose entire length did not contain a single salmon.

While operating a salmon fishing camp employing as many as forty guides, I learned a good deal about guide qualifications and guide-fisherman relations. The

The choice of a fly can make all the difference in the world. The author and Ted Bugden talk things over on the Humber River.

perfect guide for one fisherman may not be suitable at all for another. A guide becomes a confidante, a friend, a partner, or a teacher, depending upon the needs of his particular sportsman.

The best local fisherman may not be the best guide. Though he may be the most skilled in advising where to place a fly, how to handle a fish when hooked, and most able in helping to land the fish, he may fail to please because he has no room in his thoughts for others things. We had one wonderful guide who was so interested in the fishing he was always forgetting the lunch or the raincoats or some other important item. He himself did not mind in the least missing a meal or going without a raincoat in a Newfie drizzle. Another guide, less proficient in the actual fishing procedures, but who was very thoughtful, could be much more satisfactory for the average sportsman. The extra touches at the lunch, the wader-repair patches he carried, his well-fueled lighter, the small waterproof sheet to cover the food or spread out as a cloth, were the things appreciated more than an exceptional eagerness to catch a salmon, as long as the basic skills were there.

Ted and a 12-foot canoe emerge from the woods at the edge of the Lower Humber.

Any guide employed at a reputable camp will have the required knowledge of the local fishing conditions. He will know what flies are usually successful. He will know how to rig the tackle, how to cast, how to play a fish. He will be capable with his net or tailer or gaff, although on this point a very definite teamwork is required between an angler and his guide for best results. A good wild-country guide can cook, set up and maintain a clean and comfortable camp, and be responsible for the safety of his fisherman. He will keep him away from treacherous water, keep him from losing his way, and, if any unusual circumstances call for staying out unexpectedly overnight, he will be able to make a shelter and a fire to minimize the resulting discomfort.

Not all guides living on or near a given river are good guides. Many of them just happen to live there, and they feel that guiding is an easier way to make a day's pay than haying or chopping wood or digging potatoes. Such men know from hearsay what fly patterns are best, which pools the salmon lie in, and some of them know the best spots. Often they find out by asking other men, wiser than themselves, which pools contain salmon at the time they start to guide. On clear rivers where salmon can be seen readily, and they know where to look, they may be able to locate fish well, but on dark or cloudy waters, sharp eyes alone will be no help. Such a man is likely to lose your fish for you, if you are lucky enough to hook one, through lack of real interest or inexperience at the crucial moment, if you allow him to tail or gaff your fish. A dozen of them are not worth one who has a real love and respect for salmon fishing and prides himself on his tackle knowledge and salmon sense.

In the Province of Newfoundland, as the law reads today, a nonresident angler fishing on a river designated as a salmon river must be accompanied by a licensed guide if one is available. One guide may accompany two anglers, but they must be "in company" which, presumably, means they must be rather close together, either at the same pool or, at most, at adjacent pools. The only exception is that a resident angler may have not more than two nonresidents fishing with him if they are his bona fide, nonpaying guests. This is a featherbedding law since the province does not now guarantee the quality and abilities of its guides, and the hiring of one may not noticeably increase your catch. Wherever a guide is required by law, it is well worthwhile to make arrangements ahead of time for a good one.

In some other provinces and in the U.S., guides are not compulsory with the exception of such special situations as when an angler must fish from a boat or canoe, enter a forest area or for similar reasons.

An easygoing angler should be able to get along with almost any guide. The guide will be anxious to please and eager to see his angler catch fish. The life of a fishing camp revolves around the salmon that are taken. To have his sportsman bring in more fish, or a bigger fish than the other anglers is a guide's ambition, and he is often jealous beyond reason on this point. There is a certainty, however, that a guide wants his sportsman to catch fish and will work to that end.

Except in unusual cases, the guide is more familiar with the river than his sportsman. He is usually a better fisherman, as well. Even if he is not, the sportsman should show a certain deference for his opinions. It is a matter of courtesy to let the guide suggest the fly to be used when the fishing starts. If it is not successful, or if the guide's first few suggestions fail to raise a salmon, then the angler may try his own

Ted delivers the coup de grace to a 24-pounder . . .

. . . tricked by a #4 Jock Scott.

favorites without causing any antagonism. The average guide not only wants his fisherman to capture a trophy but also to be a part of its capture. If his fly selections fail after a fair try, he is usually glad to find his sportsman is able to produce a winner, and will have a high regard for his skill and judgment. When a sportsman implies the guide's advice and help are not needed, most guides tend to draw into themselves and react with the thought, "If he's so smart, let's see how well he can get along by himself. I'll live up to my duties as required, but no more."

A guide will suggest when to fish a pool and when to rest it, when to move on and when to stay. Often he will have flies of his own which he will lend you, flies he knows are effective because they have caught salmon in the past.

A good guide will follow a fisherman's fly with his eyes on every cast. He will almost use a fisherman as an instrument for placing the fly where he, the guide, wants it. He will say, "Shorten the line a little bit," or, "Cast a little more at an angle upstream," or, "Lower your rod a little now," and if the angler does his bidding, he will, in most cases, have the best possible chance of hooking a salmon.

The guide and the angler are a fishing team, and often both must work together in physical teamwork as well as in thought. The guide can take a position on a high bank or climb a tree for a good view of the pool from which the salmon in it will be visible, and from that vantage point, advise the angler just when a fish moves under his fly and what casting corrections should be made. The angler, with a low angle of vision, being unable to see the salmon move under his fly, will be able to fish much more effectively because of his guide's advice.

When both guide and angler step into a boat or canoe, the physical partnership becomes closer. The guide's contribution may be as little as propelling the boat to a good anchorage and sitting quietly while the angler fishes, or it may mean a difficult job of holding the boat or canoe in place in a fast flow with killick and pole. Some heavy waters are best fished from long canoes with two guides to man them. The mobility of the angler is an important factor in the playing of a fish. When the salmon runs out a great belly of line, and the swift and heavy flow is pressing against it, only a very stout leader will hold long against a fish. If a salmon heads seaward, the angler must follow. If the line is bent around any obstruction, a movement of the boat to the spot may be the only way to save the fish. When a salmon sulks, moving the canoe to a point downstream from the fish will most surely cause him to move. And when, at last, a great fish tires, and he can be brought to the side of the canoe and netted, there is a problem of holding both boat and fish in proper relation to the current to manage it. Simpler and safer is the practice of taking the angler to shore, where he may wade the shallow waters while he carries the struggle through its final stages, with the canoe at hand if the fish manages to work too far off shore again.

When the guide is also a canoeman or a boatman, this safe handling of his craft becomes as important as his knowledge of fishing. Then the angler's very life may well rest in his guide's hands as they shoot down through the swift and rocky flows, where inefficiency on the guide's part may spell anything from an unpleasant ducking to the possibility of drowning.

Where canoe travel is part of a trip, the fishing is usually better than where an angler can drive or fly right to a pool. With good fishing assured, the handling of a canoe and the safety factor involved naturally take on greater importance.

Some good canoemen consider the canoeing their real work. They will work hard and long in the canoe, poling upstream or poling and paddling down, but when it comes to the fishing, they will sit back and do little more than offer good advice. This may be very aggravating to the angler who feels a strong need for their help, but the remedy is a friendly approach and frequent requests for advice rather than stern looks and reproaches. In one sense, the job of running a canoe down a river, making camp, etc., is a pretty full time job. It is not reasonable to expect a guide to be working for you every minute of a sixteen-hour day, and if he does, there should be a certain gratitude on your part.

The fisherman to whom a guide is assigned should try his best to establish and maintain good relations. That does not mean he should forget, for a moment, who is employer and who is employee, or that he should be satisfied with less than a good, competent job of guiding. It does mean that he should endeavor to fish with his guide without antagonizing or embarrassing him. If a guide is remiss, he should be checked up politely but firmly, as it is in the fisherman's interest to maintain his guide's respect and good will. To antagonize him is to have his own fishing opportunities suffer. To try to change to another guide is often of doubtful value.

One of the maddest men I have ever seen came to our camp with a coast-to-coast background of trout fishing. He conversed authoritatively and frequently on the subject. His wife, who occasionally accompanied him on his fishing trips, but usually spent little time at fishing, was with him. She was a quiet woman, but had a twinkle in her eyes. Her simple comment that first night was that she did not know much about any kind of fishing but liked to be out on the water and hoped some day she would learn how to catch fish.

She drew one of the camp's best guides, a quiet man named Tom who had grown up on the river. Tom was polite but firm about salmon fishing. He would tell his charges how and where to cast and how to make the retrieve. If the cast was good and the retrieve well fished, he would say so or nod a little in approval. If not, he might say, "I believe the wind took your fly a little too far upstream that cast, ma'am, and the fly never tightened up and fished right."

Like most guides, Tom was a little touchy. If he felt his advice was being ignored, he would soon stop giving it and resort to simply answering questions from his fisherman. As it turned out, he and the lady got along famously. Whenever Tom told her she had made a poor cast, she only laughed and made a face, then tried again. Tom had it all worked out, and when she hooked a salmon, he talked her into playing it just as if it were a half-pound trout. She played it lightly and longer than usual, but she landed her first one and killed three of the five fish she hooked in her first three days.

Her husband's guide, Ned, was much like Tom, but a little younger and with more temper in his makeup. When they came in after the first morning's fishing, I could see that Ned was nettled. At the guides' lunch table, he muttered into his soup a little and passed a remark or two about "fellas that know all about fishing before they start."

One of the other guides said, "Well, anyway, your man seems to be able to cast well."

River of Ponds guide
Sam Shinnicks scrutinizes
a White Wulff, the first dry fly
he'd ever seen.

"Casting don't catch salmon unless the fly comes in right," was Ned's rejoinder. "Two salmon followed his fly, and he never even saw them and wouldn't believe me. Said he could see if a fish followed his fly. He wouldn't stay in one spot long enough to work a fish up to the point where it would take."

At the end of the third day, he had hooked one fish and lost it, so his score was nothing to his wife's three. He insisted they change guides. Next morning, he and Tom went off down the river, and his wife went out with Ned.

In 1940, a long hike through the woods was necessary to reach this outlying sod-roof fishing camp on the Serpentine River.

About midmorning, I stopped by to see how Tom was getting on with his new charge. While I watched, a salmon rose to his fly but failed to touch it. He stripped off a few feet of line and cast again. Tom sang out to him, "I think your cast is a little too long for that fish, sir." And when the angler failed to change his length of cast, Tom looked at me and shrugged.

I sat there and watched him cast for half an hour. He could cast beautifully, but he never did shorten his line quite enough. Finally I gave up and moved on.

At lunchtime, Tom told Ned where that salmon was. That afternoon Ned took the woman to the same spot and sure enough, when they came back that evening, they had the salmon and it was a good one.

I caught snatches of the couple's fishing progress over the lunch table during the next few days. He was not having much luck. He kept fishing too far beyond the fish he rose, or crowding out onto the fish itself. Salmon do not always lie in the deepest water as big trout tend to do. They are likely to hug the fairly shallow bars where the current is gentle. Instead of staying close to the shore and fishing nearby water, this man was always wading out and fishing far out into the stream where there was lots of deep and swift water but darned few salmon, if any. First thing you know, he would be standing in water over his knees right where the salmon had been lying, and, of course, the fish had taken fright and moved away. Even if he did put a fly to them in whatever spot they settled, then it would have been a miracle if one took it, according to Tom.

The thing was getting under this fellow's skin so much, and he was so ill tempered, that his wife just quit fishing altogether and went picking berries, or had Ned take her out to the old Indian campsite near the sea where they could search for arrowheads, lest she catch more fish and make the situation worse.

Miracle or not, a very big salmon finally took his fly and held it long enough to be captured on their seventh and final day of fishing. If it had not been for that, there might have been one more divorce on the books. The point is that a guide's judgment is important, and a poor fisherman can catch salmon if he or she will fish where the salmon are; the best caster in the world cannot catch one if he won't.

Guide Harry Hamilton watches the fly in the cold and rain as the author fishes.

There is a well-known story of the Scots guide, or gillie, whose angler had a nip from the bottle to celebrate each salmon as he beached it, but offered none to the guide. It ends with the gillie's refusal to go out with him again, remarking, "Him that drinks alone, fishes alone." What does a sportsman do about giving his guide a drink?

Liquor in the out-of-the-way salmon rivers is hard to come by. Some of the guides enjoy it. Some are indifferent. Some do not drink. There is no easy answer to fit all cases, but my reply to such a question, when I was running the camps, used to be, "There is no necessity to provide guides with drinks of liquor. They earn good wages and can afford to buy liquor just as they buy cigarettes, but drinks are somewhat social in their nature. If you do not drink yourselves, it is not necessary for you to have liquor for the guides. However, if you do drink, while it is not necessary that you provide any for the guides, it might be worthwhile for you to see that they have a drink in the evening, two at most. Drinking is a warm and friendly thing, a badge of fellowship, and sometimes has an appreciation beyond its worth. I would not give the guides a bottle, lest the distribution fail to be fair or lest it be emptied too quickly. I would suggest you call your guides in for a drink with you. Then, if you want to drink more yourselves, do it in the privacy of your cabins."

At the same time, my guides understood that their sportsmen owed them no drinks, no matter whether they drank inside the cabin or anyplace else. A drink together, for those who like it, can be a basis for mutual understanding. It can put employer and employee on a sound basis of companionship. Liquor also may be misused as a bribe or to loosen tongues, causing humiliation and embarrassment.

I have known men who were very reserved with their guides, who drank freely themselves yet gave the guides infrequent drinks, but who still enjoyed an excellent relationship together, while others, who shared drink for drink with the guides, have ended up with little respect for each other.

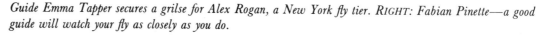

Guide Emma Tapper secures a grilse for Alex Rogan, a New York fly tier. RIGHT: Fabian Pinette—a good guide will watch your fly as closely as you do.

One guide of my acquaintance loves fishing only slightly better than drinking. He goes on a bender every so often. Between liquor bouts, he is an excellent guide. By giving him a few days off periodically, and a brief thumbnail sketch of his alcoholic proclivities to his "sports," we managed to please his charges and afford him a reasonable amount of the kind of work he loved. Any angler who insisted that he "have another" more than once, usually set that guide up for a premature drinking bout with the subsequent loss of fishing and companionship to all concerned.

Perhaps, because of the featherbedding law prevailing in some provinces that requires an angler to have a guide whether he needs one or not, there has come into being a great group of guides who are a far cry from the dedicated guides of old. As long as salmon fishermen come to their rivers, their summer's work is assured regardless of their knowledge or abilities as guides. Such men consider themselves more as companions and equals rather than temporary servants or workmen. They sometimes fish for and catch a fish that their fishermen could have caught if they had put them in their place and advised them how to fish it. On reaching a pool one such guide might say, "I'll take the upper half of the pool (the best half?), you fish the lower half. If you hook a fish I'll come down with the net."

They are being paid by the angler, and they are taking as much fishing pleasure in their day as he is and, because they are better fishermen, usually more fish. It is hard to justify cases like this but probably no harder than any other featherbedding where someone is paid for doing half a job or no job at all. If you have a good guide, treasure him.

Not only is there selfishness to consider but incompetence and lack of interest as well. A Newfoundland warden once forced a friend of mine to hire a guide who was dressed in street clothes and low oxfords and who didn't have a net. He refused to get his feet wet, and a salmon was lost in a vain attempt to beach him.

Some of today's guides have little knowledge of salmon, tackle, or techniques. They know where the pools are and simply take their fishermen to them. A novice fishing with such a guide has little chance of catching fish or learning much about salmon fishing. It is becoming more and more necessary for today's salmon fishermen to have studied the salmon, the tackle, and the techniques that catch them before they go fishing.

Reading the literature, seeking out experienced fishermen to question, joining a club discussion on salmon fishing, and attending a salmon-fishing school are becoming an increasing part of the learning process.

The indifference exhibited by "required" guides is a far cry from the customary practice, and hopefully, its spread will be slow. I like to think of the fine guides I've known. They were men and women of integrity who loved both nature and the sport. My life is much richer and my understanding of the wild world far greater for having known them.

Some sportsmen tend to take a superior attitude toward their guides because of their apparent lack of education or culture. The truth, often, is that both men are well educated but along different lines. A guide is usually a gentleman of his own area, a man of quiet dignity. I have known many guides who can neither read or write but who are educated in the things of importance and are adjusted to living in their isolated world

Maurice and Manuel Caines, Portland Creek guides, hold up a pair of mid-July salmon.

Charlie Mitchell poles up the Serpentine River in the days before outboard motors were common.

more completely than the fishermen they guide are educated or adjusted for living in theirs. How can a guide, who knows the precise habits of birds and animals of his area, who can build a snug cabin with no more to start with than his axe and the trees around him, who can travel unerringly across a trackless area he travelled only once before as a youngster, be considered ignorant or inferior?

Guides are often so impressed by the omniscience of their sportsmen they hesitate to talk much of their own backgrounds and of the interesting things around them. When the fishing is poor, as it sometimes must be, most guides, if encouraged, can add interest to the trip by showing their anglers the wildlife of the area, or by telling about the type of life they lead between salmon seasons. To a guide, the life of most sportsmen is a glamorous one. There is an interest and a fascination in the faraway cities with all their wonders. Their winters are long, and often, the mails are very slow in the north country. Anyone likes to be remembered. When the sportsman, taking his summer pictures, promises the guide a print or two and fails to send them, it may cause sadness that a friend could be so swiftly forgotten. When Christmas comes and goes and January makes its end without a Christmas card, a guide is a little more lonely than he need be. Guides themselves are notoriously poor writers, and many are shy about their inability with words on paper. Still, when the ice is broken with a card or note, it may be surprising how interesting the letters they send can be. Such as:

Dear Mr. Wulff,

The river was high all fall and the salmon had an easy time to get on to the spawning grounds. I trapped an otter and its fur was lustrous black. The snow has drifted right over the trees where you caught your big salmon and we had our lunch.

Next week my brothers and I are going into the woods to saw lumber. We'll be back before the ice goes out in time to get our gear ready for the lobster fishing. Then it will be time to think of salmon fishing again.

We talk of you often. I killed the gray rooster and made some flies. Not much to look at but when the time comes I think they will trick a salmon.

Your friend,

Jack

Barry Wulff with camp foreman Heb Caines—and his first salmon.

12

Miscellany

Releasing Fish

Of importance to anglers is the ability to catch and release a salmon, unharmed. In the early thirties, to release a salmon was considered heresy by both guides and anglers alike. Those were the days when Newfoundland had no limit on the number of salmon an angler might take and when parties fishing the Big Falls of the Upper Humber returned at the end of a week's trip with 300 to 400 fish. The general belief was that in order to bring a salmon to shore, he had to be played to utter exhaustion and would not recover. Since the great majority of fish were gaffed, it is obvious few had the chance to try.

Guides, in general, felt the played-out fish would not live after capture and were certain that, if returned to the water, they would never take a fly again. They were wrong on both counts. They were certain of one thing: salmon were good eating, and they (the guides) could use any the sportsman did not, whether they ate them themselves or fed them to their sled dogs.

In convincing guides and reassuring myself that salmon could be played out and released and would still live, I often carried fish I had captured uninjured, either by means of the tailer or by hand to pockets of water left high and dry by the falling of the rivers. When we returned to the pool a day or two later, we would find the fish fresh and lively in spite of his small enclosure and warmer-than-stream-temperature water.

At the camps, I built a dam on a tributary brook into which we put many fish that had been caught in the camp pool or nearby waters from which I could lead them upstream for a quick transfer from the main river. Not one in fifty of these fish died, and I am inclined to think that most of those that did, died from handling in getting them from the river to dammed pool, rather than from the rigors of playing and releasing.

This dam served a very useful purpose, for in the days before the icehouse or electric refrigeration, it was the best way to insure fresh salmon for the cook's unexpected demands, and for the newly arrived guests who looked down on the swimming fish from the little bridge by the cookhouse. They were exciting proof that the river held fish which were being caught.

The author brings
in a tired Adlatok
salmon for a
hand-tailing.

This Adlatok
salmon is ready for
release. Fish from
these fast pools tend
to be long and slim.

The question of returning salmon to the water brings up the usual practice of releasing grilse or small salmon to "grow up" and keeping the big ones. It is striking how notions so commonly held can be so fallacious. It is somewhat like the common fallacy of thinking a buck deer has horns as a weapon to protect the fawns and, therefore, does. His horns are growing and tender and useless from June to September when the fawns need protection most. From September to November he uses them to fight other bucks for a sexual advantage. Shortly after the rut, they fall off, and he is defenseless as a doe until September comes around again. Nature gave the doe hooves as sharp as a buck's, and those are her weapons, as they must be his, during the periods when the fawns are small and need the most protection.

Grilse rarely "grow up" to be very large salmon, as was shown earlier. There is every reason to believe that if a grilse spawns, his progeny will inherit his tendency to return to the river as a small fish. Whereas, by keeping the grilse, which have a lower commercial value in the market but which any sportsman should find equal to the large salmon for eating, and releasing the big salmon, the angler is putting back fish which should give to their spawn their own tendency of staying long at sea and returning as large fish, and which contain more spawn or milt per individual returned.

It would seem that keeping the big fish is a matter of wanting to show them off, and returning the runty salmon instead is a matter of ignorance of the salmon cycle, a situation which we can hope will be corrected in the interest of using the right breeding stock to best build up the fishing. The commercial view of limiting net mesh to "larger than a certain" size has similarly been worked out to let the commercial fishermen take the big, valuable fish and return the less marketable runts. In a thirty-year span of the records of one buyer of salmon in St. Johns, the average salmon's size had been cut more than half, and the quality of the commercial fishery, as well as the angling, dropped with it.

Race to the Fly

A remark is often made to the effect that the grilse were so thick it was impossible to catch a large salmon. Obviously, the people who say it believe it. They know salmon are present in a far greater proportion than they are being caught.

The pools below the Big Falls on the Upper Humber and on the Eagle are the main concentration point on each river in the early season for both salmon and grilse, but the fish rising to the fly are so predominantly grilse that an angler's catch may be fifty grilse to each salmon. Various reasons are put forth to explain this, but the one receiving most credence is that the grilse are faster and beat the salmon to the fly. When one considers there are often periods of half an hour without a rise in a spot where salmon, as well as grilse, are continually rolling to the surface, it is hard to believe those salmon have not had time to make up their minds and get the fly if they really want it. So, it can hardly be considered that the grilse have really robbed the salmon of all their chances at the fly. Perhaps, because the big salmon are more preoccupied with the falls they are less in a taking mood. Few who have seen the swiftness with which a mature salmon can take a fly accept as fact that a grilse can beat him to it.

Fishing Dead Waters

Many of our best salmon rivers flow through lakes. A lake is a sanctuary where a salmon can best escape from fishermen, poachers, birds, and other dangers. Rivers with

Shellbird Island Pool on the Humber River.

lakes in their flow will endure heavy fishing pressure. Those rivers in which there is no such sanctuary and where, from mouth to headwaters, salmon are subjected to a constant procession of flies, and where just one thoughtless rise can mean death, do not stand up as well.

Anglers not thoroughly familiar with salmon fishing often ask, "Why don't you fish the lakes?" The reply is, "If you find it difficult to take a salmon out there in the river where you know exactly where dozens are lying, how do you expect to catch the few fish scattered over 30 square miles of water?" Salmon may be caught in lakes just as well as in the flowing water. The problem is to find them and properly present a fly to them. The hope of trolling a fly blindly around a lake which salmon are known to cross with any assurance that many salmon will see it, is false, but wherever fish concentrate or settle in lakes, fishing can be quite rewarding.

Salmon in lakes will move to the inlets and outlets periodically, with their preference being the inlets. When the water in the rivers is very warm, the fish will often cruise the lakes during the days and nose into the current in the evenings for the hours of darkness. Salmon may be attracted even to very small brooks flowing into deep water. They can be seen cruising and jumping in the areas near any inflow but naturally tend to concentrate in the area of the tributaries they are most likely to ascend for spawning.

While a salmon in an eddy of a moving stream has the comforting effect of waters sliding along his sides, salmon in a lake must swim steadily to enjoy the same effect. They usually do. It is rare to find a salmon lying completely motionless in still water. In a still pool, they will usually make big circular swings, breaking their customary cruising to settle occasionally into whatever flow exists in a suitably deep or open section of the pool.

To fish for them, one should be able to see them or to know the pattern of their movements well enough to feel the fly is being presented to fish often enough to make the effort worthwhile. The dry fly is particularly effective when fish are in lakes and cruising near some small inflow of water. A dry fly, cast out to lie on the surface, will often draw a rise after it has rested there motionless for five or ten minutes. Salmon are caught both by twitching the fly and by leaving it alone when the fish have been seen approaching the vicinity of the floating fly. My feeling is that a really good fly, one that works well floating free on a river, will work best floating motionless on a lake. The motion of the fly also calls for motion of line and leader (which should also be sunk for best results, at least the leader). This may cause the fish to notice them and shy away. To have a fly on the water a maximum of time, cast it out and let it rest. The more casting, the more commotion, and the more time the fly is in the air. Readers may feel the insistence of keeping the fly within reach of the fish every second possible is being overemphasized. Few anglers realize how much time they waste changing flies, false casting, and unnecessarily pausing between casts. There is very little luck in salmon fishing once the spring waters or floods settle into normal flow. Salmon fishing is a sport that rewards the skillful so well that in no other fishing can one be more certain the best anglers will make the best catches, day after day.

Where only a few fish are caught in an experiment, it is difficult to make any conclusive observations. When fish are plentiful enough to experiment freely, one feels a little more certain of the correctness of the inferences drawn. There is a lake in one of the Newfoundland rivers that gave me an excellent opportunity to study still-water fishing for salmon. I first saw it while flying over the inlet in my seaplane. Looking down where the river flowed into the lake over a gravelly beach, I could see what appeared to be a dark ledge of rock extending out from the rippling of the inflow for 100 yards at an angle toward the deeper water. I circled lower and, as my shadow in the August sun crossed the "ledge," it disintegrated into literally hundreds of salmon. As always, my tackle was in the plane, and I landed.

For a while, the salmon would take almost anything. They would take a dry fly floating motionless, or one skidded across the surface, a wet fly fished slowly, or a wet fly ripped back through the water at top speed. When many of them had been hooked and released, and the catching became difficult, it was the small dry fly or the small, low-water wet fly, ragged as a nymph and fished slowly, that proved most effective.

That spot was my own private laboratory for a number of years. It was almost inaccessible except by plane, and no one else, apparently, knew the fish were there or, if so, thought they were not worth the trip. That is the only place where I have seen salmon lying motionless in still water. Often, when the lake was like glass, I have seen schools of fish showing their dorsal fins and tail tips motionless above the surface. At very first glance, they had looked like the tips of some water plant just breaking water. A bird flying over caused a flurry, and they were gone. There might be two or three tail tips in one spot and thirty in another, little groups scattered over a quarter of mile of surface. The flow of water over the shallow bar was too warm or too slow to draw them by its motion. They were listless fish, well up from the sea, waiting, waiting, waiting . . . for the waters to cool, the streams to flow full and the spawn and milt to ripen.

It was there I watched salmon rise to a dry fly in whitecaps so high the fly rarely floated more than a second or two before drowning. In fishing that slow, windswept, drifting water, the rises for the few seconds before the fly sank were many, but for the many seconds I let it drift with the flow in a sunken state, the rises were few. A small wet fly skimmed on the surface with the Portland Creek hitch was effective, but not, in my judgment, as effective as if fished under the surface conventionally. When working on any one spot, either method would produce rises after the other had been used to a point where its possibilities seemed to be exhausted.

Alain Prefontaine was the first to take a 20-pound salmon on a #16 single-hook fly, on the Moisie River in 1964.

Eventually I took a few trusted friends to the spot, some who had planes of their own. We rarely brought back any fish. A large proportion of the entire run of the river tended to gather there. To have opened it up to concentrated fishing, and the subsequent removal of those fish, would have increased the rate of decline of the run of that river, a decline which has been taking place steadily through increased accessibility and fishing pressure and a certain amount of poaching. The last time I looked over that pool on an August day, the other conditions were much as they were when I saw it first ten years before, but the salmon "ledge" was gone.

The Rise of the Tide

The dry spells mean a miserable time for the salmon. The rivers dwindle and the riverbeds become bleakly bright with their bare rocks glistening powder dry in the sun. The salmon huddle at the heads of the pools where the little bit of current can be found, or they crowd against one another to feel the soothing flow of cooler water from a trickle that was once a feeder brook. They leap little in such times, and few, if any, of them will move to chase a fly.

There was one such spell on the Little Codroy. Rain had threatened for weeks, but it never fell. Daily, I wandered along the banks and fished without much success. Occasionally, I sought the fish at the head of the tide rise without seeing them, until one evening just before my time for departure. That evening there was a high tide just at dusk, and I could not resist that one last chance at the tidal fish. Salmon, I reasoned, may try to run the river tonight, and if they do, they will come in on the evening tide, one of the highest for the month. After working the water over once without a rise, I settled myself at the head of the Spruce Pool in position to fish the deep, black water and waited. The angler who stands quietly and becomes an immobile part of the background may see, in a few hours, more live fish than the constantly moving angler sees in a lifetime.

The sun sank without a salmon having broken the quiet surface of the pool. I cast listlessly as the water rose higher and higher around my legs. The flood tide was filling the pool and exerting its farthest pressure, for above that point it could not go. At last, in the growing darkness, I saw salmon coming up the river.

At first it was just a swirl at the tail of the pool and then a few dark shapes over near the far bank. Gradually, the whole bar at the head of the pool began to fill up with them. Cautiously, I waded a little farther out on the bar until I was a third of the way across the stream with the water slightly above my knees. I waited. The salmon that had drifted away at my approach began to drift back. They even filled the water over the bar between me and the shore. I had never had so many salmon come so close to me. There were big fish, too, and the sight of so many of them set my heart to pounding. When they were fully settled and used to me, I flicked my fly out gently. The motion of the light rod was easy and, since there were no shadows, the fish were not alarmed. The dry fly floated slowly over a solid patch of salmon before it was quietly retrieved. They showed no interest and little fear on that or on any of the repeated casts following. They moved slightly if the line touched their backs; that was all. With slow, deliberate movements, I changed flies, but none evoked even the slightest response. Then, when it seemed useless to fish longer, I merely stood and watched, marvelling at the urge that drove them into

Joan Wulff shows off a salmon from the Restigouche.

The majestic Lower Humber was once a river of very large salmon.

such dangers, through all the hazards of the shallow waters, and the dangers from men and beasts and birds that might prey on them. These were Atlantic salmon, beautiful, trim fish that can lift themselves from their feeding grounds on the ocean floor to the cloud-blanketed heights where they spawn. I touched one with the tip of my rod. He stirred slightly and moved away a few inches to touch another fish and then drift slowly back to the same spot again.

I thought of the little group of fishermen who were waiting out the bad conditions of the drought up at the inn. Those men were discouraged, tired and listless, but no more so than the salmon for which they were fishing, salmon deadlocked by low waters they were powerless to pass. I watched them until the light faded, then cut across the fields to the road leading back to the fishermen's hotel, leaving the weary, blue-gray shapes to mill slowly in the waters of the Spruce Pool as the tide reached its flood, then to turn back with the falling of the tide to the cool, safe bay while they waited for rain or until an urge they could not deny again forced them to work their way upstream as far as they could go.

The Fishing Calendar

As an intensely interested fisherman who fished the inaccessible rivers alone, and as a one-time fishing-camp operator, it has been my privilege to check several of the more widely circulated fishing timetables. If any fish in fresh water is likely to be affected by tides or by any periodic earth pattern, other than the differing visibility of day and night, it should be the salmon. With no real interest in food, and a tendency to rise to a fly generally attributed to mood or whim or restlessness, it would seem no other fish could be so easily dominated by sunspots, tidal surges, or the nearness of Mars.

There have been and probably always will be fishermen's calendars which will promise to save an angler a good deal of time by assuring when he will catch the most fish. Unfortunately, as soon as an angler becomes an advocate of such a system of periodic fishing, he ceases to be an impartial judge. Since he "skips" the "poor" periods he can never know how good they are!

If one fishes for pleasure and for interest, it is foolish to sit on the porch when one could be fishing. No table will tell you when a salmon cannot be caught, for as sure as such a statement is made, its maker will as surely be surprised. At a time when fishing was slow, one dedicated addict of the sun-and-tide-table variety was offering bets at the camp lunch table that he could tell when fish would be caught. He got his timetable out and gave us the hot periods. The young nephew of one of the guests had been gazing casually out of the window. Suddenly, he piped up, "When is it you say a salmon won't be caught?"

A look at the table brought back the reply, "From noon till two."

"You'd better look over your shoulder, sir," said the boy, pointing. "There's a salmon down there that didn't read your book." While he had been watching, his uncle had hooked a salmon in the camp pool, and we all turned to look through the windows at the bending rod and the flashing leaps of the fish. No one swallow makes a summer, but one nonconforming salmon makes a man glad he did not give up that moment of fishing for *any* reason.

Guide R. Pinette holds the catch that made Lucien Rolland, left, the third member of the 16-20 charmed circle of anglers.

The Amateurs' Table

Fishing conditions were typical of early July at the camps, when the lunch-table talk began to turn frequently to the work of the guides in tailing or netting an angler's fish. Although we preferred tailer or nets to be used, there was no hard and fast rule. The old guides, who had little faith in a tailer and a lot in their gaff, continued to use them. One angler, who had lost a fish at gaffing early in the week, had started discussions on the subject. Another angler lost a fish similarly, and after the original sufferer lost a second fish when the gaff struck his leader, the problem grew serious. There was talk of a new guide to remedy the situation, and even more talk of the poor quality of the guides in the gaffing department.

These two Moisie salmon were taken on a #16 Prefontaine skater.

The suggestions were many as to how the guides should do the job, mostly along the line of sneaking out more quietly or having longer-handled gaffs. The main complainant requested that I have his guide put his gaff down into the water in a good position, hook up, so that he could draw his salmon right over it, and then the guide could come up on the fish and be sure of hitting him. That, he claimed, was the way his guide had handled fish so well at Anticosti.

I do not like gaffs for salmon, though I have gaffed a good many. I told him I would not permit a guide to gaff that way since the probability was the gaff, if it did go home in the fish, would sink into his soft belly flesh and would fail to hold and would cause the fish to die if he got off, or else would wound the fish without a real chance to hold him. My suggestion was that he should not try to hurry the guide. If they worked together, there should be no problem, and, I told the assemblage, "This is the amateurs' table. You men need a guide to go out there and catch a salmon. There is not a guide in the group who cannot catch a salmon entirely on his own without any help from anyone else. It is not reasonable to think they do not know how to gaff salmon, for they have all proven they can. It is only necessary for you to give them a good chance. Don't pressure them into taking a chance at a fish by saying you can't hold him, or for any other reason. If you play him till he's ready, I'm sure they will miss very few fish."

Running a salmon-fishing camp has its problems, but it has its interesting moments, as well. For a good angler, it sharpens his wits to take the less popular pools or the worked-over water and still produce his share of fish. The ability to go out and cast a fly into the teeth of a 30-mile-an-hour wind when a customer has just come in with a 12-foot rod and said it cannot be done, tells that man more effectively than can any words that there are few conditions under which a fly cannot be fished with some effectiveness, or that an occasional salmon cannot be caught. The salmon fisherman who thinks that because *he* cannot do a thing, it cannot be done, has ceased to learn. A return of the thirst for learning gives such a man new interest. At any rate, Fortune smiled the following day when the complainer and his guide were returning to the main camp for lunch. They passed me, waist deep in heavy water, trying my first dry-fly fishing of the season. I was using a 2-ounce, 6-foot fly rod, a #6 fly, and a 5-pound-test leader point. As they drew abreast in the boat, a fish took my fly, and the complainer pulled out his watch.

The salmon weighed 15 pounds. He made some good runs, jumped a half a dozen times, and then let me work him in close. It is easier to bring a fish close and hold him in deep water than in shallow water. He is less fearful. If you stand still and make deliberate movements, the fish are not likely to take fright. Had I tried to bring him into shallow water or to beach him, that fish would have taken much more time, but I worked him in close and, reaching down with my left hand, grabbed him securely by the tail. A fish that would not run and tire himself out, or one that would have headed for the sea, could have taken his full quota of time or more, but I had struck the right fish for the moment. Walking over to their boat, I dropped the salmon into it with a request that they take it up to camp, since I was walking and would have to carry it. The elapsed time was just six minutes. There was less talk about superior fishermen and inferior guides at the dining table for the rest of his stay.

Local Competition

Local competition in salmon fishing is the toughest sort. The visiting fisherman is hard put to take fish when there are very many local fishermen on the river. It works out this way. The local lads know the rivers from top to bottom. With a resident salmon license priced at only a few dollars, a fish or two will pay for it. If a local angler spends his spare time fishing, he may well get a fair return in valuable food, as well as his sport.

With salmon selling for sixty cents a pound and up in the local market, a 10-pound fish was worth a couple of hours of fishing. Now, with the pound price in dollars, there is more and more monetary reward to the local fisherman. Salmon fishing is a lot more productive than playing checkers, and often, more fun.

The local anglers learn all the places where salmon lie. When they cover a stretch of river, practically every salmon in it sees their fly, and sees it in a way that has drawn rises before. They waste no time on the empty spaces. The visitor fishing the same water without a guide is going to spend more than half his time fishing salmonless water, and when he does fish over salmon, he will not know the exact cast most attractive for each lie. His chance of catching a salmon is roughly one in twenty compared to a good local fisherman *unless* he has some very effective fly that is not used by the locals.

If the visitor has a guide, he can expect to fish almost as consistently over fish as the local fisherman does, but he will still not do quite as well at placing the fly. The chances are he will not catch as many as his guide would in the same amount of time. This is due to the unfamiliarity with the best casts for any given spot and the difficulty a guide has in explaining what is needed. The guide explains. The angler tries a cast. The guide shakes his head. Another cast, another headshake. Perhaps four or five casts are required before the fly swings the way the guide says it should. The guide (or local fisherman) could have done it right the first time, in one-fifth the time it takes the visitor, even though he has the benefit of the guide's complete knowledge.

How well a good fisherman with complete knowledge of the salmon's lies can take the cream off a pool is not often realized. One afternoon, I landed my seaplane at a pool that had not yet been fished during that season. I wanted to take pictures of salmon in midjump. In the afternoon hours between two and dusk, I caught twenty-eight fish and released twenty-seven of them. The next morning, I fished the same pool until noon and took two fish. After a week of rest, the fishing would have been almost as good as when I first struck the pool, but none of the salmon I played out could be expected to

A fishing camp in the wilderness.

take the fly after so short an interval, any more than if local fishermen had taken them out of the pool.

The visiting angler has the best chance when the fish are coming in from the sea or running through the river. At such times, new fish are coming into the pools each day. If the visitor gets to the pool at the same time the local man does, they share the available water and the opportunities to take fresh fish are more or less equal. If the local lad covers the pool before the visitor wets a line, the chances are far from equal. If the fish are not moving through the river, as when the water is low and clear, the fish of an accessible pool will all have been worked over, often for days, and will be very diffficult to draw to a fly. The easy fish will have been taken, and only the tough ones remain.

Manners in Fishing

Fishing manners, like social customs, are subject to change. In the last forty years, salmon fishing has changed more than in the previous century. The number of salmon anglers has grown rapidly and promises to continue its growth as long as there is room for more salmon anglers to crowd in.

Three decades ago, it was rare to have to share a pool, even on waters open to the public. Now it is sometimes a problem to find a place to step in between casting anglers, where one can both reach a fish and not tangle with other lines. There are pools where, in order to fish, an angler must join a procession of men who have spaced themselves a short distance apart and who move, continually casting, down through the pool to its tail, where each one returns to the head of the pool to start through it again. There are other pools where an angler simply seeks a station from which he can reach a salmon and stays there until his fishing time is done, for there is no other nearby water left for him to fish.

In view of such conditions, it is difficult to advise on mannerly conduct. What happens to the dry-fly angler who wants to fish upstream while three wet-fly anglers are taking turns working their way down the pool? How long should a fisherman cast to a fish he has raised, when several others are fishing toward him? Should he make them go around him, or should he give up on the fish and move on down the pool? Answers to these and related questions would try the wisdom of a Solomon.

Where an angler wades with relation to the salmon is important not only to himself but to other anglers who may be interested in fishing the same waters. Salmon frequently lie in water of wading depth at the side of deep pools instead of near their centers. A wading angler may, unknowingly, disturb these fish, causing them to move off into deeper water where they will be much harder to attract with a fly. Where an angler is fishing completely alone, the only damage is to the angler's own fishing, but where other anglers may be interested in fishing the same waters, either simultaneously or in sequence, it is damaging to their fishing, as well. Canoes or boats, especially those equipped with outboard motors often disturb the fishing in a pool.

These situations are far more frequent than one might suppose. Anglers who do not know the pools well, or are strangers to the river, often, out of ignorance, wade where the fish would normally be lying, and fish where they normally would not. If an angler is fishing strange water without a guide, it would be a courteous thing for him to ask local fishermen near whom he is fishing, whether the path on which he plans to wade

A big male (left) and a 12-pound female (right) were taken from the early run on the River of Ponds.

the pool will disturb the salmon or affect their fishing. The question will serve two purposes, prevent him from the possibility of spoiling their opportunities and will result, in most cases, in their pointing out to him just where the fish are most likely to be.

Etiquette on the salmon river depends upon the locality and the situation. The angler who can conform to the local pattern will create the least inconvenience. My hope is that you, gentle reader, find salmon fishing where you may spend your fishing hours with salmon beneath your fly and no one else impatient to get at them, where you will have time to fish thoughtfully for a fish and come back to fish for him again the following day. Unless you can do these things, you will never know quite how thrilling salmon fishing can be. I hope if we meet, we shall so share the fishing that neither of us shall have any regrets as a result.

Late Fall Fishing

The coming of fall and frosty nights can bring a change in the salmon. Their interest in flies lessens, and they seem depressed by the cold. Their taste in flies seems to change, reverting, as it were, to the bigger, brighter flies that are effective in the early cold and high waters, though their interest is nowhere near as great.

This situation was once brought home to me afresh in cold fall days on the southwest Miramichi. There was frost each night, and every morning the pails on the porch were filled with ice instead of water. As angler and adviser for a movie short on salmon fishing, I was granted a lot of good water to fish on with no competition. The pools had been rested, and the salmon should have been more than willing to take a fly. They were not.

The best hours were from eleven in the morning until three in the afternoon. Before that time, the fish would not rise to my flies. In a week of fishing, I did catch

The author and Perley Palmer hooked this late fish from the Miramichi on a Mickey Finn Streamer.

eleven salmon and fourteen grilse but, in order to take most of them, had to resort to 3/0 flies which I had not used for years but carried for just such emergencies. The Miramichi is normally a river where small flies are quite deadly, and the big, heavy irons were unusual, for the water varied from low to very low.

An angler going salmon fishing at a time when fall's first frosts may strike, can do worse than carry a few such large and heavy flies in the conventional patterns that take well early in the season: Silver Grey, Mar Lodge, Black Dose, and the like. Even though, up to that time, there had been a gradual reduction of the most effective fly size until the most successful fishermen were fishing generally with eights and tens, when the waters cooled rapidly under nightly frosts, the preferred fly size suddenly zoomed upward.

An interesting incident happened on this trip. The cameraman was Douglas Sinclair, and he wore a bulky, down-filled coat as protection against the cold winds above his waders. The producer of the RKO-Pathe film short was Early Luby, 250-odd pounds of solid strength. We were at Burnt Island Brook Pool hoping to catch a good salmon to highlight the film. Up to that time we had only a ten-pounder as our star fish.

The pool was rough and broken up by great rocks. The water was swift, and wading was difficult. I hooked a salmon of about 18 pounds and played him through his wild jumps and runs to a docile state while the camera recorded it. Turning to Doug, I asked if he could wade out close to where I stood in the fast water, suggesting that hand tailing that good-sized salmon in such difficult water would be dramatic. Doug nodded assent. Soon he reached a point within about 8 feet of me and signaled he was ready.

I turned to the fish. I worked him upstream into a good position for the camera, bracing myself against a rock to hold onto in the swift flow. I reached the tail, closed my hand in a solid grip, and lifted the fish from the water. As I turned to the cameraman, to walk past him to the shore for the shot we'd planned, I faced a lot of white water and a hand that, while holding the 35mm Eymo camera, was slowly subsiding into the waves.

For a moment there was no trace of Doug. Then he surfaced, walrus-like in his great coat, and was swept downstream.

Earl, who had been watching from the shore, waded out downstream, reached Doug as he went by, and they both waded ashore. The camera was soaked, the film ruined. In my futile effort to reach Doug I'd lost the salmon, so the star fish of that film was just a ten-pounder. Making movies of salmon fishing does involve a great deal of luck.

The Best Time of Day

As to the best time of day for best fishing, there are too many varying conditions to be considered to allow for any hard and fast rule. The evening period of activity is a general favorite. Then the air is usually warm, though cooling off, the wind has dropped a little, the salmon can mark off another day on their calendar and have night's soft blanket on its way to cover them over with her cloak of safety.

The first angler to work through a pool in the morning must also be considered to have a particularly good chance to catch fish. If this is around sunup or a little later, it is ideal. If the river is heavily fished, the first cast will probably be at the crack of dawn and may be the only one for the day in which an angler can be certain he is fishing a "rested" salmon.

In the early or very late season, when the water is cold, salmon take well during the sunlight hours and best in the early afternoon. In low, warm water, the cooler periods of morning and evening are more productive. My own choice would be, by and large, the period just after the sun strikes the water in the morning, and just after it leaves it in the evening.

Salmon will take a fly at night as well as in the daytime. I have fished late at night enough to know this is true, but not enough to make any worthwhile comparison, though it took me longer to catch salmon at night than in the daytime when I made the test. Night fishing is for the owls. I have also played quite a few other salmon hooked as night fell and landed well after dark, in addition to the three I took at midnight, but it is not much fun. An angler cannot see his fly. He cannot see where he is wading. The playing of a fish loses its precision and becomes a fumbling thing. The casting is a travesty of a good water coverage.

Transplanted Salmon

With intensive fishing, the effective fly size on a given river decreases. It is an amazing and a wonderful thing to see how quickly the new generations of salmon on hard-fished waters, particularly the smaller rivers, learn to avoid the larger flies and, with the passage of years, to rise less and less to any fly.

The Ecum Secum, a small Nova Scotia river, gave a remarkable example of this trait. A point was reached more than fifty years ago when the stock of salmon native to the river had dwindled greatly, and the remaining fish were not "good takers." A large planting of fry was made, and three or four years later, the first crops of salmon and grilse from that planting returned from the sea and brought with them excellent fishing. The new salmon were readily distinguished from the native salmon by their physical characteristics. They took large flies readily and formed the bulk of the fish caught. In another fifteen years of concentrated fishing, these new fish had learned to rise only to very small flies, and many of them had become "nontakers" also. At that time, another stocking was made with exactly the same results, producing a third type of salmon that took well at first and then tapered off to small flies or none at all in recent years. This avoidance of danger, by a fish that goes to sea with a length of 6 inches or less and no experience with artificial flies, yet comes back with its weight of full maturity and this uncanny knowledge or developed instinct of fly avoidance, after only a few generations, is truly remarkable.

Fact and Fancy

The intensity with which many anglers study salmon, and their interest in discussing them, were exemplified late one night at Mike Tompkin's lodge on the Grand Codroy. Jack Meehan and I, in making a survey of Newfoundland's west coast salmon rivers, had come there for the night, arriving just in time for a late supper. When the meal was over, we sat in the common room and talked about salmon. The minutes flew by, and at midnight we were still talking quietly. All the other men in camp had long since retired.

Apparently we mentioned the subject of grilse spawning, and I asserted that in Newfoundland, at least, I had definite proof that grilse spawned. We had gone on to another subject when we heard the patter of bare feet, and a very old man in a nightshirt and sleeping cap burst into the room.

"I've been listening to you fellows through the wall," he said, "and I want to tell you grilse do not spawn. A great Norwegian scientist has made thorough scientific tests, and there's no longer any question about it." With an admonishing shake of his finger, he disappeared behind the door, and we heard his footsteps diminishing down the hall on his roundabout way to his room.

Later on, I got to know him well. A retired clergyman, he had fished for salmon in many places, and he fished well. Unfortunately, his knowledge of the fish themselves was not up to his fishing skill, and while his catches tended to give his words the ring of authority, his concepts of the salmon were sometimes in error. In at least a dozen fishing spots in Newfoundland, I met men who passed on his ideas as gospel. Knowing he was at a nearby fishing camp one day when I caught both a grilse with milt and another with near-ripe spawn, I sent them over to him by a salesman who was travelling that way.

On another occasion, a warden supervisor, in telling of his knowledge of salmon and their interesting cycles, advised a group of sportsmen that salmon shed their skins. "They get dark and slimy and coarse by the end of the winter under the ice," he said, "and just before the breakup, they shed their old skins like a snake and have a bright new one underneath just as if they'd come in from the sea." On the grounds that a skin like that would be very valuable as an exhibit for some of the American angling clubs to see, I asked if he could get me one or two of the shed skins. He felt he could, and when I said I knew several clubs whose members would chip in 100 dollars for one for their clubrooms, he readily took an order for three.

The spent salmon's "shedding," or change from his stream coloring after spawning, to a typical sea coat for his return to the salt water in the same way the parr suddenly take on saltwater dress as smolts while still in the stream, had fooled him into thinking they must shed their skins. So it is with many theories and suppositions about this unusual fish. They are likely to be false, and the listener had best be careful to check his sources thoroughly.

A Puzzling Situation

A group of us were relaxing after lunch on the high bank overlooking the home pool one day when the spring runoff had turned Portland Creek into a wide, wild ribbon of churning, swirling water. The first salmon had been taken in the upper tributaries a few days earlier, but the chance of catching a salmon near the main camp at that time was too slim to warrant fishing. No one had yet seen a salmon jump there. Suddenly a salmon did jump near the middle of the flow. It jumped again. There was something unusual about the jumps. It did not leap normally.

With sudden inspiration, I called to the boys who were nearby, "Get a net or tailer, take a dory quickly, and go out and get that fish. He's having a fit and I think you can catch him." It took the youngsters a bit of time to get organized, and perhaps two minutes elapsed before they reached the middle of the flow. The salmon, meanwhile, had kept up its weird antics, skittering on the surface, leaping high, and falling flat to the water. It was, apparently, all but spent and unable to leap any longer and sinking when one of the boys put a tailer over its head and noosed him around the middle. He was dead when they reached shore, with no blow administered.

They brought back a female salmon. She bore no mark other than that caused by the pressure of the tailer and looked, in every respect, like a normal, beautifully proportioned fresh-run salmon of about 10 pounds. The fish not only looked perfectly normal, inside and out, but tasted in every respect as it should have. I can only assume that my intuition had been somewhere near correct. It comes as a shock that a salmon may suddenly lose its mental and physical balance and go into convulsions just as might be expected in a higher form of life. The incident is included here only because I saw it happen, and it puzzles me.

The Odds

Whenever anyone begins to think he can be sure of the action of a salmon, he is usually due for a come-uppance. The only time I ever bet I could hook a particular fish that had risen to my fly and missed, I lost. It was with a G.I. on the Gander. I had caught four grilse in the previous half hour and was as sure as I could be that the fish of the bet, a grilse, would rise again. Apparently the G.I. had not had much casting practice, and his tackle left a lot to be desired. He was one of a group who had come to the river to see what salmon fishing was like, and he had not caught a fish. He had seen me catch and release my two previous fish, and, when he saw me raise this one, said, "Bet a buck you can't take him."

It was a cinch bet, I thought. I never raised that grilse again, or, as a matter of fact, did I catch another that morning. Since that time I have not bet about salmon, except once. Some years ago, Dave Forman and his son, from Buffalo, were fishing Portland Creek and not having much luck. I explained that River of Ponds, a short seaplane flight away, was an easier place to catch fish, and, if they wanted to go over, I was sure they would have some action. In discussing just how good it was, I said I was sure we could land at a pool where, in the first three casts with a dry fly, I would have at least two rises.

Dave said, "Would you bet on that?" I felt constrained to say yes. I was not worried about winning it, but there is something about salmon fishing that makes me feel out on a limb whenever I make such a definite statement.

We slid onto the lake, taxied up to the pool and got ready to fish. I stood back waiting for them to try, but Dave insisted, "All right, now! Let's see your rises." I dropped a dry fly out onto the oily-looking water I knew was loaded with fish, and, before it had floated a foot, a grilse poked his nose at it. I did not strike because I did not want to spoil their fishing. I cast again, farther upstream, and another fish rolled up under the fly, failing to take. Dave said, "O.K., we believe you. C'mon, Jimmy, let's fish."

And fish they did. Dave was a skillful caster, and Jimmy was coming along pretty well. They covered the water thoroughly with their casts for two hours and did not raise a fish. I had been bringing my log book up to date and polishing up the plane a bit while this was going on, and as soon as I finished, Dave said, "O.K. Lee! What have we been doing wrong? Suppose you step out and catch one."

You must have guessed already that I could not raise a fish, although that is about the only time in hundreds I have gone to that pool and not caught at least one.

Timing the Run

No one knows just when the salmon will enter a river. No one knows in advance just when the fishing will be best. While this may be a headache for an angler, for a camp operator it is more like a nightmare. It is easy enough for an angler to ask for "The best two weeks of the run" and to accept the camp operator's judgment of "a good time to be here." Suppose the rivers have gone low. The early fish have pushed through, and the later runs are hanging off in the salt water. There are a few fish in the river, but the fishing is not good.

A day of rain will put the river in fine shape, draw in a new run from the sea, pep up the stale fish already in the river, and, in all probability, produce the very best days of the season. If no rain comes, the fish in the stream will become even more listless and harder to catch. Very few new ones will come in. The chances of rain are good, as such a dry period is most unusual. The customer is a thousand miles away. If the camp operator advises a cancellation, he is losing two weeks out of a six-week season for a complement of guides, a cook, and a cabin. His overhead goes on, but he gets no return. He will usually let the party come if there is a possibility of catching even a few fish. If he feels there is almost no chance for the party to get a few salmon, he will, reluctantly, cancel.

A doctor coming to a camp under such conditions and failing to catch fish, once upbraided the camp operator and demanded a return of his money, all of it, because he was sure the operator had not given him the "two best weeks." That time of season was usually good and normally produced the river's best catches, but a patient explanation of the situation did not appease the medical man who happened to be an obstetrician. In desperation, the camp owner finally explained it this way, "Doc, when you undertake a delivery, you know the woman is going to have a baby, but you don't tell her it will be delivered at three o'clock on a certain afternoon half a year away, and if it misses by a week, give your services free, do you? I know the salmon are coming in each year, and we'll have two weeks of wonderful fishing, a couple more weeks of decent fishing, if we're lucky, still another week or two of fishing of sorts and that's our season. We know when the best time should be, but it has been at the early part of the six-week spread in some years and at the tag end in others. If we knew for sure just when the best two weeks would be, we'd just open our camps for those two weeks, charge three times as much and be as happy as clams."

When a salmon angler, who has long ago made the arrangements, comes to a salmon river just as the fish are due to enter, he may face a period of waiting after his arrival. This can be difficult. I recall a case where an angler wanted some time on the River of Ponds. He had been there the previous year, from the twentieth of June until the twenty-eighth and had enjoyed what turned out to be the finest fishing of that season. Making a late decision to come again, the only space available on that river was from June eighteenth until the twenty-sixth. Our timing on the River of Ponds called for fish to be in the river for sure by the twenty-third. We had caught them as early as the seventeenth of June in one year, and the first fish had been as late as the twenty-fifth in another. I explained the situation, said I could not guarantee fish, but since he knew the risk involved and that from his own experience he knew they probably would be in, he could come if he wanted to gamble. He did. Neither he nor his guest caught a salmon. Situations like this make salmon fishing difficult. They make the good times, when the rivers are right, all the more to be appreciated.

In the case just mentioned, I believe there were some salmon in the river before he left, because the next party in caught several on the day after he went out. I do not think he fished as hard as he might have his last few days. It is easy to become discouraged under those conditions. The early fish do not jump much. One jumping fish then represents a dozen jumpers later on when a bigger percentage of the salmon will be in a mood to leap. Because the fish are rarely seen above the surface, it is hard to know

The perfect trophy.

where they may be lying. The rivers are usually flush to the banks and often flooding up into the alders and over the low, streamside meadows. There is water everywhere, and the pools exist more in the memories of the guides than in reality.

It takes a perseverance few men can claim to keep on fishing over a great flood of water after two or three days go by without a rise, without a sign of a leaping salmon, or at best, one or two sighted leaps. It is little wonder the fisherman becomes half-hearted in his fishing and tries only the guide's most certain recommendations. It is all too easy for the angler to say, "I guess they're not in yet," and for the guide to agree with "I guess not, but the tides are high, and they should be here tomorrow."

Then, when the falling waters have helped define the pools and a fish or two has been taken, and everyone is fishing with new enthusiasm, the fish will really "come in." Often, when the fish have been a week or more late in being caught, among the first few taken will be some with the hard line between blue-black back and silver side already fading and a tarnish on their sides that can only be the product of more than a week's time in the river. I am sure that in almost every case, there are more fish in the river than the early fishermen are willing to believe, but they are so spread out the chances of taking them are slim. The obvious thing to do when fish are due but not yet being caught is to fish as steadily and as earnestly as your hopes and interest will allow you. An angler can do no more.

The Toughest Fish

The most difficult salmon to play out I ever captured is covered by my notes for an August day on Harry's River. The river was fairly low, and three of us had walked in to the then-difficult-to-reach Lower-Dee Pool. Harry's is a clear river and was one of Newfoundland's finest. A large lake lies at its head, and many large salmon lay in the 20-mile stretch between the lake and the salt water.

After an unsuccessful coverage of the pool with both wet and dry flies, I climbed the high western bank and sat looking over the waters below me. I spotted salmon here and there, grey shadows above the varicolored rocks of the streambed, made indistinct by the overlapping water currents. But I saw no big ones until some slight movement drew my eyes to the far side of the stream where the water was comparatively shallow. Watching steadily while the water alternately cleared and grew blurred, I finally made out three good salmon lying close together. They weren't monsters, but it would take some good fishing or a lot of luck to beat any one of them out for top honors for the day.

They were below the area we had covered in our previous fishing. My companions had gone up the trail to the upper pool. In crossing to the far bank below the pool, the water came to the top of my waders and a little spilled over. Once against the alders, I hugged the shore, for the sun was at my back and I feared a moving silhouette might alarm the fish. As carefully as I could I eased out into the stream again until I stood 40 feet from the white rock by which I had marked down the salmon. Then I stood quietly until my eyes became used to the light on the water, and I could make out the three long, greyish shapes.

In a few minutes I could see the salmon plainly, and I knew they could see me, too. I waited perhaps ten minutes before starting to cast. Then I dropped my white fly over their heads and let it drift down about 6 feet below their tails before picking it up and dropping it down on their heads again.

The casting was steady and rhythmic. The fish showed no interest and made no movements, nor did I expect them to . . . at least, not right away. The sun was too bright and the salmon in the pool were not generally active, even though there were many new salmon among them, part of a run that had entered the lower river about ten days earlier. They were lying in shallow water rippled by some big sunken boulders. I was certain the continual drifting of the dry fly over them would eventually cause one to rise.

Time went by and I could make them out more plainly, the largest fish in the center with the two flanking fish somewhat smaller. I judged them to be from 20 to 25 pounds. I timed my casts at about ten to the minute. With the big bucktail-winged fly there was no need for false casting to dry it off. It was simply a matter of a pickup and a single cast out again for the very short float over the fish. I looked at my watch to find that twenty minutes had gone by. Still there was no sign any of the salmon had even noticed the fly passing over them so continually.

There were beautiful cloud formations to watch, whiskey-jacks scolding from the trees. There was the river itself to gaze upon and enjoy, and the broad slopes with an endless variety of patterns of sun and shadow. There was a temptation to close my eyes and listen to the sounds of summer and to doze in its warmth. But such things were not for me. My eyes stayed glued to those salmon.

Finally one moved. Not much of a movement, just the slight push of his tail to carry him a little to one side of the fly as it drifted over him. I concentrated on the fish that had moved, the one nearest me. He moved again a few casts later. Ten casts further along, he lifted up just beneath the fly and sank again after it passed over him. The following cast he lifted again, let the fly pass, drowned it with his dorsal and tail as he went down. That was all. From then on he stayed motionless as a log.

At the end of an hour he still hadn't moved, but the center fish, the largest one, left his position and leisurely poked his nose up at the fly. He did not open his mouth to take it. For another five minutes there was no movement from any of the fish. I changed to one of my smaller grey flies for fifteen minutes without result. I went back to the white one again. These were the days before I had developed as wide a dry fly coverage as I use now. After a few casts with the big white fly, the far fish moved restlessly. I concentrated on dropping it right on his nose every time. He lifted toward the fly a second time, then for twenty or more casts showed no interest. Then the fish nearest me crossed over the other two fish to take the fly, and, already turned away from me, he made his first run well over to the far bank. At that time I was using one of my early light outfits, a 7-foot, 2½-ounce rod, a 3⅜-inch reel, and 150 yards of backing. The water was heavy and deep, and it was a tough pool to wade.

Things happened quickly, and the line went off and on my reel and off and on again. My big worry was keeping the line from fouling on large rocks that came above water well out in the pool. Once the fish did curve around a boulder but when I waded out the line slid clear. The fish reeled off three cartwheels in a row, then abruptly settled to the bottom. From my position below him, I began inching him back toward me. Soon he was almost at my feet. I held the pressure of the tackle against him and he stayed motionless. I looked at my watch. Six minutes. It was too fast. He hadn't worked enough.

Unhooking the tailer from its ring, I set it up. The salmon held his position. My thought was, "If this fish is foolish enough to come this close I might as well try to tail him . . . even though I know he isn't ready." I stretched the tailer to my arm's full length and leaned down toward the salmon, expecting him to bolt away at any second. He didn't move.

If I missed him, I knew it would take a long time to bring him close to me again, but just how long I was yet to realize. He was still strong and capable of a wild, swift surge, but I rarely missed with my tailer. When it slipped up over his tail and drew abreast of the anal fin I pulled toward me sharply to release the loop.

I was prepared for his plunge ahead but it was so powerful it almost took me in over my waders. White spray flew back at me as his tail slapped and fluttered on the surface. For a brief instant he relaxed then surged ahead, and by some near-miracle escaped, the first salmon to slip through the tailer once I had him tailed. (Later I was to learn his tail was deformed with the lower half not fully filled out.) He swept off downstream. I waited for him to turn. In a few seconds, with line racing out, I realized he was not going to, and I made for the shallow water to follow him. Finally, in desperation, I broke into as much of a run as a man can manage with chest-high waders on. The fish swept over the lip of the pool and down into the ragged water below it.

Past experience told me things were going to be tough. In particular I remembered another smaller salmon on the Serpentine I had tailed, brought to the bank and then had escaped for another 15-minute fight. Once a salmon has felt a gaff or tailer, he is wary of letting anyone come close to him. Usually such fish are pretty well tired out when the first attempt is made. This one was fresh and strong.

The flow was deep and heavy and steady, and the fish kept going downstream. Three times I had to wade out into the heavy water near midflow to pass my line over rocks where pieces of pulpwood had jammed. It was half an hour before the tail end of my casting line followed my backing onto the reel again. I was as hot as I can ever remember being and dog tired from running down the shallows in heavy waders or running, more slowly but just as vigorously, through water that varied in depth from hip to knee. I still carried the tailer in my left hand since I had not had a moment of free time to refasten it to its clip. Badly as I needed the unencumbered use of that hand, I hoped I would need the tailer again and more emphatically. Pure stubbornness kept me going, for in my mind there was no real chance of saving the fish. A rough and white-capped stretch lay not far ahead, and I could hear the waters roaring.

Whenever I closed in on the salmon, he knew only too well his danger and surged off again. At the end, with one short shallow stretch lying between us and the tumbling white waters that stretched away as far as I could see, I took a wild gamble. The salmon had to cross a 50-foot stretch of water less than knee deep that rippled down over a gravelly bottom. He was 20 feet ahead of me and moving steadily. As he started across the shallows, I lowered my rod and let the line go slack while I galloped in slow motion after him and overtook him just as he was about to scoot into the deeper swirls. The shades of old Izaak must have guided my hand, because the tailer slipped up over his tail and came tight. He was mine.

It had taken a few minutes over the hour to finally capture a salmon that might have been taken in six short minutes. I sat for a while till I was reasonably cooled off and my breathing was normal again before I started back up nearly three-quarters of a mile of river with the water right to the edge of the alders, sometimes dragging my twenty-pounder up against the current, sometimes carrying him through the thickets. He was the day's trophy, all right, winning me a bottle of rum which I shared with the less-fortunate donors.

The incident with the Serpentine salmon, previously referred to, had happened a year or two earlier. It was late in June, and the water was fairly high. My tackle was a 5-ounce, 9-foot rod and a 3¾-inch reel. The fish, a seventeen-pounder, played out in about the normal time. He had risen in the second pool below the falls but had left it soon after he was hooked, and I waded well out into the wide, knee-deep flow below it to tail him. Jim White, my guide, was waiting by the shore, and I dragged the fish, which dangled from the tailer without a quiver, over to where he stood.

Jim took the tailer spring and lifted the fish high while I reached for the hook in his mouth so I could go back to fishing while Jim took the fish to the cabin. Jim was

The patterns made by a fish moving against the current are one of the beauties of salmon fishing.

unfamiliar with tailers and, to ease the strain of holding up the fish, he put up his other hand to help. I think one finger hooked in the ring of the noose and loosened it, for the fish fell into the shallow water free of the tailer. Fortunately I had not been able to free the hook before then.

What happened next, surprised me. The fish swam into the flow slowly under light pressure while I took the tailer from Jim and set its spring again. Then, when I tried to hold the fish and wade out to him, the salmon would wait till I was almost within reach and then turn with the current and move downstream a little way. This happened time after time. The fish had enough life to keep me from holding him to a dead stop in the water, and he kept using the current to gain the extra few feet he needed to stay out of reach. He kept this up through the rough water all the way to Grant's pool some 300 yards downstream. That fish, too, had to be caught twice.

These two incidents are the only times, in all of the thousands of salmon I have taken, where the playing time ran greatly over the normal rule of thumb of a minute to the pound. It is interesting to note they were both able to last because they would not let me get close to them (after each had actually been captured once). It is a strong indication that if salmon would use their strength wisely, never running far, always working downstream, and letting the current help them resist the tackle, they would get away much more frequently than they do and would always take much longer to play out. One thing is certain: it pays to secure them on the first try.

Gift Salmon

Often it is possible for one man to "give" a salmon to another. When an angler raises a fish that fails to touch the fly, there is a great likelihood of catching that particular fish, even though not another fish in the pool may be taken that day. It is common practice for experienced fishermen, when fishing with friends of lesser salmon-fishing fortune, to offer such a special chance to an accompanying friend. Normally this is a fine and generous thing, thoroughly appreciated and good for both the giver and the recipient. Occasionally, it is not.

I rate as a mistake one such fish I "gave" away. It was early in August, and the river was low and lazy. The really big fish had concentrated in a few preferred pools. Dry flies were drawing some action, but the wet-fly fishermen were having very poor luck. With a good friend who was fishing for Atlantic salmon for the first time, I sought out one of the pools where some of the larger salmon would by lying.

Because of the brilliance of the afternoon sun, the clearness of the water, the assurance that any big fish I hooked would cling to the deep water of the pool until tired and easy to handle, and the fact that none of my larger flies had evoked any interest from the salmon, I was fishing with a #16 spider on an .008 leader tippet. As I worked up along the flow at the westward side of the pool, a very large fish rose to my tiny spider and missed it. I called to my good friend and his guide across the pool, and they came over. I pointed to the spot where the fish had risen and suggested that perhaps a sparse #12 dry fly would work and would give him a good chance of landing the big fish in the deep pool. I helped him pick out a suitable fly and watched with the guide while he made his casts.

The salmon rose, took the fly, was hooked, made a run and a leap, and broke free. My friend was impressed and thanked me for the opportunity. He made me regret very much the gift of the opportunity when he added a belief that the #12 fly was too small to hold such a big fish, and that no one could have landed him on that tackle.

That salmon was not an ounce under 26 pounds, and, as surely as I write these words, there was a much better than even chance I could have landed that fish on the #16 spider. It would have been a great source of satisfaction if I had. The largest salmon it had ever been my fortune to take on a #16 single-hook fly at that time weighed 15 pounds. I had never hooked a larger fish on so small a fly. Opportunities to take large fish on such light gear are rare. In most suitable waters, a fish of such size is rarely located. I was still looking forward to another opportunity to fish over a rising twenty-five pounder or better with a #16 spider . . . where low-water conditions would give him an interest in so small a fly and me a chance to play him without the fear of long runs in a heavy current, a situation that developed later as covered earlier in the book.

Another incident ended up with a reverse twist. With Neil Marvin, another good friend also on his first salmon-fishing venture, and my youngest son, Barry, I flew to Western Brook. The water, as usual, was extremely clear in the riverbed of beautifully colored stones. The sun was bright, and a fish could be seen for a considerable distance. When we had placed ourselves around the pool and started fishing, I noticed a large salmon and pointed the fish out. Unaccustomed to distinguishing the shadowy form of a salmon from the shadowy rocks in their own tangled pattern of light and dark, he could not locate the fish.

I had on a Surface Stone fly, and, in order to show him where the fish was, I cast it out, saying, "Watch my fly! I'll drop it just below him." The long cast with which I planned to drop the fly at about the fish's tail or a little below it either lacked the final touch of accuracy or was caught by a breath of upstream wind. The fly settled just over the salmon's nose. The salmon met it with jaws agape and raced away to the sound of a singing reel.

It was a fish of about 25 pounds, and it went into a series of leaps that sent Neil rushing for his movie camera. Barry, then about ten, went to get mine. I found a quiet moment when the fish was steady to set the camera for him. Both he and Neil took sequences of the leaps that followed and, later, of my bringing the fish into shallow water and tailing him by hand. I held him up in the sunlight and then, when the cameras stopped, let him slide back into the water again, still hooked . . . while asking Barry to check the amount of the film still unused in the camera. He called back to tell me it had just run out.

Neil was not familiar with my camera and Barry had not had any experience in reloading it, so, while Barry got another roll of film, I came to the shore. The salmon was lying quiescent where I had released my grip on him. I gave the rod to Barry to hold. With the roll changed I rose to exchange the camera for my rod, but either I had misjudged the fish's degree of exhaustion or Barry inadvertently twitched the tackle and upset him. The salmon streaked out toward the deeper water and found strength for a half cartwheel and in it, striking the leader with his tail, he found his freedom. Neil's film was lost due to a camera defect and mine showed a very fine leap and just enough of the landing action to have the big tail and half the fish's body above the water before the film ended. Had I succeeded in pointing the fish out to Neil with my arm instead of my fly, we might both have fared better.

A Boy Can Do It

Just how easy catching salmon can be when there are no faults to unlearn and a reasonable approach to the sport is at hand for comparison or study showed up in the fishing of my sons. Allan, my elder son, liked to fish from early childhood and was always eager to come along with the grown-ups. I have a recollection of flying to a camp on the River of Ponds and looking down from the plane to see his tiny figure, when he was ten, way out on a bar in the middle of the river. He was casting a good line with a short, light fly rod like my own, and, as I circled, I looked again and saw his rod bent and a salmon's silvery form flashing up from the center of the flow. The guides and anglers were all back in camp for an afternoon siesta. He tailed the fish just as I taxied onto the shore of the lake below.

At fourteen Allan hooked a 25-pound fish that had been seen and fished for for about a week in one of that river's pools. The fish rose to a gray-and-black dry fly of his own tying on a #12 hook. He played it at the inlet of a lake where it had a lot of room to maneuver and, at one point, took out a great deal of his line. Taking a fish of that size on a 2-ounce rod with a fly of his own making is a feat most grown anglers dream of but don't dare try to achieve.

Allan Wulff at age 14 displays a fine trophy from the River of Ponds.

At the Falls

The leap of a salmon is a wonderful thing. It stands as a testimonial to his great energy that a salmon can hurl himself vertically 12 feet and more out of the water, farther than any other type of freshwater fish. Salmon, at many places in their upriver journeys, come to waterfalls and tumbling rapids. Whenever they can swim up through the flow, they do so. Their speed may be as swift as 30 miles an hour or more, and water sliding down rocks or falling over ledges seldom reaches that speed. Only when they cannot swim up through the flow do they leap.

On the Serpentine River there is a 12-foot falls projecting all the way across the river, yet no salmon are ever seen jumping it, because somewhere along its apparently unbroken length, there is a hidden passage, invisible to the viewer, where the salmon can swim up through. In the Humber Falls, as they used to be, there was no such channel, and all the salmon of the run, unable to swim up through the falling sheet of water, had to leap the 12-foot ledge to clear the top and journey onward. There was a circus of leaping Atlantic salmon at that point which probably has never been equalled anywhere else in the world. In 1938, when it could only be reached by a difficult canoe trip, I made some moving-picture sequences of the falls and its leaping salmon, often showing many in the air at one time. This was widely circulated in the province. Where, before, only a few had ever seen the falls, many now saw the film. One of the results of seeing the valiant efforts of the salmon to get over at a time when leaping conditions were not at their best, was a movement to put in a fish ladder. Fortunately, wise counsel prevailed, and the project was shelved.

Unfortunately, a few years later, the powers in control of such things, did blast a channel for the fish up through the falls. Now, the great spectacle of the fish leaping Humber Falls is little more than a memory. A few of the many fish leap for the waiting watcher, who can now drive almost to within sight of the falls. What kind of reasoning can have been behind it? When the white men first came to Newfoundland, the river was full of salmon. There were many times as many fish then as now, and the falls were there, weeding out the weaklings and permitting only the strong to reach the spawning beds and reproduce their kind. There is always the possibility that humans, in their effort to help a species of wildlife, will lack the all-encompassing wisdom and understanding of the Creator. For the sake of a few salmon that might have died attempting the falls, a number which could not possibly have exceeded half of 1 percent of the run even in a very bad year, the world lost a magnificent spectacle, and the salmon of the Humber dropped down a notch or two in their quality. As one U.S. Marine remarked, "It's like putting us back in the Navy."

Salmon Pictures

Falls are a good place to get pictures of leaping salmon, especially still photographs. To get a truly good moving picture of salmon, the sequence should start before the fish comes into sight and continue until he disappears into the water again. When the photographer cannot control the timing, it may mean the wasting of a great deal of film in order to get perfect movie leaps.

To get first-rate moving pictures of salmon leaping while being played on tackle, the photographer should have his camera running and focused on the water before the

An aspiring movie maker captures the spectacular leap of a salmon at the Humber Falls.

salmon breaks through the surface and comes out into his leap. To do this, angler and cameraman must work together.

The angler, under certain circumstances, can make a salmon jump at will. He can then tell the cameraman where to point his camera and when to start it, in order to get the complete jump. In this manner, I was once able to let *Life* photographer Howard Sochurek photograph over 100 jumps from seventeen salmon in a single afternoon. Salmon can be controlled best in deep water rather than shallow, and in a smooth or a slow flow rather than a very swift and turbulent one. The shorter the line, the more effectively are the angler's controls felt by the salmon.

A salmon can be made to jump, as a usual thing, by a sudden tension when he has momentarily relaxed. To get him relaxed and then put on the tension is something dependent upon the pool, the particular fish, the type of water, and other factors.

Teamwork is essential in attaining good pictures with any degree of regularity. The camera must be set and aimed when the jump occurs. Judging the available light, the speed of shutter, and depth of field must be set before the salmon comes into view. The fisherman is the key to success. It is one thing for a fine fisherman to put an inexperienced cameraman on a rock and say, "I'll make a salmon jump in front of that ripple. Set the camera at F8 to focus at 15 feet," then he makes the fish jump in that spot. It is quite another for an expert cameraman to sit on a rock and say to an inexperienced angler, "Make a salmon jump 15 feet away. Right there. *Now!*"

Being skilled in both fields, I long ago wished I could be twins at such times, and in 1941, I decided to try it. With two Leicas strung around my neck, one with a standard lens and one with a long telephoto, I operated the cameras as I played my salmon. I came up with more dramatic salmon jumps than I had ever been able to achieve with cameramen assisting me. The best of the leaps shown in this book were obtained in this way. To do it, one need only be sure enough in the handling of his fish, to have one hand and arm free to use the camera when the fish is ready to jump. This, I believe, is the first time an angler ever took pictures of a fish he was playing.

The next step was to take movie sequences of a fish I was playing myself. It is not too difficult when the camera is light enough to be held in one hand. The lightest of the 16mm cameras are the types using 50-foot magazines. (Any of the 8mm cameras are light enough to use for this purpose.) It takes good muscular control to keep a movie camera steady. Setting the camera at slow motion helps make the jumps smooth. Taking a movie camera out from one's wader pocket and photographing one's own salmon while playing it adds a thrill to a sport already thrilling and gives a permanent record to help make pleasant memories more real.

Flies and Fish

The importance of color and pattern of a fly to a salmon comes in for endless discussion. Conclusions are usually based on tests or experiences in which personal variations of the element of chance still play an important part. In one case, although fishing was exceptionally good on the Upper Humber (1938) and catches of fifty grilse or salmon in a day were being made, there were still some anglers in the small group at the falls who were having very little action. The old argument about the importance of fly patterns came up, and we were divided in opinion. Accordingly, I tied up as weird a concoction as I could, a fly with a sheer silver body, a bright red-orange tail of good size, a hackle of brightest blue and wings of jet black squirrel tail. It was a bizarre creation, but on a #6 hook, which was our favorite size. I named it Liver Trouble and put it to work.

The fish were very anxious to prove fly presentation was more important than color that day, and my catch was as good as ever. I tied up more flies of the same pattern and still use it occasionally, often as an ace-in-the-hole fly when normal patterns have failed. Sometimes it works.

A fisherman should never use the word "never" about the flies a salmon will or will not take, as long as they are smaller than a full-sized herring. My friend Okey Butcher, in his second year of salmon fishing, arrived well armed with strange flies. One of them was a #2 hook covered with a great ball of white polar bear hair. It looked like nothing his fishing companion, Frank Frazee, had ever seen before. When Okey tied it on and made his first cast, Frank said, "If you catch a salmon on that thing I'll eat it." The sound of his words was still on the air as a 12-pound salmon sucked it in. At lunch the next day, in order to make it a little more palatable, Frank filed the hook into small shavings, cut the polar bear hair into half inch lengths or shorter, and put a liberal supply of sugar and cream on it.

In some areas guides have a dislike for red in a fly. On some rivers they will not use such a fly, on others they pull out the red feathers. There was one such discussion going on while some sportsmen were resting, having given up fishing for lack of action. When I came along, the discussion was at full heat. One of the men said, "We had some rises, but we can't catch any salmon out there. Can you?" Another asked, "Can you catch one on a red fly?"

Anybody who falls for a sucker deal like that should have his head examined, but I said I was sure I could. Accordingly, we went through all the fly boxes in the assemblage. They picked out a #6 Red Ibis trout fly. I think it would have been the very last one I would have chosen if I had had a million patterns. On the third cast, I caught a fish. The story could end there, but in fairness, I should add (1) there were a lot of fish in the pool, although they had fished it hard, and (2) they had fished it as it was normally fished, from the far side where the angler could stand on the beach or in shallow water and reach the fish. By wading out within an inch of the top of my waders, I moved into position to cast from the near shore.

It looked as if I were just doing it to save time, but actually I was sure that pool had not been fished from that side since I had fished it that way the season before. Reversing the direction of the fly's approach to a salmon will cause a reluctant, short-rising fish to take about once in five or six times. Figuring there were thirty or more fish in the pool, most of them with an inclination, however slight, to rise to something, the odds were all in my favor. I could count on at least one very foolish fish among them that would take the reversed fly out of a pent-up, but until then, restrained desire to take something. The moral, more important than the debunking of a salmon "never" taking red, is to cross over to the other side of the pool to fish before you leave, when you have raised fish that will not latch on to your wet fly.

Why More Grilse?

The proportion of grilse to salmon has been growing. Some rivers in which only mature salmon used to be found in the spawning runs of fifty years ago, now have runs made up predominantly of grilse. In almost all rivers the situation is the same. It is relatively easy to guess why this has happened, but it has been very difficult to prove.

The larger salmon have a higher commercial value and the netters of the sea originally set large-mesh gill nets which held the fish from 10 or 12 pounds weight on upward but which let anything smaller pass through. Some nets used would hold only fish of 20 pounds or over. These were the prime stock of the salmon run. They were the fish staying long in the sea, and the practice of taking them and allowing the smaller fish to pass on through would be comparable to a cattle breeder sending his best breeding stock to the slaughterhouse and keeping his runts to produce his future stock. It is reasonable to assume that salmon with a quick, freshwater development habit and long sea life tend to transmit it to their offspring.

Instead of letting these very large salmon breed and taking the small ones for commercial use in order to benefit the future of the industry, the largest fish were most sought after. If the regulations had called for the taking of salmon of all sizes for a certain period of time and none for another period during the run, the same balance of salmons' sizes could have been maintained. It seems likely that a reversal of the process and the heavy taking of grilse in the sea, with a concurrent cessation or reduction of the taking of the larger fish, would reverse the trend and, eventually, lead to a return to the situation where most rivers would have a run made up predominantly of big salmon. A decision by the anglers to keep only the grilse and return all mature salmon to the rivers unharmed would aid greatly in this problem.

Another factor in the predominance of grilse has often occurred to me. In the days when only the salmons' other enemies took their toll, before man's nets and rods oppressed them, the rivers were producing parr to full capacity. There must have been the keenest sort of competition among the parr to stay alive. Under such circumstances, only the roughest, toughest, fastest-growing parr could survive. Such fast-growing parr were almost certain to have matured and gone to sea early as smolts; they have a tendency to stay in the sea for a period of more than a year. Being fast growers and rapid feeders, their sea growth would have been greater than our present average. Everything indicates we should then have had the best specimens the normal evolutionary process could produce.

But when the nets began to operate and the spawning run was cut and cut again, the parr in the streams were not as competitive. Where before a parr had to battle for enough food to survive, there soon was enough food for all. The weak alevins and the puny parr could live and eventually breed. They were the slow growers, the weaklings. As a class, they are more likely to produce grilse than larger maiden salmon. Even natural stream processes of evolution have been disturbed, disadvantageously, for the angler who would like to catch large salmon.

Some anglers feel too much emphasis is put on the size of a salmon. It is certain that if all salmon return as grilse, and there was no such thing as a salmon of more than 7 pound weight, salmon fishing would still be considered a remarkably fine sport. There still might be no other fishing to compare it to, but we would not have the great sport we have today. The big salmon are more difficult to raise and are much more exciting to handle once they are hooked. To catch a salmon is so much greater an achievement under most circumstances that where there is a large salmon to fish for among many grilse, it is the large fish toward which the angler's casts are first or most emphatically directed.

Seals

The problems salmon fishermen encounter are of endless variety. Consider the time when an aging druggist from St. Johns was fishing the lower section of the Gander River not far from the sea. Mr. McNamara had fished for salmon many years, and a very considerable number had taken his flies and been killed. But the biggest of them had never surpassed the 20-pound mark. It was a dream of his to some day land a twenty-pounder . . . and that day on the lower Gander promised to be the day.

He hooked a fish both he and his guide were absolutely certain was well above that seemingly unattainable mark. He played it carefully and well through half an hour's time and then, as the fish had lost most of its original speed, he let it swing from the current down toward some deep and steady water. The fish took out some line in this maneuver while the angler moved along the rocky shore. Then, just when he was well positioned and started to bring the fish back, disaster struck in the form of a seal that took his salmon firmly in its teeth and swam off with it, breaking the tackle as he went.

The loss of any other fish might have been tolerated on a live-and-let-live basis, but to lose so fine a prize caused McNamara, who was well loved by everyone in the government seat at St. Johns, to complain bitterly to the head of the warden service. Seals were already being pursued for the value of the bounty placed upon them, but in the following months they were hunted relentlessly by the wardens of the area, as well.

Bay seals frequently travel long distances up rivers. In the Gander they have travelled up through 30 miles of river to Gander Lake. At Portland Lake, every summer found at least one pair of seals raising their young in the big lakes through which the waters flowed. Occasionally they would appear in the camp pool and, when sighted, the camp gun, for which I held a special permit, would appear, and we would hope against hope the small target a seal's head makes in the distance would be big enough to hit. We potted one almost every year while I was there. The salmon were always badly frightened when a seal appeared, and the pool would have to be rested for a while. Seal, especially the young ones, are palatable enough if all the fat or blubber is removed from the flesh. The meat was relished not only by the guides but often by the visiting anglers who were on hand when a seal was killed.

Sanctuary

One of the greatest needs of the salmon is a sanctuary area near their spawning grounds where they can be safe. When a great fish has made his sea voyages and returned up the long and tortuous way to his spawning grounds, when he has been through the nets, evaded the sharks and otters and eels and seals, and the flies of anglers, it is only reasonable that man, after helping to oppress him so heavily, should give him a place to rest and feel secure.

Anglers have a saying that is almost a slogan. It says: "You can't hurt a salmon river by fishing it with a fly." It is a foolish statement. If there are so few salmon coming into the river (and it takes two salmon to bring four back in five or six years' time, even when there are no nets or anglers) that the run is barely holding its own, or is losing ground over the years, which has been the case on almost all rivers, then, even if only *one salmon* is taken on a fly, it has cut down the number needed to maintain the run by that one fish. If a hundred are taken, the damage is more serious, and if it runs into thousands, the damage may be very great. This is not to say anglers are getting their proper share of this resource. But the closer to the spawning grounds a salmon is, the surer he is to make it. The Miramichi salmon netted in Newfoundland's coastal waters may have but one chance in five of returning to their Miramichi spawning ground. The salmon in the river's pools may have one chance in two, in which case, the taking of one fish in the river is more damaging than taking two in a faraway net at sea.

In past times, only the lower pools of the salmon rivers were fished and, once the run got by these pools, the fish were relatively safe. Now roads parallel the streams to their sources. Trails go up each branch. Airplanes fly anglers to the source lakes. There is no safe resting place. I remember sackloads of salmon that were brought out of White Creek, a small tributary of the Humber, 90 miles above the tide. They were taken by legal (?) angling in small pools where they were packed in like sardines. There was no place for them to run, no place to hide. It was not sport but a murderous sort of play.

On many rivers there is nowhere a salmon can escape the angler's flies. They pass over his head in a tormenting parade, hour upon hour, day upon day. If, during the whole of the summer under constant fishing, a salmon makes one mistake and takes a fly, his chance of surviving is cut nearly in half (allow that 50 percent of the fish hooked are landed, and that 90 percent of the salmon landed are killed). No matter what his chances are of surviving a single rise, his chances of surviving two or three successful rises to a salmon fly are very small indeed. To his fishing dangers add the poacher who finds him in a small, exposed pool or in any exposed position, and it becomes clear the salmon's stream survival is being jeopardized.

It seems a great shame on all of us that this should be so, especially on anglers who blame the net men for taking too many. Every salmon river, I believe, should have a sanctuary for the salmon. It should be toward the headwaters but could not help but include some excellent fishing water. Fishermen would be called upon to make a sacrifice. Camp operators and guides would cry bitter tears. I'm reminded of a Department of Natural Resources secretary who, relative to my asking for enforcement of a regulation to lift the commercial nets one day in each week, once said, "The sea fishermen claim they have only two weeks to catch the salmon before the run is over, and they can't afford to miss a day." My reply was, "Turn that around and look at it from the salmon's point of view."

Large or Small Water

Is there more charm to fishing on big waters than on small? That depends largely upon individual taste. It depends upon the size of the fish and the degree of bigness or smallness. To compare the great sweep of the Lower Humber River sliding its smooth and deliberate way beside the 1,000-foot limestone cliffs rising steeply from its shores, or the Moise where it bends its great flow through the level land near the Gulf, with the small waters of the Little Codroy or an Anticosti river is not just a matter of size. It is a matter of the spirit of angling, for both rivers may have good-sized fish and both have interesting, if different, fish problems.

Barry Wulff on Portland Creek.

Big salmon are hard to come by, and, though they may give a greater thrill than the lesser fish, there will be long waits between rises. Any angler who likes action should choose a river where fish are plentiful, even if most of them are small. The man to whom a big fish is of greatest importance should pick a river where big fish are taken frequently. He should settle into a campaign of fishing for big salmon. Usually this means choosing a big river, but a few specially blessed smaller rivers have very large salmon in their runs. Where water is under lease, money can buy fishing rights where big fish are the order of the day.

Big rivers are more windy, as a rule, than the smaller, more protected waters. Wind makes casting more difficult . . . but it blows the insects away. A salmon angler can pretty well assure himself he will have either black flies and mosquitoes or a wind hard enough to blow them away wherever bright salmon fishing is good. Big rivers call for a boat or canoe as a rule, and that means a guide. If you plan to fish without a guide or share a guide between two or more people, the big rivers are not for you.

If you want to wade in order to handle the capture of your fish entirely on your own, then the rivers of medium size are best. Rivers as big as the Lower Humber are fished successfully by wading anglers but most wadeable rivers are smaller. Many are wadeable in the normal summer run but require a boat for fishing the best pools in high water when the salmon first enter the river.

There is a charm to the small waters. Casting coverage is easy. There is a little problem in locating the fish for there is only sufficient water for their safety in the occasional deep pools. There is little wind to worry the caster, and the mood and setting are much like that of trout fishing.

There is one drawback to the very small rivers from the point of view of sport. The salmon are handicapped in a small pool. They have nowhere to go. The angler loses the thrill of a long run that will bite deep into his backing.

Rough waters normally permit heavier leaders where, because of the turbulence, fish cannot see them as well. An angler seeking delicacy of tackle and fine-tackle problems will prefer the quieter streams or the low-water periods when rivers flow most peacefully.

There is a charm about all salmon waters, a thing tying them all together, for the fish have come into them from the great mother of all life, the sea, and in their coming have somehow brought the basic problem of a difficult, swift, and restless fish to the small waters of angling. I like big salmon, but I like them best in rivers where a tall man can wade and perhaps, when the waters are low, handle the biggest fish he can hook on the smallest fly in his vest.

13

Salmon Fishing in Europe and Iceland

ountless old timers have always known that the salmon of each river or major branches of a great river are different. Although they are all the same species, *Salmo salar*, the salmon of Iceland are different from those of Canada, and those of Norway are different from both those of Iceland and Scotland. Similarities between all salmon are great, the differences minor . . . unless you're a dry-fly enthusiast.

In Iceland salmon fishing is made much more pleasant because there are no mosquitoes or black flies to create the annoyance those pests cause on the "New World" rivers. Those who gladden at the thought of avoiding the insect bites may sadden to learn that because of the very scarcity of insect life in Iceland, the salmon there have almost no interest in a dry fly. With the decline of salmon fishing almost everywhere and the good salmon management of Iceland, salmon fishing in Iceland is judged by many as the best in the world. But, good as Iceland's fishing is, for those who draw delight from the rise of these great fish to a dry fly, there is something valuable lacking.

The salmon of Iceland seem to jump nearly as much as Canadian salmon do when they are being played, but the salmon of the British Isles and Norway are far less likely to break into the flashing, exciting leaps the Canadian salmon anglers have come to expect. I do not know why this should be so. As with the basic reason for the salmons' free leaping, many theories can be advanced. The truth, so far, escapes us.

The differences of the European fishing methods are far greater than the differences of the fish. In order to protect and conserve the salmon on this side of the Atlantic, we, having access to mostly public waters, have ordained that salmon must be taken only on unweighted flies cast in the customary manner, which happens to be the most challenging and most sporting manner. The Europeans, who *own* the salmon rivers, do not have the same management problems we do. Since the rivers are privately owned, each owner has the option of choosing the angling methods by which he and his guests may take salmon and to what extent he wishes to limit his catch. The allowable methods usually include not only fly-fishing but other casting methods and hardware and baits, such as shrimp and angleworms.

Rivers are very valuable, and no owner of fishing waters wants its run of fish to diminish and its value on the market to fall. He wants to leave it to his heirs in as good or better shape than when he received it. So, though the methods may be more deadly, every owner has both the right and the responsibility to maintain his salmon runs. He, therefore, makes sure his salmon runs do not diminish. The most important thing is the number of fish that reach the spawning grounds, and the owner makes sure that the number is adequate.

The freedom of an individual to fish in many ways and to keep large numbers of fish in a daily catch upsets many Americans who feel that the keeping of more than one or two salmon a day is morally wrong. The other side of the coin is that, while one angler may take twenty fish a day on a European river, the owner may limit the total catch to a certain number like 300, whereas on a Canadian river with a daily limit of two and public fishing the anglers may take many thousands, a number far above that which the river's run can spare if it is to maintain itself.

There are many variations within European salmon management. Where a number of owners control a river, although they may agree on certain management practices, they may vie with another to get the greatest share of the total catch. Rod-caught salmon in Europe are sold in the market. A man may lease a section of a salmon river and hope that he and his guests (technically the catches belong to him) will be able to catch so many fish that they'll bring more money in the market than he has paid for his lease. He will not want to limit his guests to fly-fishing only because the fish they do not catch (because of such a restriction) will move on up the river and out of his reach. He might agree to fly-fishing-only restrictions if all the owners agree, but this happens rarely. Those who have paid for a section of river want their guests to catch fish, and most realize that few of their guests will be good fly fishermen and that if they want the others to catch fish they will have to allow hardware, bait and methods other than fly casting.

It is the experience of most American and Canadian anglers who go to Europe to fish that their chances of catching salmon on a fly aren't too good. They're likely to come back saying, "Some fine fish were caught while I was there. They were caught on spinning gear. I fly fished for a while and then broke down and used a spinning outfit. I caught a seventeen-pounder."

The joy that fly fishermen get from fishing with their favored tackle, and their willingness to pay for it, is changing this attitude somewhat. Some rivers in Iceland go to fly-fishing-only rules during long periods of the season. The owners make more money, and the American and European fly fishermen who are their customers are happy. The Icelandic owners, who take over their rivers after the fly fishermen leave, are happy to have the extra fish left, because of the fly-only regulations, to take by any angling method they choose.

Most of Norway's rivers rise in the high mountain range that runs, as if the spine of the country, from north to south. The rivers that rise in these high, generally snow-capped mountains are different from those in Canada. In the hot summer days the cold snowmelt from Norway's snowcapped mountains runs into the rivers and brings their temperatures down low. In Canada, without that snow backup, hot days simply mean warmer water in the rivers. This cold water running into most Norwegian rivers mitigates against surface action by the salmon and against success with dry, surface-skimming flies.

One of the great salmon rivers of the world is Norways's Alta. The Alta is different in that it rises in a broad valley north of the main Norwegian range and is not affected to any great extent by snowmelt in the summer. It is more like the Canadian rivers, and it has a run containing very large fish.

It is an interesting river to fish because it lies so far north that daylight never ends during late spring and early summer. Our guides, Hjalmar and Kaare, preferred to have us fish from eight in the evening until five in the morning with an hour's break for lunch at midnight. The darkest time was the best fishing time.

The river is owned collectively by the farmers along it and the guides, some of whom are also owners, work an eight-hour day. They were extremely capable in their long, narrow, outboard-equipped boats. The Alta is a big and scenic river, like the Moisie, the Lower Humber, and the St. John. There is enough white water in the upper fishing areas to make the river runs interesting. In our few days there I caught two salmon weighing between 27 and 30 pounds, both on a 5/0 Jock Scott. I used my usual light 6-foot rod which amazed the guides but, also as usual, did not make them converts to ultralight tackle. One of the guests at the lodge brought in a forty-four-pounder during our stay. It, too, was caught on a fly for the Alta is designated as a fly-fishing river during the period it is open to nonresidents for fishing. The late season is reserved for the owners, and they fish with baits and spoons, as well as flies.

The Alta is one of the most expensive rivers in the world to fish. The cost may approximate 5,000 dollars per week per angler. While he fishes that river, the angler knows his fly is passing over salmon in the 40- to 50-pound class. Two of my friends have caught salmon weighing over 50 pounds on the Alta. It is truly a river to dream about and remember.

The Laerdal is one of Norway's most beautiful rivers. It flows down a gorge and into a fjord with some flatlands in the valley where the river meets the sea. On the upper beats there are places where an angler literally clings to the cliffs in order to dance a fly or flash a spoon in the foaming waters. It, too, has large salmon in its run but not as large as those of the Alta, the Vossa, or the Aero.

My trip there was to make a film, and therefore, it was important that we catch at least one good salmon on a fly. Olaf Olsen, tyer of classic salmon flies, lives there and he helped to guide and advise us. Our hosts, Kirsten Mustad and Frederik Thrane, were also fishing with flies, and I felt sure we would have plenty of salmon to film. I was disappointed.

We did see a forty-three-pounder caught on a prawn and a few other fine fish taken by spinning by Lady Sopwith, but it was not a week for fly-fishing. I cast and cast, hour after hour, day after day, using my light 6-footer and flies that were more often 7/0s than anything smaller. We all caught grilse, and I did hook one big salmon. I played him to near exhaustion when, as fate dictated, the hook pulled out and he drifted slowly back to the deep water. Cheray Duchin's photo caught my expression at that moment and it shows exactly how I felt.

With but two days remaining, I asked some of our party to fish with spinning gear, hoping that I might get a good salmon catch on film. Unfortunately, between the evening of that decision and the following morning, it rained heavily in the upper valley. The river rose up out of its banks. Water was knee-deep on some of the fields, and it swirled around the tree trunks that stood on the bank at the river's edge. Casting into an eddy behind one of those trunks, the film's star, Peter Duchin, caught a 12-pound salmon on a spoon. We did make a satifactory film for the *American Sportsman* TV Series but we didn't have a big salmon on a fly. My expression in that photo will always remind me of that failure.

The Dee, one of the storied rivers of Scotland, in Aberdeenshire, was a great pleasure to fish. It was there that A. H. E. Wood devised the greased-line method of fishing for salmon. It was there, also, that he ran his tests on flies and narrowed down his own choice to three, the Blue Charm, the March Brown, and the Silver Blue. There, too, he fished with bare hooks, whose only adornment was some paint on a section of their shanks, and caught salmon.

Watching Donald Rudd, equipped with his 16½-foot Grant's Vibration rod, and my gillie, Alex Cowie, with his 16-footer, roll out their long spey casts was something to remember. There is a great feeling of tradition on that river which one accepts and respects. Above Ballater, where we fished, is the water of Balmoral and the Royal Castle. There was a great pleasure, too, in my taking of salmon on both a dry fly and a hitched fly when such flies were considered by the gillies and anglers alike to be far beneath a Dee salmon's dignity.

The Dee flows through a land in which the sunshine is more than equalled by the fog and rain. On one of my two trips there we had only one day of sunshine in more than ten. On the other trip the sun shone almost all day, every day, through an equal period of time. Rain makes things green, and the countryside was a perfect setting for a great salmon river. The Scots have a way with words, as well as with salmon, and a big part of any trip is the enjoyment one finds with the people.

One of my Scottish friends, the late Alan Sharpe, was not only expert in his fishing but eloquent in his comment when I lost a Dee salmon that was just about ready to let me slip my hand around his tail. Alan was standing nearby when the hook pulled. As the fish drifted off, a few quick steps brought him to my side. His arm slipped around my shoulders and he said, "Too bad! But we're not defeated, lad. You'll land the next one." And in another pool he had led me to, I did.

One of the most interesting salmon rivers of the world lies on the north shore of Iceland. It is the Laxa Adaldal. This river rises in mountains and has a dam which holds back its upper waters for controlled releases into the lower plain. On first hearing of it I thought, "Ah! The perfect salmon river. A controlled flow which would never have either floods or drought periods." The salmon range up to, and occasionally over, 30 pounds. The river flows through gentle slopes and meadows in beautiful pools. There are no black flies and mosquitoes to inflict their particular poisons. Truly a wonderful salmon river. And yet there is a flaw.

Because of the steady flow, and because there are no spates or dry spells, there grows on the streambed a very special moss. It grows luxuriously, and by late spring it has grown to a height where, when the wind blows, its soft stems break in the waves and drift downstream in matted bunches. When a salmon takes a fly and starts to move about the pool, the line and leader pick up soft, clinging gobs of this dark-green moss. They stick to the line, not even sliding along it very well. This puts a great drag on the fish as he pulls it behind him.

Because of the moss it is almost impossible to land a big fish on fine gear and unwise to use fine leaders and very small hooks. It is still a great river, but after having fished it, one is still looking and hoping for that perfect salmon river, the dream that doesn't exist.

European salmon anglers tend to be more traditional than the Canadians and Americans. It is fun to surprise them with some of the flies we have tried and found successful on the western side of the Atlantic. I'm fully aware, as all anglers should be, that your guide on a new river will know more about it and the characteristics of its fish than you do. When I arrived at Pool number 2 on the Laxa Adaldal, I took from by box a special fly and showed it to Hermodur, my guide, who was also one of the river owners.

It had a bright yellow plastic body, paired, light-mallard breast feathers over its back with hackle fibres coming down from beneath them, and the length of the body was shrimplike. A black eye was painted on each side at the head of the feathers. It was on a #6 turn-down-eye trout hook. Helmer looked it over disdainfully and said something like, "Salmon will never take that."

Instead of trying to find one he liked I simply turned and, wading out, began to fish. Within five minutes I had a salmon. When he played out I hand-tailed him and brought him in to the bank. Then I opened two of my fly boxes and said, "How about picking a fly that will catch me a bigger one?"

For the rest of the afternoon I fished with *his* choices, fishing especially hard with a couple of flies he took from his own small stock to lend me. On one of them I caught a salmon that was bigger than the wild, shrimp-fly fish. We got along famously after that.

I learned a great deal about the river and its salmon from him, and was able to surprise him several times with flies that he looked at with the greatest of skepticism. He liked double-hook flies of which I had only a few, all quite small. I sensed a logic in his preference. Those Adaldal fish, as parr, had not been used to chasing hard to catch nymphs, I reasoned, and their rises were more likely to be short with the fish hooked in the forward part of the mouth where the flesh is softer and the hold not as good as when the hook settles into the corner of a salmon's mouth. A single hook in the soft forward flesh will probably pull out easier than a double.

ABOVE LEFT: Alan Sharpe of Aberdeen is shown fishing the Dee with a two-handed rod. ABOVE RIGHT: River moss entangling the line is the curse of fishing the otherwise perfect Laxa Adaldal in Iceland. Photos by Joan Wulff

RIGHT: Joan Wulff brings one in on the Lierasveit River in Iceland.

I was reminded then of the Sandhill River in Labrador where the fish also tended to come short on wet flies and to pull free more often than usual. Once, on the first afternoon of a trip to the Sandhill, after fishing the Moisie and taking ten big fish without losing one, I had the hook pull free on the first seven fish that took it. By the third fish I was a little upset. By the seventh I was ready to say that it was more than coincidence, to believe that the rising pattern of the Sandhill fish was different from that of fish of most other rivers. Returning to that river last summer I found, again, that I had hook-pulls more frequently there.

In Iceland that year we fished four rivers, the Laxa Adaldal, the Nordura, the Haffjardera, and the Grimsa. Each was different, and each gave us fine fishing. At the end of our trip, on the last afternoon, I came to the realization that in every morning or evening fishing session of our fifteen fishing days, regardless of the river or the length of the period, I had caught at least one fish. We were set to spend that final evening session on the Grimsa on one of the lower pools. As we walked down to the stream I saw several good salmon jump and thought, "This will be wonderful. We'll go out in a blaze of glory."

So I fished with enthusiasm and confidence. The salmon leaped frequently and porpoised a bit less frequently all around us, but none rose to a fly. Three hours went by during which time I lost faith in my most favored patterns. I tried a good many that hadn't been in the water for years and years. Finally, in desperation, I tied on a strange fly of Jock Scott character that I'd picked up on the beach of a pool in Scotland. It was about three inches long, yellow and black, and fortified by large jungle-cock eye feathers. At the tail of its twisted wire and along its wool-wrapped body was a #6 treble hook, legal, of course, in both Scotland and Iceland.

It landed with a plop and had scarcely begun to move when a grilse took it and was hooked. "Ah," I thought, "my luck has finally changed, I've found something they'll take."

A minute later the hook pulled out. I cast on with confidence but not another salmon looked at the strange fly. Nor would they look at any others, loved or unloved, that I put out to swim before them. As Joan and I walked back to the car as the twilight was fading, I pondered, again, the problem of catching these mysterious fish. Surely the wisest salmon fishermen can be counted on to be most successful over the long period. Yet, was there ever salmon a fisherman who has not found himself completely bewildered more often than he likes to admit?

There is a special challenge new waters and strange conditions hold. A fly fisherman going to Europe to fish for salmon would be wise to check into the records of any river he plans to fish. Records are well kept on most European rivers. They can tell you, very accurately, what methods, what flies or lures (of which sizes) are most productive, and what part of the season offers the best chance.

The anglers of Europe, too, are trying hard to restore their salmon rivers. In Spain, because Francisco Franco had been a salmon fisherman and had had the necessary authority, the Spanish salmon rivers were restored during his tenure. Organizations of anglers in France have been making progress in the restoration of their rivers, and they hope for a brighter future for salmon anglers on their waters. The British Isles have recovered from the "Irish" salmon disease of a decade ago and are generally productive, save in Ireland, which has been plagued by drift netting. The Irish salmon runs are generally at a low ebb at this time.

France

Regarding Atlantic salmon fishing in France, Pierre Affre writes from Paris: "Fifty years ago many of our rivers were as good as those of the British Isles, and the fly then must have accounted for a great percentage of all salmon caught by rod and line. After World War II the fixed-spool reel and nylon became this country's 'salmon public enemy number one.' Today most of the French fly fishermen for salmon cast their flies in Scottish, Norwegian, or Icelandic waters.

"In the late nineteenth and early twentieth centuries many English fishermen used to cross the channel and fish the nearby French Brittany. The rivers Ellé and Aulne were extolled by British writers of the time. When the salmon guides on these rivers began to tie flies they lacked the exotic feathers the ships of Queen Victoria were bringing in to England from far parts of the world and they made their flies of poultry, pheasant, and woodcock feathers together with hare and wild boar's fur. These became known as the 'Mouche Bretonnes' and outfished the British patterns like the Silver Doctor, Wilkinson, and Green Highlander.

"Rivers of the Pyrénées like the Gave D'Oloron and the Nives were, at the turn of the century, as famous among British salmon fishermen as the Laerdal or the Driva of Norway. In the years immediately following World War II most of the Gave D'Oloron was taken over for salmon fishing by British anglers. After a few years the fishing became public and fell to low quality.

"The British brought a fly-fishing tradition to this area which is still very much alive today. Casting is done with very powerful two-handed rods (now of carbon fibres) up to 20 feet long. Most of the fly fishermen of today use variations of the Jock Scott, Lemon Grey, Black Doctor, and other standard British patterns in sizes 1 to 3/0. Even in July the Gave D'Oloron is big and powerful.

"Fly-fishing was brought to the Allier River, which flows into the Loire near Nevers, after World War II by the British. Here, as in Brittany, local anglers soon learned how to dress their own flies. Badger, wool, and mallard feathers were the most common materials, and the sizes ranged from 4 to 1/0. The most famous of these flies is the Bonnefant series named after Lucien Bonnefant, one of the great salmon anglers of all time who, although now seventy-five, is still fishing actively. His flies are very simple: body of wool (red, black, brown, grey, or green) with tinsel—wings of badger hair with mallard fibres. No throat. No tail.

"In 1946 Lucien Bonnefant caught some 150 fish on the fly in a three-month period on the Allier. Now fewer than fifty fish are caught annually on a fly in this river, representing less than 5 percent of all fish caught there on rod and line."

Affre goes on to describe the situation of the salmon in France as of today, 1981: "After the really black years of the sixties and the early seventies when fewer than 2,000 salmon a year were caught by all means (commercial and recreational) in *all* French rivers, the French Government finally decided it was time to do something.

"In 1976, under the pressure of ecological and conservationist groups, the Government set up a 'Plan Saumon 1976–1980' with a budget of 70,000,000 francs (15,000,000 dollars). As usual, most of these funds went to bureaucratic studies in the different ministries and commissions involved. However, the small amount of this fund that finally went into concrete realizations had a very positive result on the remaining stocks. From an average of 2,000 fish the number climbed to about 6,000 for 1980 and 1981.

"Perhaps even more important than the overall increase in numbers is the fact that in rivers like the Dordogne and the Gave de Pau a few fish are showing up again after fifty years of complete absence. Along the same line word comes from West Germany that about 200 Atlantic salmon were caught by rod and line in the Rhine this spring and summer (1981).

"In 1981 there are three areas in France that support some salmon fishing. The first is Brittany and Lower Normandy. These are short coastal rivers from 10 to 50 km long. These catches are listed by the Association Pour La Protection du Saumon en Bretagne for rod and line in 1981.

						(Lower Normandy)	
Ellé	525	Jet	220	Elorn	160	Selune	450
Scorff	280	Odet	70	Penze	90	See	350
Blavet	250	Steir	110	Leguer	400		
Aven	130	Aulne	150				

"The total catch for all the rivers in the area was 3600. For certain more than 95 percent of these catches fell to 'hardware,' prawns, and worms. The season starts the first week in March and ends in mid-June. So most of the fish, fresh from the sea in March and April, are on the take and in the high water are easily caught on worm or spoon. June, July, and August, which are the months most countries fish with the fly, are closed in France to all types of fishing. As in the British Isles we have more and more grilse in our salmon rivers and they come in in the summer. No one but a few poachers fish for these generally male salmon. On the contrary the big fish (mostly female) of the early run are almost all killed off.

"The rivers of the Pyrenées. The D'Oloron is the main river of this area. The Nives is now almost empty. Where in the early seventies, only a few hundred fish were being caught annually in the D'Oloron the last three years have been considered good with almost a thousand caught each year, two-thirds by net, one-third by rod.

"The D'Oloron can compare with the most powerful of the Norwegian rivers. Having fished the George and the Matapedia in Canada, Norway's Laerdal, the great Scottish Classic rivers, and having seen the Restigouche and the Grand Cascapedia, I think the D'Oloron is the river most suited of all for fly-fishing. It offers more than 100 km of fast-flowing water with huge, deep pools where the fish can rest. The season opens the first week in March and goes to the end of July which gives a good month of fly-fishing. May and June are usually snowmelt months.

"On this river, also, most of the fish fall to hardware in March, April, and May. The average fish in the D'Oloron during the early season weighs 8 to 10 kilos with a few 12- and 14-kilo fish taken. However, during the last years more and more small fish of 2 and 3 kilos, which were unknown in the river twenty years ago, have been caught. Since 1970 this river has been stocked with parr from the Thurso and Polly rivers, and I fear that in the nearby future the race of big salmon will be absorbed by these dwarfs.

"Thirdly, there is the Allier River which may well be the longest river ascended by salmo salar in the world today. The spawning grounds, above Brioude, are almost 500 miles from the sea.

"Due to flooding conditions all spring this year only an estimated 400 fish fell to rod and line and twice as many to commercial netting in the Loire. A good stock of fish, perhaps more than a thousand, was seen on the spawning grounds in mid-November.

"The Allier salmon are big, averaging 8 kg and most of them, too, fell to big

A beautiful small river in Scotland. Photo by Joan Wulff

spoons and Devons in March and April. As in Brittany, when in mid-June it is time to fish with a fly in this big, beautiful river, the season closes.

"Under the new Socialist Government's Ministry of Environment the 'Plan Saumon 1976–1980' has been transformed to a 'Plan Migrateurs' for the period 1980–85. Not only the salmon but the sea trout, shad, and sturgeon are designed to benefit from it.

"This year has seen the first Atlantic salmon in the Seine in many years. It was caught by an eel fisherman in Rouen Harbor. Perhaps one day they'll be seen rolling again under the Pont Neuf.

"There is little hope in the near future that salmon fishing in France will favor the tourist fisherman, whether he be Canadian, American, or from Paris. Public fishing with all kinds of bait and hardware will be permitted. The seasons do not favor the fly fisherman. Salmon is the *only fish* an angler has the right to sell to a restaurant or fishmonger. This year in Brittany at Eastertime the price, in spite of a glut of fish was fifteen dollars per kg. On the Gave D'Oloron or the Allier the price went up to twenty-five dollars per kg or 250 dollars for a 10-kg fish. In these areas where unemployment is a big problem many industry or agricultural workers are paid 500 dollars a month in wages so one can easily imagine the urge to take and sell salmon.

"It is good to know that the Atlantic salmon is rebuilding in France and that our rivers will support them. We can hope that in the far future the opportunity to fly-fish for them on these beautiful rivers will improve, but hopes in the immediate future seem slim."

Time changes things on salmon rivers. This year's best river may fade and, a few years hence, be considered more or less ordinary, although the character of the fish, large or small, will change slowly. Even on a good river one may run into unfishable spate conditions . . . or drought. Salmon fishing is a chancy thing.

14

Salmon Management

he Atlantic salmon runs many dangers and is subject to predation all along the line of its travels from birth to spawning redd. It can be taken in nets far out in the sea, hundreds of miles from its native river.

It can be trapped and killed anywhere along its route to the sea feeding grounds, particularly at the bottlenecks where salmon must concentrate as they travel their lifetime routes. The salmon has been preyed upon by natural enemies ever since its beginnings, and has always managed to survive and thrive in spite of them. However, when man, the most deadly of all predators, developed his boats, spears, nets, and other salmon-taking devices the salmon began to lose ground, and so deadly has been man's attack that only a remnant of the great hordes that once swam the sea and crowded the rivers still remains.

As it is with all wild things, the time of greatest danger is the time of reproduction, of laying eggs, or of giving birth. The mature spawners endeavor, despite all dangers, to see that the fertilized eggs are placed in the best location and at the best time for the young to survive. In the case of the salmon it is necessary to come into small rivers and shallows and go through the spawning ritual in these places where it is next to impossible for them to hide. This is the key point in the salmon's preservation. We must make sure there are enough salmon spawning in suitable habitats to continue the species. From there we work both forward and backward to protect the growing fish through their cycles from alevins to smolt in the rivers and from smolt to their spawning runs back to their streams of origin.

The closer they come to their time and place to spawn, the more valuable they become. Thus it has fallen to the anglers to make the greatest sacrifices. No matter how many fish are taken in the sea or in nets at the mouths of rivers, the angler knows that if he takes all he can, *no one* will have any salmon at all. He is the first to make the sacrifice, the first to limit his catch and establish strict controls.

Poaching on the rivers has been a major problem ever since conservation laws were established. Originally, poaching was done to provide food for the families of the poachers, but more and more, as the value of salmon in the market increased, it has been done in order to sell the salmon for cash. To a very great degree the early wardens appointed were picked for political reasons: to reward a good campaign worker or to give a job to a deserving veteran or a cripple. While some of these men were of good character few of them were trained and most were neither industrious nor efficient. The job of salmon warden was a summer job, often terminating at the end of the fishing season but before the most vulnerable time for the fish—that of the spawning redds. The realization is growing that if we are to have viable salmon runs we must protect them all year round and protect them well.

A great damage to the salmon run is being done at this time by Native American Indian groups, sometimes under treaty rights and sometimes permitted because of sentimental feelings of past injustices. This situation has not yet been brought into a hard-and-fast schedule of quotas for various tribes on certain rivers. The fishery managers and the Indian managers have failed to agree and jointly ask for strict enforcement. The tribes have often gone ahead with unconscionable catches of threatened salmon runs. The determination of "Indian" is yet to be spelled out completely. Must he be living on a reservation in essentially the style of his ancestors in order to deserve the right to take salmon as a right of heritage? Must he be of more than "half" Indian blood? Must he have a real need for the food, or can he be engaged in another business which gives him a good living yet still qualify to take salmon? Can he use nylon nets and other deadly devices which were not used by his ancestors at the time of the treaty? We can only hope that these questions will be answered satisfactorily and that the "take" of Indian tribes will fit a pattern in which the salmon can be restored.

We have eliminated some, but not all, of the salmon's natural enemies. We have brought the seals that preyed upon them to a low level. The fish hawks and eagles are also at a low level. The mergansers, relatively inedible fish-eating ducks, have been protected and not harvested by hunters. Their great numbers still seriously threaten the parr of the salmon streams. It is a rule of good management that when one harvests a natural crop one eliminates its enemies in a proportionate amount. Nature changes, old enemies die out, and new ones appear. Salmon management must be able to change with the times to be effective.

The salmon-angling methods in Canada have been restrictive compared to those used in Europe, because Canada's streams are largely public. Almost none are "owned in their entirety." European countries can afford to leave the control (by numbers) to the owners of the salmon waters because those owners can be counted on not to damage a valuable resource and thereby suffer financial loss. If the Canadian salmon suffer depletion, the loss is felt by the citizenry as a whole and, consequently, very little by each individual and practically not at all by the civil-service fishery mangers.

In order to try to limit the salmon catch by instituting laws to govern the methods of fishing, we, on this side of the Atlantic, have opted for fly-fishing as a means of giving the fish a reasonable sanctuary in the deep water and of preventing the foul hooking of the fish which could easily be done if weighty lures were permitted. We haven't gone far enough. Treble hooks and double hooks are far more effective for snatching salmon than are single hooks. On this issue we have hedged. Treble hooks are barred, save in Quebec where small trebles are permitted. Double hooks are permitted almost everywhere even though they are almost as deadly as trebles if an angler wants to foul hook a fish. This is regrettable since a double hook is not necessary to hook and land a salmon, and the fact that a large share of our salmon are taken on dry flies, which are always single-hooked, proves this point. A heavy double hook will sink readily in slow or

This salmon was still full of life as darkness settled on a Serpentine salmon pool.

normal water, and a great many salmon are presently foul hooked and taken from the streams by this *legal tackle*. The taker could say, "The fish made a pass at the fly and was foul hooked" and therefore, be safe from prosecution. It is my hope that, eventually, *both* double and treble hooks will be eliminated from salmon angling for the good of the salmon runs and to make the game as sporting as possible.

Fines and punishments have been minimal for salmon-fishing offenses. While big-game managers have been able to establish stiff fines, and often jail sentences, judges have not yet been convinced to strictly enforce the salmon laws. The legislatures, too, have not yet decided that the salmon resource needs tougher laws and strict protection to survive and be of maximum benefit to the population as a whole.

As mentioned earlier, salmon have home rivers but are a wandering, anadromous fish. In a sense, the salmon "belong" to their rivers, but only Iceland, of all the nations, has seen fit to manage those rivers under the essentially fair and sensible premise that salmon should be harvested only at the rivers of their origin. In Iceland the salmon are both netted and caught by rod and reel *only* in their native rivers, and thus, each river can be managed independently according to its needs. It follows, logically, that of all the nations, Iceland has had the best salmon management.

The other nations let individuals and companies, who have not in any way provided salmon, harvest them on their migrations in the sea. There is some validity in a nonriver harvest if the harvesting nation provides food for the salmon as in the case in the feeding grounds off Greenland and the Faroe Islands. Except for those feeding grounds, it has been both foolish and detrimental to the salmon stocks to allow them to be netted in the sea.

Sea netting of salmon is indiscriminate. The take may be too heavy in a river badly in need of conservation of its salmon run and very light in a river where the salmon run is in excellent shape. At long last, the idea of harvesting only in the rivers of "origin" is being considered seriously on this side of the Atlantic.

Our Atlantic salmon managers have considered salmon caught by sportsmen to be in a different category from those caught commercially in nets. In Europe (Iceland included) rod-caught salmon are considered a commercial crop and are normally sold by the owner or the angler to whom they belong. If we were to bring that viewpoint to this side of the Atlantic we might benefit from it.

At present we *pay* commercial fishermen to go out in their boats, often in miserably cold and rainy conditions, to set nets, and to capture salmon for food. Yet we have hordes of anglers whose main interest is in *catching* rather than eating salmon who would *pay* to be permitted to catch salmon and turn their catches over to the government to sell. Obviously, it would be more sensible to *make money* by having salmon angler-caught for food consumption than to have to *pay* commercial netters, as we do now, for the same service. How long it will take for the salmon managers to admit this and agree to it is anyone's guess.

They will say that salmon taste best when caught in the sea. Tests, I believe, will prove that any difference between a sea fish and one taken in its first week or two in the river (when salmon are most vulnerable to angling) is minor indeed. This "angling only for commercial catches" has been tried in Canada with success. The scarce big, bluefin-tuna catches were limited to fishing tackle as specified by International Game Fish Association rules (130-pound-test line) and certain tackle limitations. This commercial catching of food fish on specified angling tackle worked well for years. Finally, perhaps because the U.S. did not bar hand lines and harpoons, Canada recently also made hand-line fishing for these big fish legal again.

Back in the early 1960s, when the sea feeding grounds of the Atlantic salmon off southwest Greenland had been discovered, there was a great catch in that area which threatened the salmon runs of both continents. Nations with no salmon rivers at all, like West Germany and Japan, were free to come and net these fish on the high seas. It was a free-for-all with everyone hoping to get as many salmon as possible while the resource lasted.

Sport-fishing organizations, particularly the Committee for the Atlantic Salmon Emergency, headed by Richard A. Buck in the U.S., worked with all interested parties, and the result was a move by the U.S. Congress to boycott the fisheries' products of the Danes if they allowed this anticonservation high-seas salmon fishery to go on.

A treaty resulted with a gradual phasing out of the high-seas fishery. Then the various world governments moved their territorial boundaries out to the 200-mile limits, which brought the heretofore high-seas salmon fishery within the territorial waters of Greenland. While there may be disagreements as to the amounts of salmon captured by the Greenlanders or the Faroese, they are sure to be reasonable about the allotments since both will want the resource to prosper.

There is an international Atlantic salmon treaty ready for finalization at this time. It is causing thorny debate among the nations involved in the producing of and fishing for salmon. It is hoped that this treaty can remedy the interception by one nation of another nation's salmon, and since the salmon of both continents go to southwest Greenland, it is also hoped that such a treaty will limit the take of each continent's or each nation's salmon proportionate to its own run. Such a treaty is needed and will, I am certain, come to pass in good time.

Platforms are an advantage when fishing on wild and turbulent waters.

One great salmon mystery remains. Where do the grilse congregate when they go to sea? It is important for the angler to realize how important this discovery can be. These fish, probably between 2 and 3 pounds in weight as they congregate on their feeding grounds, might be preferred over any other stage of salmon for food. One can imagine these mackerel-sized salmon being caught by the ton and their numbers brought to near depletion before action could be taken. Inasmuch as our management regulations changed the runs in our salmon rivers from a make-up of predominantly large salmon to one of predominantly grilse, the taking of grilse in the sea would have a disastrous effect on angling. We had best be ready for quick action when the grilse "pockets" in the sea are found and devastation begins.

Although the numbers of salmon in the runs and the suitable fishing waters have diminished, the number of salmon anglers has been growing, and their organizations are becoming more and more aware that their problems are political (salmon management is controlled by politicians). In addition to establishing meetings and publications which promote friendship and understanding among anglers, they are feeling the need to organize so that their influence on all those who seem not to be doing a good job of salmon management can be increased. The two major conservation organizations of this continent, the Atlantic Salmon Association of Montreal, Canada, headed by Lucien Rolland and directed by Michael Price, and the International Atlantic Salmon Foundation, headed by Joseph Cullman III and directed by Wilfred Carter, are, as of this writing, merging. They will now be able to work more effectively just as conservation groups from Canada, the U.S., and Mexico have worked together through Ducks Unlimited to the greater benefit of all the water fowlers on the continent.

It is certain that better management will follow when those interested in salmon angling, who outnumber and can outvote those who commercially net salmon, can prove that salmon taken by angling are more valuable to society than those taken in nets far from their native rivers. It will take time. It took many years before the U.S. fishery managers accepted the premise that by making catch-and-release regulations, which are applicable on good trout waters, they could have the greatest number of fish available and provide the best trout angling possible for the fishing public. This management technique is now spreading rapidly to all the U.S. trout waters, and trout angling in the U.S. is constantly improving while angling for other species, of which more fishermen are steadily taking more annually, is getting worse.

No-Kill, the returning of angling-captured fish to their streams to live for another angler to catch or to go on to spawn, has a real value in Atlantic salmon management. Take the case of a river where the salmon are few and need maximum protection. At a time of low water and great salmon vulnerability, it is better to have anglers on the stream to help protect it while they play fish and return them without damage than to leave it empty of anglers, giving poachers free rein.

Reuse, when possible, was the policy regarding salmon at the camps I ran. We returned a great many of them after capture, unharmed, to the rivers, much to the dismay of the guides who always wanted fish to take home. I tried to explain that our customers came to catch salmon, and that if the run diminished because of fishing pressure, where there had been none before, they'd be less likely to come. I explained that we must return all the salmon possible to maintain the run or the camp would fail to attract as many anglers, in which case some of the guides would lose their jobs. I didn't reach them and they fought the release program until I started *buying* salmon from the commercial netters nearby to give them to take home, and I insisted that they aid in putting back any salmon we did not really need. When they realized how seriously I felt about releasing, they cooperated and, from then on, began checking the mouths of the salmon as they came in for earlier hook marks. They were impressed at the number of salmon that had been caught and released previously.

If a salmon is played with reasonable pressure and speed and then released unharmed, it is almost certain to survive. On the Margaree, Nova Scotia regulations permit angling and the keeping of grilse, but stipulate the returning of all large salmon during the early-summer fishing in order to build up the percentage of big fish in the run. By using such innovative regulations this exceptionally beautiful river is being restored to its former glory.

An Icelandic salmon still strong after capture is released into the Grimsa River. Photo by Joan Wulff

On the Grimsa, in Iceland, fly-fishing-only and catch-and-release are the orders, as determined by the owners and managers for the period, when the river is open to fishing by non-Icelanders. Anglers are given fresh or smoked salmon from commercial sources to take home, and they are satisfied with this arrangement. When the Icelanders have their turn, toward the end of the season, they find more fish in the pools and they, too, are happy with the arrangement. The owners and managers believe that more of this increased number survive the Icelanders' fishing and give the river more fish on the spawning beds. Scientific study of the released and tagged fish is giving valuable information on the high survival rate and the actions of played and released fish.

With an ever-increasing number of devoted salmon anglers we are bound to see new and better management techniques to derive the maximum combination of recreation and food from our salmon rivers. It always seems darkest just before dawn, and I believe that we are about to see better salmon management within the next few years. It is my hope to live long enough to see the kind of progress that will rebuild, to their old-time averages, not only the size of the runs but the size of the fish that make up the runs.

15

Flying for Salmon

The great Atlantic salmon explorations were made by the British navy. The Royal Navy covered the world. They charted the coasts. They measured the depths of the harbors, and, because many of the officers were salmon fishermen, they fished the salmon rivers that were readily accessible from the sea. There's an old saying to the effect that the reason the British let the Russians have Alaska was because the salmon there wouldn't rise to a Jock Scott.

After covering Newfoundland's salmon rivers by train, road, boat, canoe, and on foot for that Colony's Tourist Development Board, I decided, after World War II, to open a fishing camp on the wild northwest corner of the island. I soon found I needed a plane to make the operation go, so I obtained a J–3 cub, a 65-horsepower, two-seat, tandem monoplane on floats, to do the job. I rushed through training, getting a pilot's license in just under three weeks, and I flew to Newfoundland five weeks after my first lesson.

It was against the advice of every experienced pilot I knew. Bill Turgeon, chief pilot for Maine's Fish and Game division, said I'd be blown away. Air Force pilots I'd known said that light planes like my Piper cub, which took off and landed at just over 30 miles an hour and were delicately made of doped linen fabric and light steel tubing, couldn't take the gales that swept Newfoundland every summer.

I had some exciting moments as a new pilot when great gales threatened to lift me into the clouds . . . when the fog swept in suddenly . . . when the waves seemed too high for my fragile "bird" to light on. I was lucky. I learned fast and, at forty-two, had experience in the bush and the judgment of maturity rather than youth's resilience and extrafast reactions. Caught by a sudden wind on a short trip I remember coming into my base at Portland Creek when the anemometer at the nearby Daniel's Harbor station was reading 52 miles an hour.

For one who had travelled the bush so long on the slow ground routes, flying was like heaven. I used my plane as a hunter or fisherman would use a jeep. I turned on the switch, swung the prop, hit the sky, and in a few minutes could land at a salmon pool that would have taken two days of earthbound travel to reach. Great areas were made up of soggy bog and tundra through which walking was impossible except when winter froze it over. I could fly to pools that were practically never fished and have them all to myself. The British may have explored the reaches of the rivers near the sea but they

Something that happened on my first flight back to my home at Shushan, New York, at the end of my first flying summer in Newfoundland opened up a great new vista for me. I was in the air over Wedgeport, Nova Scotia, where I had enjoyed some exciting giant bluefin-tuna fishing. In fact, it was my great luck in having caught the most and the biggest tuna in the First International Tuna Tournament at Wedgeport that had led to my work in Newfoundland. I was exploring for giant tuna, but I was also covering the hunting and the fishing, as well as the salmon rivers, in order to write stories that would bring sportsmen to the island.

The sun was bright and the sea was very blue. I could look down and see the sport-fishing cruisers, many of whose crews I knew, and watch their trolling baits flashing in the wakes behind them. In one boat I saw a captured tuna lying in the cockpit. Then, as I turned for a closer look, I saw three great tuna swimming lazily along the surface. Turning again for an even better look, by accident, my plane's shadow fell on the fish and with a flash of white spray they disappeared into the sea beneath them.

Why should tuna weighing 600 or 700 pounds take such fright at a shadow? No bird alive had been a threat to them since they were babies of 5 pounds or less. But frightened they were. I mused about it as I flew on across the sea from Nova Scotia to Maine. If those great fish were needlessly frightened by a shadow, wouldn't salmon, lying in a pool, with much more to fear and a much longer period of real vulnerability, be even more frightened by my plane's shadow?

The next season, on a bright, sunny afternoon, I flew over a pool in Western Brook. I could see no salmon. Then, at about 250 feet, I swung my plane's shadow across the pool.

The results were startling. Five salmon left their invisible resting places and darted swiftly about the pool before settling down again. The fish themselves, because of their somewhat protective coloring, were not really easy to see but the hard, black shadows they cast on the gravel of the streambed were. I could count the fish and make a pretty good guess as to their size.

That capability opened up a whole new world of salmon exploration. In the past I had to reach a pool on foot, fish it for a period of time, and, judging by the rises I got under the conditions at the time, estimate the number of fish in the pool and, from that, determine how great that stretch of river's potential was for angling. Now I could simply fly over a river on a sunny day and know a lot more about it. I did need relatively clear water. When the dark rivers of peat-bog drainages ran low and relatively clear I could see the fish and the rocks of the streambeds by low-level flying, but when they were in spate I could see no fish.

Just flying a river was great fun. There were no telephone wires, no radio towers, no sudden bridges to worry about in the bush. I could fly below treetop level, twisting as the rivers twisted, flying a river as a skier might ski a narrow trail, alert because of the danger but sure of the capability to make each turn or to power up into clear air above the trees and slopes that lined the racing water under the wings when the turn was too sharp.

ABOVE: *Exploring for salmon in 1947.* RIGHT: *The author had good fishing fortune on Western Brook Gorge when it was wild. The Link canoe was flown in on the floats.* BELOW: *When a bush pilot landed where a plane had never come before, it was an event for the whole settlement.*

There were no weather services, and the storms seemed to breed at a moment's notice. I listened to the old timers who had to decide on which days they would venture offshore in their frail dories. Whenever I saw an old fisherman I asked his opinion of the weather and remembered whether or not his prediction came true and the basis on which he'd made it. "A build-up of clouds to the southeast on a bright afternoon and you'll have a storm coming in that night." "Morning fog and no wind give a clear day by ten." "Two decks of clouds and the weather won't clear." I listened and I learned. I flew to the places I wanted to reach with surprising regularity. It was a time when about half the bush pilots I knew died flying—Pink Henderson at Gander, Tommy Mantinon at Buchans, Bill Webster out over the Gulf. Though I had a share of grim experiences, I lived to follow the salmon north up the Labrador Shore, ahead of all the other planes and future fishing camps I knew would come behind me.

I'd made flights north to Labrador in my J–3 cub, making gas caches to extend my range from the base at Portland Creek. My Supercub, new in 1955, with an extended range was the first light plane based in Labrador. It, too, was a two-seat tandem like the J–3, but it had 150 horsepower for twice the thrust of the old J–3, a speed of 95 miles an hour, flaps for better control in slow flying, and in it I had installed an auxiliary tank that gave me a range of 750 miles. A 95-mile-an-hour airplane crossing one of the empty reaches of the Labrador bush and bucking a sudden, surprising 50-mile-an-hour head-wind either has to have range or the pilot must sit down and wait, perhaps for days, for the wind to change.

My job in the summer of 1957 was to explore and recommend fishing campsites for the U.S. Air Force at Goose Bay.

Through the long northern days of that summer I checked out the rivers and lakes within reasonable flying range. Minipi and McKenzie and No Name were great for trout. The Adlatok and the Sandhill and a host of others fine for salmon. Some didn't have dependable fishing; some couldn't provide enough fishing at one spot for enough anglers. I came to know that country well. I could lift off, see the far mountains, and by their mass and the shape of their peaks, know the courses to the watersheds I learned to love.

The following year I flew that country making films of trout and salmon fishing, which appeared later on CBS-TV's *Sports Spectaculars* and ABC's *American Sportsman* TV series. In 1959 I was commissioned by the Newfoundland Government to report on the Labrador salmon rivers.

I followed the rivers up to the Davis Strait, not far south of Nain, the northern limit of the salmon runs on the Atlantic coast. My floats drew only about 8 inches of water. I could land on any of the lakes and on the pools or flow of most of the larger rivers. Once on the water, I could often taxi my way upstream or down, following the main channels between the rocks and bars, to reach otherwise isolated pools.

A seaplane is something like a sailboat—difficult to handle in a mixture of wind and current. Often I'd have to get out and pull my plane through shallow runs or wade it along a bar when the wind wanted to blow it to deep water or against a rocky shore. For that reason I wore chest waders when I flew to explore. I recall taxiing up the Jem Lane, one of the far northern rivers, and having a salmon of over 20 pounds come downstream as I went up, passing under me, between my floats.

One summer day in 1958, the year of the great forest fires when all of Labrador seemed made up of smoke and flame, I flew to a pool I knew on the Paradise River. A long, rapid run, split at a rocky ledge, that flared out into a long, deep pool on either side of a wadable gravel bar. Salmon runs, moving up through the slow water between that point and the river's mouth at Sandwich Bay tended to hold there for a while before tackling the long stretch of white water that lay ahead. Ted Rogowski was with me.

The Paradise is the most southerly of three big salmon rivers that flow into Sandwich Bay. The Eagle comes in from the West and the White Bear from the North. The other two were closer to the Settlement of Cartwright, more accessible, and better known. I had flown the river 60 miles or more from its mouth to its source and found that the flow was generally swift with only one small lake at its head. Landing in that lake I'd found no salmon at the outlet and not many parr. Indications were that it wasn't as good for salmon as the other two. However, I knew salmon ran it and, on that mid-July day, I wanted to see if I could catch a run moving through at that long pool.

When we reached the pool we found forest fires alive there on both sides of the river. The river banks were low and relatively swampy. The trees were mainly black spruce, the thinnest of the evergreens. The fire was working through the dry surface peat from tree to tree. Periodically we could see one of the spruces catch fire at the base and the flames tower upward until the whole tree was a spear of light.

When I'd landed there earlier I'd tied up at the little clump of rocks above the long, submerged bar, and those rocks, at the river's center, were 150 feet from the trees on either side. Downstream the steady water was even wider. I realized the danger of flying sparks should they land on the flammable fabric of my airplane. The air was still. I decided to land and fish till the wind came up. I looked down at the pool, a great river of dark water with a dark streambed. It was one of the few rivers where the salmon would not be visible even though the river itself was low.

The fish were there. Where my first trip had given me only four salmon, this time there must have been hundreds holding in the flow on either side of the bar. These were salmon that had never seen a fly. A local boat might come to the mouth of the river to set a net, but no one came there to cast. We waded down the bar from the rocks, Ted taking one side and I the other, changing sides occasionally for variation. We caught over a dozen fish before the water began to ripple with a developing wind, and I felt the need to get out before the sparks from the burning trees on the shore could reach us.

A little over a quarter of a mile of fairly steady flow lies below the main falls of the Eagle before it spills over a lesser chute of white water to reach the placid flow that takes it to the tidehead half a mile away. That quarter-mile stretch was loaded with leaping salmon and studded here and there with rocks and an island that broke the surface. Two friends, Gordon Woods and Buzz Duhamel, had invited me to go fishing.

I flew over that pool a long time before I landed the first plane ever to land there. I always carried a lot of tools in my plane to take care of emergencies, even though I hated to lose that weight capacity for fuel or other things. I carried a small buck saw and a hatchet tied under my front seat with a bow knot for quick release. I had the simplest tools—pliers, a wrench, and screwdrivers—set in a strap beside me where I could reach them readily even though the plane was loaded to its fullest. Behind me, on the floor between front and rear seat, was a folding anchor, big enough to hold a plane far bigger than mine, with a coil of heavy nylon rope attached to it that I could grab, extend, throw over, and tie to the halter between my floats in a matter of seconds.

Salmon from a wild Labrador River, caught with the aid of the author's Super Cub.

That pool is generally too deep to wade, and the anglers normally fish from small boats, two to a boat. The camp, as it happened, was full and all three boats were in use. After a welcoming lunch, in order to give us fishing, Ted and I were taken to a big rockface on the true right bank of the river not far below the main falls. It sloped to the water's edge at a 30-degree angle, and the salmon came in close enough to the shore to be cast to.

Ted and I fished the afternoon through, wishing we had a boat so we could reach the main runs, catching some fish nevertheless. When it was time for the evening meal one of the boats headed over to pick us up. The motor started up, ran a bit, then died and had to be started again. It stopped again, momentarily, as they crossed below the falls to reach us. The boat was 10 feet long, built deep, and rounded like a bathtub. Doc, the angler at the outboard, weighed well over 200 pounds. His companion was not much lighter. It was with trepidation that we added my 185 pounds and Ted's 140 to the load. The boat had about 3 inches of freeboard which, if we stuck to the smooth water, would be enough.

As we started, Doc complained that the motor had been a bit uncertain, so Ted and I suggested that we cut across immediately to the smooth, slow water on the far side and follow it down to the landing. Doc was from Minnesota where the waters are flat, and he just headed straight down through the main flow, the shortest route. We were hardly halfway down when the motor cut out and wouldn't restart. I threw over the small "grapple," a typical fisherman's anchor made of an iron shaft with five equally spaced hooks at the end. The anchor dragged.

Gordon and Buzz, who were in their boat, hauled in their anchor and raced over to throw us a line. I tied it to the bow, and they tried to tow us up and across the stream to safety. Heavy laden as we were, they didn't have the power to hold us against the flow. Doc's frantic efforts failed to restart the motor. Both boats were being pulled steadily down to the lower chute. At the brink of the white water I cast the towline free in order to let Gordy and Buzz pull away to safety. We were doomed to go through the tumbling chute, water that would almost assuredly turn us over, with our anchor dragging, and if the dragging anchor caught, even momentarily, on the streambed it would pull our nose under and swamp us.

I thought of jumping over to lighten our load, having no fear of being able to swim in my waders, something I'd done before, on occasion, to prove a point, but decided the act of my jumping would probably upset the boat. I sat and thought, "How stupid! To risk us all when it was so needless."

High waves threw some water aboard. The light anchor scraped a ledge, caught for a second, dragged free. We passed within inches of the rough rock wall rising and falling in the foamy sweep. It was over in seconds. Miraculously we were drifting, barely afloat, in the smooth water of the lower river. Buzz broke out of the woods, out of breath and white faced at what he expected to see. As thoughts raced through my mind, I realized I had been more worried about the others than myself. I felt capable of coming through that wild water in waders as long as I wasn't struck on the head by the boat or a rock, but the others, not being as strong or as secure in their minds, might have panicked and swallowed some water and gone drifting downstream, and we had no boat to follow and reach them.

We were all fishing again that evening. I guess it pays to be lucky.

I was flying back to Goose Bay from the Sandhill when I decided to land on the White Bear River. My tanks were as light as they were ever likely to be, and I had no passenger and no load. I could fly my slowest, take off fast, and climb at my best. I'd often looked down at that long, rough river tumbling its way from the Mealy Mountains to Sandwich Bay with only one break in the steady ribbon of white water it presented from source to mouth. It was a long way from anywhere overland. It had no lakes to land in, only one elbow in the river where it smoothed out for about 300 yards. I'd looked down at it often realizing that the pool was too short to carry passengers into or to carry in materials to build a camp. Yet I was curious about the fishing possibilities.

It is a funny thing about flying—you're constantly looking at the ground below you, wondering where you'd land if your motor quit. If there's a place you even think of as a possible landing spot you study it hard every time you fly over it. Sometimes you lie awake at night, calculating in your mind the capability of your plane, the wind or lack of wind conditions you'd need to try it, the danger from rocks or current, and above all, your judgment and your ability to make your plane do its absolute best.

After a good, low look in which I checked out a gray ledge of rock that extended part way across the streambed, feeling sure I would pass safely over its deeper end, I came in with the seat of my pants telling me I was just above stalling. The touchdown was within 50 feet of the tail of the pool, and I started to settle with lots of room to spare when I felt a sudden shudder and knew I'd touched a rock. There's a rule that if you're still on the step and in takeoff configuration when *anything* happens to you, you pour on the power and fly, if that's possible. I put all my 150 horses to work and lifted off against the current but into the wind, just clearing the rocks at the head of the pool, climbing back into the safety of the sky.

Even if I had had put a hole in my floats they were compartmented and I could land at the No Name camp where I could pull the plane up out of water and make a field repair. The White Bear could wait for another time when I thought conditions were right and I felt lucky—a time that never came.

The aluminum of the big float compartment was dented but not punctured, and there was no structural damage to the floats. No repair was necessary that time, but I remember one field repair I had to make while I was on the Hawk River, a big lonely river flowing into the Atlantic, south of Sandwich Bay.

I was still based in Newfoundland. We went up there in two planes, Frank Frazee in a Stinson and I in a Piper Pacer, each with a guide for company. One of the guides, Mañuel Caines, had trapped that country years before and had seen and speared some salmon in the river. The only people for 50 miles around were his uncle Ase and his wife, who lived on Deer Island, one of the fringe islands on the outside of the big bay 25 miles away. Ase moved everywhere from his doorstep by boat, netting salmon in the summer, catching cod in traps, and killing seals on the pack ice and ice flows in the winter.

The river was in flood, something we hadn't counted on because the rivers at our base at Portland Creek were, at that time, very low from lack of rain. In those days, with no radio communications, such surprises were not uncommon. Mañuel could hardly tell where the pools were or where the salmon used to lie. We tried several possible pools and had only one salmon follow a fly. Deciding that further fishing was a waste of time, we took off for the home camp.

I went first and was airborne and circling Frank's Stinson "Station Wagon" as he made his takeoff run. Suddenly he stopped and headed his plane for a shallow sand beach on the shore. I watched him get out and wave me down.

Frank had hit a rock, hit it while he was still "plowing" along at about 15 miles an hour, low in the water, before he could get the plane up on the step. There was a long gash in his main float compartment which would let that float sink so low he couldn't get up enough speed to take off.

Had it been a lone pilot doing the work, he'd have had a big job. One man would have had to use a block and tackle and a long rope to dead-end on a tree. We quickly cut spruce poles to slide the plane out and with four of us pulling it came easily. When the floats were high and dry and we could get at the bottom, I brought out, from one of my float compartments, a coke-sized can of tar and some rags I carried for just such emergencies. It was remarkable how quickly we patched that hole.

A fire heated the tar, and tar-coated rags were stuffed into the hole as tightly as possible. The rags were trimmed on the outside as neatly as possible, and a piece of hot, tar-soaked rag was spread out over the hole and the surrounding metal to give a smooth outer skin. The whole area was being heated by a small fire on the ground beneath it, to warm the metal and give a good bond. Sliding back to the water its coolness hardened the tar thoroughly, and such a bond would hold for a takeoff or two and get us back to Portland Creek where, with rivets or stove bolts and sheet aluminum, we could fashion a repair as good as new.

The evil genie of flying can show up when it is least expected. I took off from our base at Portland Creek with a guide and Neil Marvin, a good friend and salmon fisherman. I was flying a four-seat Aeronca Sedan, a broad-winged bird that flew at about 90 miles an hour and had a gliding range like a pelican. I'd had the tanks filled before our takeoff right after lunch. We would be fishing 20 miles north in the river of Ponds. It was a milk run. I made it often. We were halfway there when the motor suddenly stopped.

The dead silence that replaces the steady drone of a cruising motor comes with a

ABOVE: The author reached the then-wilderness pools of Newfoundland and Labrador by seaplane in 1947. RIGHT: Lee Wulff with his Aeronca "Sedan" and his ever-present 6-foot fly rod, 1950.

chilling shock. I had just looked at the gas gauge and it read almost full. I looked again. It read empty. I set up my best glide angle and made a small circle to see where I could land safely. There was nothing under me but unbroken forest and as I looked I was warmed by the thought that I had followed my habit of rising up to 1,500 feet or better when crossing that stretch of forbidding forest. Off to the north I spotted a lake, the closest water, out at the limit of my gliding range. Close to it, and slightly closer to us, was an open bog which I knew I could reach and where I could bring the plane in with nothing more than a hard bump for my passengers.

The seconds ticked by, and the forest slid by slowly under my wings. I was headed for the lake with the bog off to one side. I realized finally that making the lake would be too great a risk and started a turn toward the bog when I remembered something an old pilot had said at one of the hangar bull sessions, "There's always a drop or two of gas in your priming line for a few seconds of flight in an emergency."

The prop was windmilling. I pumped the primer knob. The engine caught with a roar. I swung back toward the lake. We climbed for perhaps a dozen seconds, then went into a final silent glide which carried us over the last of the trees with 50 feet to spare. We settled on the lake and I paddled the plane to the shore.

We found out later that that model Aeronca had gas tanks of a new type. They were of a heavy, collapsible, gasoline-proof material inside an aluminum case. When the lad who had filled my tanks had failed to put on the gas cap, the gas siphoned off as we flew. Both tanks were connected so all the gas siphoned off. The gas gauges were of the liquid type that showed the gasoline level visually. The collapsing tanks kept the pressure up and kept the gauge level at practically full until the last moment.

We were a 15-mile hike through raw bush from the gulf of St. Lawrence, where there'd be a path to walk, to Belle Burns. Once there we could get a boat to run the 12 miles to Daniel's Harbor and walk the remaining 5 miles to the camp. Neil's wife, Connie, was in camp and, knowing she'd be worried, Neil decided to beat his way through the brush with Heb, the guide, who knew the country from his winter trapping expeditions. I settled down to wait.

I spent the afternoon fishing, but it was one of those rare lakes with few fish in it. I managed to catch a few small trout that I saved for breakfast. Spending the night in the plane wasn't uncomfortable because the right front seat could be bent back to make a place for a makeshift stretcher I used when taking an injured person to the hospital. I dug out a little salt for the trout which I cooked over a small fire, but I touched none of my survival rations.

In my view, anyone forced down shouldn't eat from his precious store of food for at least a day or two, coasting on his usual well-fed condition. The survival food, if that's all he has, will do him a lot more good if he waits to use it till his body is really crying for it. I think survival rations should be very nourishing, but they should taste like sawdust soaked in gasoline so a downed pilot will put off using them till they'll do him the most good, and, even then, stretch out their use. My own survival rations were about a dozen small, very hard sea biscuits and two boxes of raisins, both things I love. I counted on will power to keep me from eating them too soon in an emergency.

Late in the second day Heb came back with three gallons of gasoline in his pack. Fifteen minutes later we were back at camp for lobster chowder, veal stew, homemade bread and honey, black tea, and apple pie—all the fixings. They knew I'd be hungry.

I remember some of the rivers of Labrador for special reasons. Once, flying back from Hopedale, I stopped at the Makkovic River. The river was clear but I could see only a few fish in the pool near the steady water I could land in. I caught one and then we flew on southward. I always remember the Makkovic because during World War II an Air Force C47 went down in the hills just behind the river where I fished it. The village of Makkovic was only ten miles eastward across some low land. The crew, following procedure, had stayed with the plane for shelter, counting on being found by Air Search & Rescue. Apparently they were far off course, for the plane wasn't found for years. They kept a diary and there were many days between the first and the last entry when the last crew member gave up to cold and starvation. It was particularly sad because if one of them had climbed one of the high peaks he could have seen the sea and if he had walked east a dozen miles he would have seen the village or at least the lights of Makkovic. That was one of the reasons why I always knew what watershed I was on and how I could reach the sea and, somehow, get to a village. I was in good shape to travel and chances are no one would know just where to look for me.

Flying south we stopped at the Big River, which, until that time, was just a name on the charts. There is a long pool where it hits the salt water after a rapid run following another long pool as the river comes in from the southwest. Dave Burchinal, who was with me, began to cast into some attractive heavy water partway up the run.

Within a minute or two I saw Dave's rod bend, and I watched a 12-pound salmon break out into the sunlight. It was his first, and I knew how thrilled he was. I turned to cast again and just as my fly hit the water a great black shape came up from below and half cleared the surface. I was thinking only of salmon and was nonplussed for a moment. At first glance I thought it was a monstrous salmon . . . but realized instantly it was too big and too dark to be a salmon. I'd seen a seal. That meant there were fish there for the seals to feed upon so it was bound to be a good river. It meant, too, that the fish would be scared, and I marvelled that the seal, so close to Dave's fish, hadn't scared him back to the open brackish water where he'd have the best chance to avoid being food for the seal.

After watching Dave beach his salmon I walked up along the southern shore of the river to the pool that I'd seen from the air, to lie just above the fast run. Two seals waddled into the water from the shore, and half a dozen heads stuck up above the surface of the long pool, looking at me. They all swam to the head of the pool and stayed there, keeping low in the water. There was a bounty on seals because they are a host to a cod parasite, and the Newfoundlanders fought bitterly against anything that threatened their mainstay, the cod.

I fished near the tail of the pool but rose no salmon. Putting on a big streamer fly, I took several large sea-run trout, fish of about 5 pounds. They were relatively fresh from the sea, brook trout with silvery sides but a back that was more gray than the usual greenish color a brook trout brings back to his stream from the sea. We had a long way to go to get back to Goose so we couldn't stay long on that beautiful river.

The jewel of all the rivers I flew to in Labrador was the Adlatok. The first time I saw it I was with Tommy White; it was mid-August. Labrador can be as cold as the ice in the sea drifting down from Greenland or as warm and dry as the dog day weather of the middle of the continent. 1954 was one of the hot, dry years of southwesterly winds. The great river was low, and we hiked up to the big pool just below the falls. The water was crystal clear, the pools nearly dry, and we saw no salmon in the pools we passed going up. At the big pool, a bit below the falls, we saw a few fish and Tommy caught one. The fishing was far from good. The boulders of the streambed were polished granite covered with a thin coating of slime making the slipperiest wading I'd had in a long, long time. We left after three hours fishing, a bit discouraged and with a relatively low opinion of the Adlatok as a salmon river, although we were impressed with the majesty of the steep cliffs and dramatic rock faces that lined the pools. Little did I know how really bad those conditions were. I was never to see it anywhere near as low in all the years that followed.

I went back in 1957, in my search for recreation sites for the Air Force, more out of duty and doing a thorough job than any great hope of finding a special river. It was near the distance limit for a suitable site.

This time conditions were at the other extreme. It had been a wet season and the river was high. There were salmon in all the pools, practically all of them 10 pounds and over with some around 30. I fished each pool on the way up, raising or catching a salmon in each one and lingering a little too long at each pool, so that when I reached the big pool we had fished on my previous trip, where the water was now racing through its solid rock basin, I had little time left. Instead of a placid pool spilling easily over its lip at the tail, I found a torrent pouring into a 30-foot-deep pocket of stone and sweeping around in a great circling eddy on one side while the main flow carried over a spillway into a fierce white race to the pool below.

This was dangerous water. I found myself thoroughly fearful of falling into that pool and being carried over that lip to the rocks below. It was nothing a man could swim in. Anyone falling in would be more than lucky to come out alive. It was a hard pool to fish for the banks were sheer with little room for back casts. The turmoil of the waters was such that the salmon had to keep moving. They could not settle lazily into a steady eddy in an easy flow.

I cast out into the circling water and made retrieves I thought should be attractive to a salmon. I couldn't see any, but twice salmon had leaped and they were big ones. I started out with a normal fly, a #6 Jock Scott. When I had no rises to that one I began working up in size and changing patterns. At the end of half an hour, with the sun getting low and daylight dwindling, I put on the largest fly in my vest, a 7/0 Jock Scott, and made a cast.

In midretrieve I saw a dark shape behind the fly. I kept up a slow retrieve and the salmon followed. I went through that most excruciating time a salmon angler can have. A really big salmon was following a foot or two behind the fly but wouldn't take it. If I stopped the retrieve he'd lose interest, yet I knew that if he followed on and didn't take the fly he'd come in too close, see me, and take fright.

The great salmon's interest held. He followed the fly, just inches behind it, almost to my feet, before some motion of mine gave him fright. He flashed a broad band of silver as he turned away.

A storm was brewing, which may have been why he was hesitant to take the fly, and I dared not stay the night for fear of being fogbound there for days. I was already close to running out of daylight before I could get back to my base at Goose Bay. I cast a dozen times and then raced down the river to my plane, knowing I'd found a future recreation camp and a river I'd love to fish.

The early bush pilot had a vast wilderness at his feet; he could fish where no one had fished before.

The Adlatok is unique among Labrador rivers. Not far above that wonderful pool the river has a forks. It is not a normal forks, where two flows join to make a larger river, but one where the flow of a great river rising a hundred miles or more inland divides and takes two separate courses from there to the sea. The fork I was on was called the Adlatok, and that name was given to the entire length of the river above the forks as well. The other branch that veers off to reach the sea in a different bay many miles to the south is called the Ujitok. It is the larger of the two branches and would also be a great salmon river if it did not drop over a great falls far higher than any salmon could surmount. It has no salmon run. All the salmon of that great, long river are pent up below the falls in this lesser Adaltok branch, where anglers can fish for them, till a certain water condition is reached.

The salmon can pass through the falls only at one particular water level. That first time I'd fished it there had already been enough water to let the run of fish climb the falls and go inland, leaving only a very few in that one big pool. In 1957 the water was just too high all season for the fish to make it, and all the salmon for the whole river were still below the falls in high water providing good fishing into September.

I was lucky enough once to be there when the water was lowering to the right level for the salmon to run it. The fish had left the big pool and moved up into the swift sluice just below the falling water. They were there in the hundreds. I climbed to a precarious position on a ledge with a sheer drop to the fish below. I managed to hook one and almost fell in trying to work around, in a vain effort, to land him. The next morning, when I came back, the fish had all gone through, and I saw none and raised nothing either in that sluice or in the wonderful pool just below it.

Flying for salmon was the highlight of a long fishing career. From my plane, I had the great feeling that the world I looked down on was mine. That far northern country could be forbidding when the gales swept in or the fog smothered the land, and it could be utterly beautiful with bright sun on blue waters and green mountains stretching in clear air to the far horizons. It brought a special rapture to just being alive and being there. I felt as the mountain men must have felt with a new, wild, world all their own, and my plane was to me as their horses were to them. It was a part of me. I cherished it for, if it failed me, I might perish.

One friend, looking into my small plane and seeing the fly rod, the tools, and the flies I had hooked into the inside fabric said, "Ah! Lee. This smells of happiness."

As I write this in our home in the Beaverkill Valley, in my seventy-seventh year, that Supercub, spawned in 1955, is still with me. It stands in our meadow by the river, on wheels instead of floats, and from time to time, I climb into it and take off from the short strip to the sky—to feel the wind and remember the wild flying and the unspoiled salmon rivers I knew when it was young.

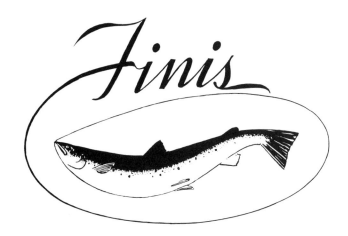

Index